Studying Service-Learning
Innovations in
Education Research Methodology

Studying Service-Learning
Innovations in
Education Research Methodology

Edited by

Shelley H. Billig
RMC Research Corporation

Alan S. Waterman
College of New Jersey

Routledge
Taylor & Francis Group
New York   London

Camera ready copy for this book was provided by the editors.

First published by Lawrence Erlbaum Associates, Inc., Publishers
10 Industrial Avenue
Mahwah, New Jersey 07430

Transferred to digital printing 2010 by Routledge

Routledge

270 Madison Avenue
New York, NY 10016

2 Park Square, Milton Park
Abingdon, Oxon OX14 4RN, UK

Cover design by Kathryn Houghtaling Lacey

Library of Congress Cataloging-in-Publication Data

Studying service-learning : innovations in education research meth-
    odology / edited by Shelley H. Billig and Alan S. Waterman.
        p.   cm.
    Includes bibliographical references and index.
ISBN 0-8058-4275-6 (cloth : alk. paper)
ISBN 0-8058-4276-4 (pbk. : alk. paper)
1. Student service. 2 Education—Research—Methodology.
    I. Billig, Shelley H.   II. Waterman, Alan S.
LC220.5 .S795   2003
373.119—dc21   2002192546
                                                     CIP

Contents

Introduction

Studying Service-Learning:
Challenges and Solutions

Although individuals have been studying service-learning for decades, most would agree that research in service-learning is still in its infancy. Many fine evaluations of service-learning have been conducted, such as those by Melchior (1999), Furco (2002), and Eyler and Giles (1999). Several summaries of studies have been compiled, such as those by Conrad and Hedin (1991); Billig (2000); and Eyler, Giles, Stenson, and Gray (2000). Volumes of collected research have begun to appear, such as those by Furco and Billig (2002), Waterman (1997), and Anderson, Swick, and Yff (2001).

Those efforts to gather and disseminate what is known about service-learning are important first steps. They represent efforts to understand the basis for the passion that many educators feel for the practice of service-learning. These works collectively provide glimpses into the factors that help build the quality of service-learning practice. They begin to identify key variables needed to maximize desired outcomes and the effects of various contexts on the impacts that participation in service-learning may have on different stakeholders.

Given the prevalence of service-learning, however, it is surprising to see so little actual research. Service-learning has been estimated as being performed in nearly one-third of all public K–12 schools and one-half of all high schools (National Center for Education Statistics, 1999) and up to 88% of all private schools (Genzer, 1998). Participation in service-learning for faculty and students in higher education is equally strong (Eyler & Giles, 1999). Yet the vast majority of published studies on service-learning are of program evaluations or anecdotal descriptions, not research (Billig, 2000; Eyler, Giles, & Gray, 2000). Having a body of evidence comprised primarily of evaluation studies severely limits the ability to make generalizations about service-learning impacts and restricts the ways in which the studies can be used to improve practice. Furthermore, program evaluations are less likely to be built on strong theoretical foundations. This means that their explanatory value is also restricted. Finally, the definitions of service-learning being used, the program designs being studied, and the populations of students and community members being examined vary so broadly that the discussion of service-learning research must always occur in the midst of multiple qualifying statements.

SERVICE-LEARNING RESEARCH CHALLENGES

Clearly, more rigorous, replicable research in service-learning is needed for both K–12 and higher education populations. In studying service-learning, researchers will need to grapple with seven challenges: definitions, theoretical foundations, methodology, interpretation of results, dissemination, practitioners' use of research for improvement, and funding for research.

Definitions of Service-Learning

The challenge of defining service-learning is discussed throughout this volume. The issue of definition is complex, and arguments about conceptions of service-learning have plagued the field for years. Although most service-learning researchers, evaluators, and practitioners would agree that service-learning involves both service to the community and learning tied to academic curriculum, the definitions of service, community, learning, and academic curriculum all vary widely. Although most agree that the process of service-learning involves planning, action, reflection, and celebration, the content and relative stress placed on each of these components are greatly divergent. The context in which service-learning occurs, such as whether service-learning involves the environment, senior citizens, young children, community agencies, or other recipients of service also varies greatly along with characterizations of the relationship and degree to which mutuality occurs. The populations providing the service, the individuals facilitating knowledge generation and/or skills application, and the frequency and duration of the service-learning activities also differ. The definitional problem, then, is layered and complex. The authors in this volume offer several suggestions for dealing with the definitional challenge.

Lack of Strong Theoretical Foundations

The second challenge, basing the research on strong theoretical foundations, is thornier than it appears at first glance because so many theoretical perspectives seem appropriate. For example, understanding service-learning through the lens of developmental theory can illuminate the ways in which service-learning program designs can be tailored to match students' age and grade levels. Theories of the development of cultural sensitivity, citizenship, and civic responsibility teaching and learning, development of cognitive complexity, nature of schooling, and career exploration could all be used to promote a greater understanding of the way in which service-learning works. For example, theories that address the socially constructed nature of comprehension and "meaning-making" could be drawn upon to understand the role of reflection within service-learning processes and the differential outcomes associated with varied reflective practices. Theories related to conceptions of social justice and/or social action could be used to strengthen collective understanding of motivation to participate and differential impact on student identity formation. The opportunities to connect service-learning to theories in psychology, sociology, anthropology, political science, education, and so on, are seemingly boundless, yet too few of these opportunities are seized since so many service-learning studies are evaluations.

Research Design and Methods

The methodological challenge is also daunting but is not unusual. The study of service-learning needs to increase the robustness of study design, whether using quantitative, qualitative, or mixed method approaches. Currently, too few studies use control groups, too few are longitudinal in nature, and too few validate results through triangulation. Very few studies use the same data collection instruments and fewer still are replicated so that results are confirmed. Random assignment is extremely rare, and, as several authors in this volume point out, service-learning practitioners often inadvertently undermine study designs because they seemingly cannot bear to withhold service-learning from control groups. The issue of methodology is also addressed by several authors who offer descriptions and insight into the use of multiple ways of knowing. Several discuss the value of the teacher-as-researcher and action research approaches and variants such as portraiture. These methods often provide greater insight into the thinking and processes by which service-learning is implemented and offer rich texture to help readers understand the phenomenon. However, these approaches also have drawbacks, and authors describe the ways in which research designs using these approaches can avoid common pitfalls associated with their use.

Interpretation of Results

The fourth challenge, data interpretation, has some aspects that are relatively unique to service-learning perhaps because of its nature as a field of study. Challenges associated with data interpretation include the tendencies to overclaim and/or overgeneralize, ignore alternative explanations for outcomes, overanalyze data and, conversely, underanalyze data. In addition, some researchers argue that service-learning can only be understood as an individualistic phenomenon because it is perceived and experienced so differently by the individual having the experience. This stance argues for a very different interpretation of data. Conversely, interactive effects are too often underanalyzed. Researchers often do not examine covariance and the nested nature of the activity that occurs.

The overclaiming problem is the most insidious since it undermines the credibility of the field. Overclaiming tends to occur when researchers or respondents appear to be saying that service-learning does it all and is superior to any school-based intervention. This advocacy position may be important for the field, but it has little place in research. The authors in this volume discuss these interpretation challenges in detail.

Dissemination

The fifth challenge, dissemination, is common among relatively young fields of study. Because service-learning is defined generally as an approach, philosophy, pedagogy, or program and not as a content specific field, it has no natural home for research. Although the good news is that service-learning can be legitimately claimed as a field of study for many academic disciplines, having no single area for affiliation, dissemination, and publication inhibits the ability to build the body of knowledge. There is no single venue where researchers gather to share research, build foundations, and replicate good studies. The recent development of the annual International K–H Service-Learning Research Conferences begins to address this problem. However, even though there is a quarterly journal (*The Michigan Journal of Community Service Learning*) devoted to service-learning in higher education, there is still no well-known peer-reviewed monthly journal that primarily addresses research in service-learning at all grade levels and for all academic subject areas. The lack of relatively easy access to multiple dissemination vehicles with strong credibility may keep some young scholars who are seeking tenure and promotion from studying service-learning and clearly keeps researchers from replicating many studies and validating results.

The sixth challenge is the use of research for improving service-learning practice. Researchers and practitioners often have difficulty achieving two-way communication. On the research side, too often results are published using sophisticated research jargon that is not easily accessed or decoded by practitioners. Researchers do not often listen to practitioners with regard to their needs for information, but instead, select something that is of interest to their funders or the researchers themselves. On the practitioner side, too often access is restricted or study designs are undermined, through lack of candor, cooperation, or understanding. Practitioners sometimes do not see the need for research because they are "true believers" and are concerned that research will undermine their ability to do their work. On the other hand, practitioners demand that research quickly prove the efficacy of service-learning practice. Clearly effective communication between the research community and the practitioner community has strong benefits to each, particularly in helping to improve practice. This challenge, however, requires mutual understanding and respect, and multiple formal and informal ways to communicate, particularly for the purpose of sharing priority needs for information and results.

The final challenge is funding. Service-learning research is relatively unique in that the field was built with little research, and its history is that the research that exists was conducted with little or no funding, with foundation funding, or as program evaluations. There are few funders that have service-learning as part of their funding agendas. Given the call for accountability in education in combination with the prevalence of use of service-learning in K–12 schools and higher education, this lack of research funding is surprising. Yet at the time of this writing, neither the Corporation for National and Community Service nor the U.S. Department of Education spent any funds on service-learning research. Without sufficient funding, none of the necessary research, especially the longitudinal experimental studies with random assignment, is likely to be accomplished.

CONTENTS OF THE VOLUME

In the first chapter, Howard frames many of the important issues that emerge when studying service-learning. By way of introduction, he discusses the nature of service-learning, provides a brief history of service-learning research and the early results of research performed in the 1980s and 1990s, the rationale for conducting research in service-learning, and common research problems. He calls for a new research paradigm and poses several questions to help guide future research.

In chapter 2, Furco expands upon Howard's introduction by analyzing the research issues that emerge when there are varying service-learning definitions and program designs being utilized in the field. Furco shows that because service-learning definitions and program designs are so idiosyncratic, results of studies are often difficult to generalize. He offers multiple suggestions for improving the study of service-learning and urges researchers to develop a more comprehensive approach that addresses the broad range of outcomes and appropriate units of analysis. Furco's proposed "grand-design approach" addresses the research challenges by combining the best available research methods, instruments, and data collection and analysis techniques into one large design that employs the meta-matrix as a framework for analysis.

In chapter 3, Waldstein addresses epistemology and service-learning research. He discusses the need for a better understanding of the methodological vocabulary for the research on service-learning, both within the contexts of disciplinary and multidisciplinary research, and urges researchers neither to split hairs nor leave terms undefined. In addition, he provides an explanation of the roots of empiricism and the scientific method and shows their relevance to current service-learning research. Finally, he strongly recommends researchers to base their studies of service-learning on a stronger theoretical base.

Bradley provides insight into two sets of theories that are especially promising as guides for service-learning research and evaluation in chapter 4. Bradley examines three theories of human development and two learning theories that could be used, either individually or in combination, to design and evaluate the effectiveness of service-learning programs. The developmental theories by Erikson, Chickering, Selman, Kohlberg, Gilligan, and Perry, and the learning theories of Jung and Gardner are compared. These theories are also discussed in terms of their appropriateness for use in planning service-learning activities.

In chapter 5, Waterman tackles the thorny issues regarding the selection of variables for study in the context of diversity of possible student outcomes of service-learning. Waterman makes a compelling argument that no student experiences service-learning in exactly the same way due to the confluence of individual personalities and histories, actual service experiences, and other confounding, idiosyncratic variables. He discusses challenges associated with the selection of outcome variables for study and the selection of research instruments to measure the variables selected, and strongly recommends the use of continuous rating scales and other techniques that address the student as the unit of analysis.

Fertman and Yugar examine how to create and utilize databases on service-learning in chapter 6. They provide examples from their work in the state of Pennsylvania and describe a rich array of resources available for service-learning researchers and evaluators who wish to conduct secondary research.

In chapter 7, Hecht discusses the issues of research design and statistical analysis that emerge when studying the impact of service-learning on student participants. She describes the limitations of current empirical approaches and specific challenges associated with data analysis. She offers many recommendations regarding the selection of service-learning programs to study, research and evaluation designs, the use of constructs and assessments, and approaches to data analyses. Bailis and Melchior in chapter 8 discuss the practical side of conducting large-scale, multisite research and evaluation. Drawing from their experiences in conducting 10 national studies, Bailis and Melchior make a cogent argument for involving those to be studied in evaluation decisions at every stage of the study. They describe what could go wrong and how to solve emerging problems from the perspective of those who have experienced many research challenges. Many of these challenges were best addressed using the researchers' participatory approaches.

In chapter 9, Shumer discusses the potential utility of service-learning self-assessments. He describes the ways in which his service-learning self-assessment tool was developed, and stresses the need for input by service-learning researchers and practitioners for the instrument to have validity. The development process involved multiple iterations, each of which served to improve the instrument. The self-assessment tool can be used as an important method for the improvement of service-learning practice.

Chapter 10 presents Root's discussion of teacher research in service-learning. Root suggests that teachers can provide great insight into the variables that may mediate participants' understandings of their service-learning experiences. Root discusses the value of teacher research and argues that the very nature of service-learning with its emphasis on voice and democracy, predicates the inclusion of teachers as valued contributors. She provides a matrix that explains the knowledge domains in which teacher research on service-learning can contribute, and gives an example from a project conducted in Michigan in the early 1990s.

Anderson discusses students as service-learning researchers in chapter 11. Reflecting on the experiences of students in Seattle University's Master in Teaching (MIT) Program, Anderson demonstrates the type of learning that can occur when students and teachers engage in action research. Case studies are presented, along with an analysis of the benefits and pitfalls of the approach.

Seven suggestions are provided to faculty who wish to undertake the student-as-researcher approach.

In chapter 12, the final chapter, Hill, Pickeral, and Duckenfield explore an emergent form of research called portraiture. These authors explain the characteristics of portraiture and how it differs from other forms of qualitative research, particularly with regard to the unabashed advocacy/caring stance and a technique called *outside in* writing wherein portraiture writers strive to make context come alive to the reader through extensive use of imagery. They present portions of four portraitures from the Service-Learning 2000 projects in which they have worked. The authors feel that the use of portraiture is one important new technique for improving service-learning practice since it provides deep insight into activities and outcomes.

ACKNOWLEDGMENTS

I would like to extend appreciation to Mary Ann Strassner for her work in helping to edit, proofread, and format this volume and to Christine Kwak of the W. K. Kellogg Foundation for her unending support. This volume was in development for many years. The chapter authors' dedication, passion, and willingness to persist helped to make this project a reality.

The majority of the chapters in this volume originated in discussions held at the 1996 National Service-Learning Conference in Detroit, Michigan. The National Service-Learning Conference is sponsored annually by the National Youth Leadership Council. The co-editors wish to express their appreciation to James C. Kielsmeier, NYLC President, and to the staff of NYLC, for their continuing efforts to promote research and scholarship on service-learning. Through their pioneering efforts, evaluation research has become an integral part of the development and advocacy of service-learning pedagogies.

—S.H.B.

REFERENCES

Anderson, J., Swick, K., & Yff, J. (2001). *Service-learning in teacher education.* Washington, DC: AACTE ERIC.

Billig, S. H. (May, 2000). Research on K–12 school-based service-learning: The evidence builds. *Phi Delta Kappan, 81*(9), 658–664.

Conrad, D., & Hedin, D. (1991, June). School-based community service: What we know from research and theory. *Phi Delta Kappan,* 743–749.

Eyler, J., & Giles, D. E., Jr. (1999). *Where's the learning in service-learning?* San Francisco: Jossey-Bass.

Eyler, J. S., Giles, D. E., Jr., Stenson, C. M., & Gray, C. J. (2001). At a glance: What we know about the effects of service-learning on students, faculty, institutions, and communities, 1993–2001 (3rd ed.). Washington, DC: Corporation for National

Service, Learn and Serve America and Scotts Valley, CA: National Service-Learning Clearinghouse.

Furco, A. (2002). Is service-learning really better than community service? A study of high school service program outcomes. In A. Furco & S. H. Billig (Eds.), *Service-learning: The essence of the pedagogy,* (Vol. 1, *Advances in service-learning research*, pp. 23–50). Greenwich, CT: Information Age.

Furco, A., & Billig, S. H. (Eds.). (2002). *Service-learning: The essence of the pedagogy,* (Vol. 1, *Advances in service-learning research*). Greenwich, CT: Information Age.

Genzer, D. (1998). *Community service and service-learning initiatives in independent schools.* Washington, DC: National Association of Independent Schools.

Melchior, A. (1999). *Summary report: National Evaluation of Learn and Serve America.* Waltham, MA: Brandeis University, Center for Human Resources.

National Center for Education Statistics. (1999). National Household Education Survey. Washington, DC: Author.

Waterman, A. (Ed.). (1997). *Service-learning: Applications from the research.* Mahwah, NJ: Lawrence Erlbaum Associates.

Service-Learning Research: Foundational Issues

Jeffrey Howard
University of Michigan

Many signs point to the expansion of service-learning as an educational innovation in contemporary American schools and colleges (see list in Howard, 2001, p. 5). Instructors, from elementary schools to graduate and professional schools, are turning to the community as a laboratory to strengthen students' citizenship preparation and academic learning. With student partners, communities are solving individual and community-wide resource and advocacy problems. At the same time, researchers have been studying the effects of this pedagogical model on the multiple constituencies of service-learning—students, instructors, educational institutions, and communities—and have been publishing their findings.

Some recent markers lend credibility to this burgeoning interest in service-learning. In 1984, the Campus Outreach Opportunity League was formed to encourage student leadership in community service on college campuses across the nation. In 1985, Campus Compact was established as a national organization with a similar mission and has grown to more than 750 college and university presidents whose membership implicitly declared their commitment to involving students in community work at their respective colleges. In 1990, the National Youth Leadership Council began offering an annual national conference on K–12 service-learning. In 1994, the peer-reviewed *Michigan Journal of Community Service Learning* began to publish articles devoted to research, theory, pedagogy, and practice of service-learning. In that same year, a special issue of the *Journal of Adolescence* (1994) was devoted to service-learning, followed by *Education and Urban Society,* (1994) also devoting an entire issue to service-learning. In 1995 Campus Compact's Invisible College held its first National Gathering on service-learning in higher education. In 1997, a series of 18 monographs devoted to service-learning in the academic disciplines was spawned by the American Association of Higher Education. Today, students of all ages are participating in service-learning at their schools and colleges. The National Center for Education Statistics estimates that more than half of all public high schools engage in some form of service-learning. Increased participation rates, national organization memberships, and scholarly publications reflect the growth of service-learning in America today.

As the field of service-learning continues to flourish, it is essential to develop a knowledge base for, and evidence of, the outcomes and impacts of service-learning. Every field and every educational innovation is bolstered by research and evaluation.

THE NATURE OF SERVICE-LEARNING

What exactly is service-learning? Although there has been a plethora of interest in and development of service-learning opportunities across the country in the last decade, there is, nevertheless, a great deal of misinterpretation about it. Jane Kendall's (1990) introduction to the three-volume set, *Combining Service and Learning: A Resource Book for Community and Public Service*, provided more than 140 terms used in the literature to describe and define activities that involve service and learning. Although it is beyond the scope of this chapter to review or evaluate existing definitions, it is imperative to be clear about how the authors in this book understand the practice of service-learning.

There is broad-based agreement that service-learning is a form of the broader model of experiential education, with community service as the fulcrum. There is general agreement that what distinguishes service-learning from other experiential education efforts, such as internships, practica, simulations, and the like, is its focus on community efforts, which makes a difference for individuals in the community and for students' commitment to the general welfare of society.

Beyond that, there is considerable disparity in people's understanding about this pedagogy. Is service-learning any combination of community service and some kind of learning or does it entail more? Real examples can inform the search for clarity. For example, week-long alternative spring-break programs invariably involve students in daytime service to the community and in evening reflection. College courses across academic departments at universities around the nation involve students in service to the community as a requirement or option. Are these examples of service-learning?

To reduce the confusion about the conceptualization of service-learning, it has become useful to make a distinction between co-curricular service-learning and academic service-learning. The aforementioned alternative spring break trip exemplifies co-curricular service-learning, that is the combining of service and learning outside the formal school curriculum. In this prototype, the student learning that results from the community service is outside what is traditionally thought of as the province of the academy. In contrast, academic service-learning is bound to the curriculum, so that the service is connected to an academic course. The learning in the community and the learning in the classroom are complementary.

Although there is growing agreement about this conceptualization, there remains a wide range of academic service-learning practice. Although all service-learning courses require community service, some instructors intentionally integrate the learning from the community with the learning in the classroom, whereas others do not. The latter practice is a compromised interpretation of academic service-learning, largely because the community service and academic learning of the course function as parallel, rather than integrated, activities. High quality, academic service-learning initiatives in which the learning informs the service and the service informs the learning create a reciprocal and synergistic relationship between the two.

Perhaps the best way to think about academic service-learning is to identify its necessary defining or essential features (Howard, 2001). A review of definitions and conceptualizations finds three essential elements of service-learning: First, there is a service provided in the community, one that responds to a need that originates in the community (Honnet & Poulson, 1989); second, students' academic learning is strengthened (Howard, 1993); and third, students' commitment to civic participation, active democratic citizenship, and/or social responsibility is advanced (Barber, 1992).

Having identified these three essential elements, it becomes apparent that service-learning stands in stark contrast to more traditional forms of pedagogy (Howard, 1998). It is different from traditional pedagogy in many ways, including the role of the student, the role of the instructor, the kind of learning that is valued, and the emphasis on social rather than individual responsibility. This non-traditional nature of service-learning makes not only the practice of service-learning, but also the study of service-learning, that much more subtle and complex.

A BRIEF HISTORY OF SERVICE-LEARNING RESEARCH

A range of positive outcomes has been attributed to service-learning, including gains in self-esteem, career knowledge, social responsibility, and academic performance (see Eyler, Giles, & Gray, 1999, for an annotated review for higher education; Billig, 2000, for a review of K–12 outcomes). The last five years in particular have seen a substantial increase in research on service-learning.

Years ago, much of the data about outcomes, particularly student outcomes, was anecdotal. Anecdotes would come from students, teachers, administrators, and community members, and these respondents served as the sole sources of data. However, in research circles, anecdotal evidence on its own is considered inherently subjective and subject to severe threats to validity and reliability.

In the 1980s, researchers primarily studied outcomes from community service for pre-college students. Conrad and Hedin (1982, 1989, 1991), the most cited of the pioneering researchers, found that students engaged in community service demonstrated gains in social and personal responsibility as well as in academic performance. Newmann and Rutter (1983), Calabrese and Schumer (1986), and others found additional positive results from their studies of student participation in the community.

In 1991, the *Research Agenda for Combining Service and Learning in the 1990s* (Giles, Honnet, & Migliore, 1991) ignited service-learning research, primarily the study of single courses at the higher education level (see e.g., Boss, 1994; Cohen & Kinsey, 1994; Kendrick, 1997; Mabry, 1998; Markus, Howard, & King, 1993; Osborne, Hammerich, & Hensley, 1998; Vogelgesang & Astin, 2000). Additionally, the Corporation for National Service and Community Service and its predecessor, the Commission on National and Community Service, began multisite evaluations of the programs they were funding (Gray et al., 1999; Melchior, 1999). This flurry of research was followed by a top ten set of questions in academic service-learning (Giles & Eyler, 1998); a comprehensive, national study (Eyler & Giles, 1999); and the development of a national strategic platform for service-learning research (Howard, Gelmon, & Giles, 2001).

KNOWLEDGE FROM PAST STUDY ABOUT SERVICE-LEARNING

Although a comprehensive literature review is beyond the scope of this chapter, a few snapshots of recent research may be illustrative. Regarding subject matter learning, most studies have used student self-reports, that, although assailable, have demonstrated some positive correlations between the use of service-learning and students' acquisition of academic knowledge and skills (Cohen & Kinsey, 1994; Eyler & Giles, 1997, 1999; Gray et al., 1999; Markus et al., 1993). Research has also clearly demonstrated that service-learning has a strong effect on students' personal development, including self-esteem, confidence in political and social skills, and building relationships with others (Eyler & Giles, 1997, 1999; Kendrick, 1996). Service-learning research also demonstrated that participating students' had an increased sense of social responsibility, expressed as feeling connected to their community. Students were found to have greater racial tolerance, value the role of service in communities, and perceive communities as having capacity for solving their problems (Eyler & Giles, 1997 1999; Gray et al., 1999, Kendrick, 1996; Markus et al., 1993; Myers-Lipton, 1996). There is also some evidence that service-learning positively affects cognitive moral development, which is related to complexity of thinking about social issues (Boss, 1994).

Eyler and Giles (1999) demonstrated that certain service-learning program characteristics, including quality of the service placement, structured reflection opportunities, and intensity and duration of the community service component, can affect the student outcomes. Finally, a small number of studies has shown that faculty's primary motivation for using service-learning is related to pedagogical improvement (Hammond, 1994), that institutional support facilitates utilization (Holland, 1997; Stanton, 1994), and that, in most cases, resistance is related to problems with implementation (Driscoll, Holland, Gelmon, & Kerrigan, 1996). To date, unfortunately and ironically, researchers have only scratched the surface about the impact of students' service on local communities (Cruz & Giles, 2000).

WHY CONDUCT SERVICE-LEARNING RESEARCH?

The inevitable question related to service-learning research is, "Why conduct research about this educational practice?" Three purposes are typically cited for conducting research around service-learning, most of which are pertinent to any educational innovation.

The most important reason to conduct research is to improve practice. Researchers are in a position to collect and analyze data that can help shape both existing and new service-learning courses and initiatives. Examples of practice questions that research can answer include: What kinds of service-learning placements are developmentally most appropriate for K–12 and college students? What are the best reflection methods for strengthening academic learning? What are the best ways to crystallize students' lifelong commitment to civic participation? Whereas evaluation can be helpful in answering these questions for specific programs, research can provide generalizable conclusions that can inform the development and implementation of all service-learning courses and initiatives. Research can determine if service-learning benefits students and communities, in what ways, under what conditions, and for how long.

A second reason that is frequently cited for conducting research about service-learning is to develop a knowledge base about this educational practice. A knowledge base not only contributes to the improvement of practice, but it also confers a perception of scholarliness and therefore has a legitimizing function. A knowledge base commands respect and is more likely to draw others to it, either as practitioners or researchers.

A third reason for conducting service-learning research is advocacy. Largely due to widespread confusion of academic service-learning with voluntarism and community service, the latter of which is generally perceived as outside the academy's domain, academic service-learning seeks legitimacy in the academy. Research, as the currency of the realm in higher education, enables advocates to provide acceptable forms of evidence about service-learning's benefits. Positive outcomes from a well conducted research study can turn skeptics into champions.

THE PROBLEMS FOR RESEARCH
ABOUT SERVICE-LEARNING

Most studies of service-learning, as well as those of any educational innovation, attempt to discern cause and effect (i.e., whether a treatment, in this case service-learning, leads to changes, however that may be defined, and if so, to what degree). The methodology usually employed for such experimental or quasi-experimental studies is the treatment/control group design. A simplified description of this traditional methodology lays the groundwork for identifying the limitations of this design for service-learning research.

In this experimental research methodology, the treatment group is subjected to an intervention that is absent or withheld from the control group. All members of the treatment group receive the same treatment. The use of random selection maximizes the chances that the groups are equivalent at the beginning of the process, vis-à-vis extraneous factors that may influence outcomes, and minimizes the chances that any changes can be attributable to the differences in the groups. The control group can then be used as a benchmark for determining whether the treatment has led to change, and if so, by how much. If two groups start out as comparable on potentially influencing factors (e.g., gender, race, academic achievement), and if the post-tests reveal differences between the treatment and control groups in favor of the former, then one can conclude with some degree of confidence that the differences may be attributable to the treatment.

According to social science research standards, this traditional research design is sound. Service-learning as a subject of study, however, poses multiple challenges for researchers who would like to undertake this approach to the research. The most significant threat is that this research design relies on equal treatment across individuals in the treatment group, and in service-learning there are many variables beyond the control of the researcher that can compromise this need for treatment equalization. Whereas a study about a new classroom intervention purported to encourage student learning collaboration could introduce some control because the classroom intervention can be planned by the researcher, service-learning students are involved in community experiences that are sometimes beyond the control of the researcher.

For example, in his study on students' perceptions of power and efficacy as a result of participation in service-learning, Miller (1997) said, "Reviewing the findings on differential student characteristics and experiences not only deepens our understanding of the students' changed perception of the power of people, but also significantly supports the importance of attending to these variables as mediators of service-learning outcomes" (p. 19). He goes on to say, "In the research area, this study reinforces the need to continue to empirically evaluate these experiences in light of their vast complexity," and that "whole group comparisons, across diverse sets of students and experiences, are likely to obscure important impacts on particular students, and lead to misunderstandings of the service-learning enterprise" (p. 20). Because the experimental research design necessitates a constancy of experience within the treatment group, and because this is beyond the control of the service-learning researcher, it is problematic to generalize cause and effect.

In addition to the methodological problem of lack of control over students' community-based experiences, other challenges to service-learning research abound. For example, most past studies have focused on a limited number of student outcomes. One study might look at academic issues as the dependent variable, while another may look at personal development issues. Furco (1994), for example, has found there are six educational domains that past studies have shown to be positively correlated with participation in service-learning: academic, career, social, personal, ethical, and civic responsibility. But most studies have not attempted such a comprehensive assessment covering all domains. Therefore, the limited selection of outcomes variables in past research has short-changed the study of service-learning.

Another confounding issue for service-learning research is that most past studies have examined very specific courses or programs. This creates questions about generalizability. Even one of the most widely cited service-learning studies (Markus et al., 1993) has questionable generalizability. In that study, students in a political science class at a large, Midwestern public university were divided into two groups, using random selection: one that was required to perform 20 hours of community service related to the course of study and one that was required to do a time-comparable library research assignment. The students in the community service group reported greater academic gains, received higher grades, and demonstrated stronger social responsibility gains from the beginning to the end of the class than their library research counterparts. The degree to which researchers can generalize findings from this study is not clear. Do the results generalize to all political science classes, or is there something special about the study of Contemporary Political Issues that enables community service to serve a strong academic and social responsibility function? Do the study results generalize to other academic disciplines, such as history or engineering, or were the results influenced by the compatibility of community service with the study of political science? Perhaps it worked with this set of instructors, or this set of students at a large public university, but might not work with other instructors, students, or at other kinds of higher education institutions. It is difficult to generalize from this study due to the limitations of academic discipline, instructor, student, and institution samples. This study's weak generalizability is common to many past studies of service-learning.

Other problems for service-learning research are discussed in this volume. These include the lack of agreement on a definition of service-learning; the inherent variability among courses and initiatives; the lack of representative sampling of programs; problems with sample selection, randomization, and control groups; failure to investigate impacts subsequent to the service-learning experience; and inconsistent findings across studies for some of the dependent variables.

Beyond the idiosyncratic issues, service-learning research suffers from many of the same limitations as other educational research. For example, naturally occurring conditions, such as length of the semester; variability in the students' personal interests, abilities, and values; and variability in the site placements (individual vs. group activity, high vs. low intensity of the community work, etc.), can each have a dramatic effect on outcomes, thereby limiting the generalizability of any single-site study.

CALL FOR NEW RESEARCH PARADIGMS

Given the problems with, and limitations of, past studies and the use of traditional research methods to study service-learning, the authors in this book raise the question about appropriate research methodology for the study of this educational practice. Some have argued that the use of traditional quantitative methods alone underachieves in its discernment of service-learning outcomes; that pencil-and-paper measures are insufficient for capturing the depth and subtlety of outcomes from service-learning experiences (Eyler, 2000).

Some researchers have insisted that quantitative methods should be supplemented with qualitative efforts (Bringle & Hatcher, 2000), such as personal interviews or focus groups, in order to adequately study service-learning. Others have gone further, arguing that the inherent nature of service-learning challenges traditional social science research. They assert that service-learning values learning beyond the classroom and ways of knowing that go beyond textbook and teacher expertise, and that the study of service-learning must use methodologies that are epistemologically consistent with its subjectivistic orientation (see, Liu, 1995; Palmer, 1987; Shumer, 2000).

UNANSWERED QUESTIONS ABOUT
THE STUDY OF SERVICE-LEARNING

What directions should future efforts take in studying service-learning? Researchers currently know the most about the effects of service-learning on students, a bit less about service-learning's effect on faculty, less still about its effect on schools, colleges, and universities, and virtually nothing about the effects of students' service-learning efforts on communities and community members (Giles & Cruz, 2000). Furthermore, researchers know a fair amount about the effects of service-learning on students during their period of participation, but much less about the long-term impacts of participation. Do students become lifelong civic participants as a result of their involvement in service-learning? How else are they influenced over the long run?

Beyond these kinds of specific research questions, what are the unanswered questions about the study of service-learning? One question has to do with the relationship between K–12 and higher education. Service-learning has penetrated both sets of institutions, and therefore, has begged the question about the relationship between these two sets of institutions, especially around their service-learning initiatives. Further, can service-learning function as a catalyst for discussions about creating seamlessness between K–12 and post-secondary education?

Another matter pertinent to service-learning research has to do with ensuring the continuation of research in this field. If researchers seek to improve practice, build the knowledge base, and extend the capacity to advocate, then it is important to cultivate the base of new researchers and to encourage further work by current researchers. At least three contributing strategies have been identified. First, cognitive and learning scientists must be enlisted to strengthen the direction of current efforts (Eyler, 2000). Second, because practitioners far outnumber researchers in the service-learning community, one strategy would be to build the capacity of practitioners for conducting research (Stanton, 2000). This might be accomplished, for example, via regional technical assistance centers (Furco, 2000). Third, current researchers' practice can be encouraged by making available funding opportunities and publication outlets (Furco, 2000). If research is to continue to flourish, then intentional efforts must be made to build capacity.

Another issue has to do with insuring that the findings of research and evaluation studies are disseminated widely. Because improvement of practice and strengthening of advocacy are primary reasons for conducting research, it is imperative that findings be disseminated throughout the service-learning community, both on campuses and in K–12 schools, as well as in local communities. When the dissemination of research or evaluation has only a limited reach, the field of service-learning suffers. How can results from research and evaluation studies be certain to be disseminated? Perhaps an accessible clearinghouse could serve as a repository for all research pertinent to service-learning (Furco, 2000).

Finally, how can communities contribute to the generation of knowledge about service-learning? This is a call for co-generative scholarship. After all, since the community is involved in the practice of service-learning, shouldn't the community play a role in the development of knowledge about service-learning? Of course, this too, like the pedagogy of service-learning, would be nontraditional, and a stretch for those who argue that only those credentialized can conduct quality research.

As interest in service-learning continues, there is likely to be a concomitant demand in understanding its potential impact on students, teachers, schools and colleges, and communities. More research is needed to understand the power of service-learning.

REFERENCES

Barber, B. (1992). *An aristocracy of everyone.* New York: Ballantine Books.
Billig, S. H. (2000, May). Research on K–12 school-based service-learning: The evidence builds. *Phi Delta Kappan, 81*(9), 658–664.
Boss, J. (1994). The effect of community service work on the moral development of college ethics students. *Journal of Moral Education, 23*(2), 183–198.
Bringle, R. G., & Hatcher, J. A. (2000). Meaningful measurement of theory-based service-learning outcomes: Making the case with quantitative research. *Michigan Journal of Community Service Learning,* Special Issue 2000, 68–75.
Calabrese, R. L., & Schumer, H. (1986). The effects of service activities on adolescent alienation. *Adolescence, 21*(83), 675–687.

Cohen, J., & Kinsey, D. (1994). 'Doing good' and scholarship: A service-learning study. *Journalism Educator, 48*(4), 4–14.

Conrad, D., & Hedin, D. (1982). The impact of experiential education on adolescent development. *Child and Youth Services, 4*(3/4), 57–76.

Conrad, D., & Hedin, D. (1989, December). *High school community service: A review of research and programs.* Madison, WI: University of Wisconsin, National Center on Effective Secondary Schools.

Conrad, D., & Hedin, D. (1991). School-based community service. What we know from research and theory. *Phi Delta Kappan, 72*(10), 743–749.

Cruz, N., & Giles, D. E., Jr. (2000). Where's the community in service-learning research? *Michigan Journal of Community Service Learning,* Special Issue 2000, 28–34.

Driscoll, A., Holland, B., Gelmon, S., & Kerrigan, S. (1996). An assessment model for service-learning: Comprehensive case studies of impact on faculty, students, community, and institution. *Michigan Journal of Community Service Learning, 3,* 66–71.

Eyler, J. (2000). What do we most need to know about the impact of service-learning on student learning? *Michigan Journal of Community Service Learning,* Special Issue 2000, 11–17.

Eyler, J., & Giles, D. E., Jr. (1997). The impact of service-learning on college students. *Michigan Journal of Community Service Learning, 4,* 5–15.

Eyler, J., & Giles, D. E., Jr. (1999). *Where's the learning in service-learning?* San Francisco: Jossey-Bass.

Eyler, J., Giles, D. E., Jr., & Gray, C. (1999). *At a glance: What we know about the effects of service-learning on students, faculty, institutions, and communities, 1993-1999.* Nashville, TN: Vanderbilt University.

Eyler, J., Giles, D. E., Jr., & Schmiede, A. (1996). *A practitioners' guide to reflection in service-learning: Student voices and reflections.* Nashville, TN: Vanderbilt University.

Furco, A. (1994). A conceptual framework for the institutionalization of youth service programs in primary and secondary education. *Journal of Adolescence, 17,* 395–309.

Furco, A. (2000). Establishing a National Center for Research to systematize the study of service-learning. *Michigan Journal of Community Service Learning,* Special Issue 2000, 134.

Giles, D., Honnet, E. P., Migliore, S. (Eds.). (1991). Research agenda for combining service and learning in the 1990s. Raleigh, NC: National Society for Internships and Experiential Education.

Giles, D. E., Jr., & Eyler, J. (1998). A service-learning research agenda for the next five years. In R. A. Rhoads & J. Howard (Eds.), *Academic service learning: A pedagogy of action and reflection: New directions for teaching and learning #73* (pp. 65–72). San Francisco: Jossey-Bass.

Gray, M., Ondaatje, E., Fricker, R., Geschwind, S., Goldman, C., Kaganoff, T., Robyn, A., Sundt, M., Vogelgesang, L., & Klein, S. (1999). *Combining service and learning in higher education: Evaluation of the Learn and Serve America, Higher Education program.* Washington, DC: Rand.

Hammond, C. (1994). Integrating service and academic study: Faculty motivation and satisfaction in Michigan higher education. *Michigan Journal of Community Service Learning, 1*(1), 21–28.

Holland, B. (1997). Analyzing institutional commitment to service: A model of key organizational factors. *Michigan Journal of Community Service Learning, 4,* 30–41.

Honnet, E. P., & Poulson, S. J. (1989). *Principles of good practice for combining service and learning*. (Wingspread Special Report). Racine, WI: The Johnson Foundation.

Howard, J. (1993). Community service learning in the curriculum. In J. Howard (Ed.), *Praxis 1: A faculty case on community service learning* (pp. 3–12). Ann Arbor, MI: OCSL Press.

Howard, J. (1998). Academic service learning: A counternormative pedagogy. In R. A. Rhoads & J. Howard (Eds.), *Academic service learning: A pedagogy of action and reflection, New directions for teaching and learning #73* (pp. 21–30). San Francisco: Jossey-Bass.

Howard, J. (2001). Service-learning course design workbook. Ann Arbor, MI: OCSL Press.

Howard, J., Gelmon, S., & Giles, D. (2000). From yesterday to tomorrow: Strategic directions for service-learning research. *Michigan Journal of Community Service Learning*, Special Issue 2000, 5–10.

Kendall, J. (1990). Combining service and learning: An introduction. In J. Kendall & Associates (Eds.), *Combining service and learning: A resource book for community and public service*, (Vol. 1, pp. 1–36). Raleigh, NC: National Society for Internships and Experiential Education.

Kendrick, R. (1996). Outcomes of service-learning in an Introduction to Sociology course. *Michigan Journal of Community Service Learning, 3*, 72–81.

Liu, G. (1995). Knowledge, foundations, and discourse: Philosophical support for service-Learning. *Michigan Journal of Community Service Learning, 2*, 5–18.

Mabry, B. (1998). Pedagogical variations in service-learning and student outcomes: How time, contact, and reflection matter. *Michigan Journal of Community Service Learning, 5*, 32–47.

Markus, G., Howard, J., & King, D. (1993). Integrating community service and classroom instruction enhances learning: Results from an experiment. *Educational Evaluation and Policy Analysis, 15*(4), 410–419.

Melchior, A. (1999). Summary report: National evaluation of Learn and Serve America. Waltham, MA: Brandeis University , Center for Human Resources.

Miller, J. (1997). The impact of service-learning experiences on students' sense of power. *Michigan Journal of Community Service Learning, 4*, 16–21.

Myers-Lipton, S. (1996). Effect of a comprehensive service-learning program on college students' level of modern racism. *Michigan Journal of Community Service Learning, 3*, 44–54.

Newmann, F. M., & Rutter, R. A. (1983). *The effects of high school community service programs on students' social development*. Final report to the National Institute of Education. Madison, WI: Wisconsin Center for Educational Research.

Osborne, R., Hammerich, S., & Hensley, C. (1998). Student effects of service-learning: Tracking change across a semester. *Michigan Journal of Community Service Learning, 5*, 5–13.

Palmer, P. (1990). Community, conflict, and ways of knowing. In J. Kendall & Associates (Eds.), *Combining service and learning: Resource book for community and public service* (Vol. 1, pp. 105–113). Raleigh, NC: National Society for Internships and Experiential Education.

Shumer, R. (2000). Science or storytelling. How should we conduct and report service-learning research? *Michigan Journal of Community Service Learning*, Special Issue 2000, 76–83.

Stanton, T. (1994). The experience of faculty participants in an instructional development seminar on service-learning. *Michigan Journal of Community Service Learning, 1*(1), 7–20.

Stanton, T. (2000). Bringing reciprocity to service-learning research and practice. *Michigan Journal of Community Service Learning,* Special Issue 2000, 119–123.

Vogelgesang, L., & Astin, A. (2000). Comparing the effects of community service and service-learning. *Michigan Journal of Community Service Learning, 7,* 25–34.

2

Issues of Definition and Program Diversity in the Study of Service-Learning

Andrew Furco
University of California, Berkeley

One of the greatest challenges in the study of service-learning is the absence of a common, universally accepted definition for the term. The overarching educational goals of service-learning are subject to numerous interpretations. The programmatic features of service-learning (e.g., duration of the service experience, degree of student choice, etc.) vary widely among classrooms, and sometimes across service-learning experiences within classrooms. All service-learning activities, regardless of their overall design and programmatic goals, involve a complex interaction of students, service activities, curricular content, and learning outcomes. What results are highly idiosyncratic, situational experiences for which there is minimal predictability of how each service-learning experience will unfold. Indeed, no two service-learning activities are alike.

Such idiosyncrasy and unpredictability has significant implications for how one should approach the study of service-learning. Because of a high degree of program diversity, it is often difficult to generalize the findings from a service-learning investigation beyond the particular programs studied. In addition, because service-learning is an inherently complex enterprise, traditional research designs and methodologies cannot easily capture all the aspects of the service-learning experience. Most of the more than 100 published studies of service-learning have been unable to make definitive statements about the impacts of service-learning on students, teachers, schools, and communities.

CHALLENGES IN THE STUDY OF SERVICE-LEARNING

The lack of an existing, universal definition for service-learning, coupled with service-learning's idiosyncratic nature, brings severe limitations to studies of service-learning. This section explores some of these limitations and the particular challenges they pose to the study of service-learning.

13

Definition of Service-Learning

Although there have been many attempts to define service-learning in specific terms, there is no one universally accepted definition for service-learning. Over the last 10 years, at least 200 different definitions of service-learning have been published, casting service-learning as an experience, a program, a pedagogy, and a philosophy (Jacoby & Associates, 1996). To complicate matters, various terms such as *community service, community volunteer learning, community-based learning, service-learning internship*, among others, often are used interchangeably with *service-learning*. Although the differences in these terms initially may appear to be simply semantics, some practitioners and researchers have sought to make clear distinctions among these and other experiential education terms (Schine, 1997; Wade 1997). In particular, differences among various forms of experiential education, especially with regard to who benefits from the experience and what outcomes the various forms of experiential education foster, have been noted (Furco, 1996).

In its earliest manifestation, service-learning was described as a community-based *internship* experience in which students explored careers in nonprofit agencies (Hamilton, 1989). Conrad and Hedin (1989), whose early research played a significant role in raising the visibility of service-learning, described service-learning as a community service program that includes a formalized reflection component. More recent descriptions have focused on depicting service-learning as a *pedagogy*. Jacoby and Associates (1997) wrote, "As a pedagogy, service-learning is education that is grounded in experience as a basis for learning and on the centrality and intentionality of reflection designed to enable learning to occur" (p. 9). Similarly, Bringle and Hatcher (1996), Wade (1997), Zlotkowski (1999), and others described service-learning as a teaching strategy that uses community service to teach students about the academic curriculum.

Without a firm definition of what service-learning is and is not, it is difficult to decipher from previous research the degree to which study findings truly are outcomes of service-learning. Indeed, reviews of so-called "studies of service-learning" have explored investigations that reflect a broad range of community-based learning and community service activities. For example, whereas several literature reviews have attempted to focus exclusively on studies of service-learning (Billig, 2000; Eyler & Giles, 2001), most of the research reviews that appear in the service-learning literature include studies of community service, field education, youth service, and community service-learning programs (Andersen, 1998; Root, 1997). Collectively, these reviews have provided a varied set of the potential service-learning outcomes for students.

Individual studies of service-learning, as they are described in research reviews, are based on varied and oftentimes inconsistent sets of incongruous assumptions, constructs, and definitions. Such inconsistencies have made it difficult to identify and pinpoint the outcomes service-learning can and cannot foster. If there is to be a full understanding of the effects of service-learning on students, schools, and the community, then some agreement must be reached as to what encompasses a service-learning experience.

In particular, there must be a clear understanding of how service-learning differs from similar forms of experiential education, such as community service, project-based learning, unpaid internships, and so on. To do this, there first must be a comparative analysis among the various programmatic forms of experiential education in order that the commonalties and differences among the forms can be clarified, and the specific programmatic features of service-learning can be isolated. Then, the field must begin to distinguish between studying the effects of service on the educational development of students and studying the effects of service-learning on the educational development of students. This will help researchers discern the interaction effects of integrated service and learning experiences from the singular effects of service experiences.

Unlike most other fields of study in which one research study is used to form the next, the service-learning research field continues to be a mass of disconnected investigations that have focused on variety of issues related to a broad array of idiosyncratic service activities. There continues to be little consistency in the methodologies, instruments, and data analysis approaches employed in these studies. A more concerted, comprehensive, and systematic approach to studying the effects of service-learning can advance the service-learning field's understanding of how the various forms of service-learning impact students.

Issues of Program Diversity

Along with the lack of a universally accepted definition for service-learning, service-learning research is confounded by the inherently diverse and situational nature of service-learning experiences. The idiosyncrasies of individual service-learning activities make it difficult for researchers to develop a set of common instruments that can be applied to a variety of service-learning contexts. Service-learning researchers have indicated that one of the main challenges to studying the impacts of service-learning has been a lack of well-tested instruments and protocols that are able to capture comprehensively the multiple outcomes of service-learning across various school and community sites (Billig, 2000; Furco, 2002; Gray, 1996). Although there are instruments that have been designed specifically to measure particular service-learning impacts (e.g., increased social involvement, development of a service ethic), these instruments are not designed to capture the full range of potential impacts of a complex, individual program. Several studies of service-learning have incorporated instruments and protocols designed to capture outcomes that are particular to a specific type of program, such as a social studies service-learning course that focuses on issues related to homelessness. However, these program-specific instruments make it difficult to replicate studies and to conduct cross study comparisons that involve different types of service-learning activities. As Bailis and Melchior (chapter 8, this volume) suggest, the situational variations of service-learning practice pose numerous methodological challenges when conducting multisite, large-scale studies.

A further complication to this scenario is the fact that outcomes from students' participation in a particular service-learning program are influenced by students' personal interests and abilities, the length of their involvement in the service activity, and the degree to which they reflect on their service experiences (Conrad, 1980; Eyler & Giles, 1999; Morton, 1997). The outcomes are also likely influenced by the varying intensities of the service projects (e.g., degree of personal investment that is required, the length of the service activities); the nature of the students' working groups (e.g., individual service activities versus small or large group service projects); the degree of choice students have in selecting their project; and a host of other variables (Ammon, Furco, Chi, & Middaugh, 2002). For example, in a recently developed comprehensive framework for assessing outcomes for service-learning students, Billig (2000) identified more than a dozen programmatic variables that might influence the outcomes of service-learning for students. And, as a number of researchers have noted, many outcomes of service-learning for students are unintended and unanticipated (Furco, 2002; Gray, 1996).

Multiple Outcomes of Service-Learning

Reviews of the research suggest that school-sponsored service programs can produce a broad range of outcomes for students. However, there is a lack of consensus among reviewers regarding the particular areas of impact. Because each reviewer has applied a different definition of service-learning, only those studies that meet the criteria of that definition are included in the review. Depending on the reviewers' definition of service-learning, certain studies of service programs are included or excluded from the review. As a result, there is substantial variation in what are purported to be the overall effects of *service-learning* on students.

For example, one of the most frequently cited research reviews in the service-learning field is Conrad and Hedin's (1989) review of studies of youth community service (p. 9). In their review, Conrad and Hedin identified personal growth and development, intellectual development and academic learning, and social growth and development as the impact areas for programs that combine service and learning. In contrast, in another widely cited service-learning research review, Williams (1991) provided a report of field education programs. In this review, Williams identified positive impacts of these programs on students' personal, career, affective, and academic development.

In a review of K–12 school-based service programs, which included community service and service-learning programs, Root (1997) identified outcomes in six domains: cognitive development, academic engagement, civic development, social development, moral development, and personal development. Similarly, Furco (1994, 2002), who reviewed research on K–12 school-sponsored service programs (which included community service, service-learning, and unpaid internships), identified outcomes in six domains. However, unlike Root, Furco's categories (academic, career, social, personal, ethical, and civic responsibility) included career development as an outcome. In another review of school-sponsored service programs, Yates and Youniss (1996) identified impacts on students' interpersonal, intrapersonal, moral, and social responsibility development.

In reviewing K–12 service-learning programs, Wade (1997) identified academic and intellectual development, social and personal development, and political efficacy and participation as potential outcomes. These outcome areas were affirmed in a more recent comprehensive review of service-learning outcomes for students, conducted by Billig (2000). In her review of K–12 service-learning research, Billig identified impacts in three domains: students' personal and social development, civic responsibility, and academic learning.

Overall, the service-learning research suggests that the range of service programs (i.e., community service, service-learning, internships, field education) can foster positive outcomes for students across a variety of domains, many of which overlap across the various programmatic forms. For example, personal development of students (e.g., self-esteem, self-confidence, and resiliency) is an outcome area that has been noted in all of the various programmatic forms of service. However, there remains little understanding as to which types of service programs foster which outcomes. As Billig (2000) pointed out, not enough quality research exists to know "which types of students are most affected, which specific program designs are most powerful, what type of reciprocity with service recipients is needed, how connected to the community service needs to be, and what impacts occur on the school as an organization or on the community as an entity" (p. 663).

Several individual studies of service programs suggest that even within a single program, a broad range of outcomes can be manifested. For example, in their study, Calabrese and Schumer (1986) found that students in one community service program exhibited significant decreases in alienation, behavior problems, and isolation. In addition, they found that the students who engaged in service showed significant gains in their ability to work with others through collaborative and cooperative work. Similarly, in a later study, Batchelder and Root (1994) found that students who participated in the school's service-learning activities gained in their ability to make prosocial decisions and also demonstrated gains in their overall moral and ego development. More recently, Scales and Blyth (1997) found increases in students' sense that, after engaging in service-learning, they had something positive to contribute to the community as well as their perception of social competence. Singularly, each of these studies' findings suggests that one service program may produce multiple outcomes for students. This implies that studies of service-learning that measure only one or two constructs might miss some of the important impacts (intended or unintended) that service-learning has on students. In order to understand the full impact of service-learning, researchers should consider designing studies that include a broader range of constructs.

Further complicating the issue is the fact that the outcomes of service-learning may vary among individual students engaged in the same service-learning activity. The importance of accounting for this individual student variance was first noted by Conrad (1980), who in his study found that experiential education program outcomes are predominantly based on students' individual experiences. A similar finding was identified by Furco (2002) who, in his study of 529 high school students in California, found that students benefited uniquely from the same service project. His study findings suggest that the individuality of the student should be taken into account when investigating the impacts of service programs on students. The interplay of a student's prior service experience, motivation to do service, enthusiasm for particular service activities, and personal interests and talents appear to strongly influence the outcomes for individual students (Furco, 2002). Thus, can individual student outcomes be captured when the unit of analysis of a study is the school or the classroom? If the outcomes for students are as individualized as Conrad, Furco, and others suggest, then careful consideration needs to be given to the unit of analysis in the study of service-learning.

IMPROVING THE STUDY OF SERVICE-LEARNING

Given the lack of definition for service-learning, the inherently idiosyncratic nature of service-learning program activity, and the range of possible outcomes of service-learning, researchers need to explore new design models that can better manage the complexities of service-learning activities. These new design models provide a first step to systematize the service-learning research field and help garner findings that can inform and shape future research studies.

One way to improve the research on service-learning is to improve on the limitations of previous studies. Although the existing studies of service-learning have been helpful in shedding light on the various potential outcomes of service-learning, the studies have not been conducted through any collective, systematic approach. Rarely have the studies been based on prior research findings. With few exceptions, the existing studies of service-learning have been independent investigations based on different theoretical frameworks and assumptions. Moreover, to date, no study of service-learning has been fully replicated. An exploration of the limitations of the existing research on service-learning can provide insights into the research areas that need to be improved.

Limitations of Previous Studies

While the presence of limitations can severely weaken a study's validity and generalizeability, methodological limitations are present in any study of education phenomena (McMillan & Schumacher, 1984). Within a single study, educational research deals simultaneously with many variables that are often ambiguous, unpredictable, and methodologically uncontrollable. Although previous studies of service-learning have helped provide a better understanding of the vast array of possible outcomes that can be fostered by engaging students in service-learning, the overall strength and generalizeability of the findings of individual studies can be strengthened by reducing the various limitations fostered by the studies' designs.

Collectively, the limitations of the studies of service-learning have been varied, with some limitations appearing more often than others. Table 2.1 highlights the areas within which these limitations have occurred most often and presents suggestions for reducing and eliminating these limitations in future service-learning studies.

TABLE 2.1
**Implications of Limitations of Previous Studies
for Future Study of Service-Learning**

Limitation Issue	*Previous Studies*	*Future Studies*
Constructs included in the study	The impacts studied focused on only one or two constructs or educational domains (academic, career, personal, etc.) although a broad range of service-learning activities with varying intentions and purposes were studied. The design did not consider the full range of possible educational outcomes that service-learning might foster or did not focus on constructs that were well-aligned with each program's primary intended objectives.	Service-learning research studies should incorporate multiple measures that can determine how various different outcomes (intended and unintended) manifest themselves among different populations and within different settings. Studies need to consider the goals and objectives for each service-learning unit (working group, classroom, etc.) included in the study.
Scale of the study	The findings were based on small scale studies whereby the outcomes of a very specific service program or service activity (e.g., a ninth-grade social studies service-learning class in an urban school that provides assistance to seniors with Alzheimer's) were studied.	Service-learning research needs to include multisite and cross-programmatic analyses so that stronger generalizations of the findings can be made.
Control groups	The study did not include a control or comparison group.	Service-learning studies need to include comparison or control groups in order that stronger evidence about outcomes and impacts can be more firmly attributable to service-learning.

Continued on next page

TABLE 2.1
Implications of Limitations of Previous Studies (Cont.)

Limitation Issue	Previous Studies	Future Studies
Control groups	The study did not include a control or comparison group.	Service-learning studies need to include comparison or control groups in order that stronger evidence about outcomes and impacts can be more firmly attributable to service-learning.
Sampling	The study did not include a random sample; the sample involved in the study chose to engage in the service-learning activity.	Service-learning studies need to employ random sampling to eliminate self-selection bias.
Instrumentation	The study findings are based on data collected from a limited number of instruments (e.g., one pre-/post-survey).	Service-learning studies should employ multiple instruments that measure various constructs and utilize a variety of data collection approaches in order that data from various data sources can be triangulated.
Data sources	The data for the study were collected from a limited number of data sources (e.g., students only).	Service-learning studies should collect data from a comprehensive array of relevant data sources; data that are corroborated among the data sources can add power to the finding.
Data analysis	The study's data were analyzed through one approach (either quantitatively or qualitatively).	Service-learning studies should employ a variety of data analysis techniques; qualitative data can be used to support the findings from the quantitative analyses and vice versa.
Program length	The study findings are based on short-term impacts (e.g., 10 weeks). Such short time frames might not be ample time for the impacts to manifest themselves.	Service-learning studies should investigate outcomes and impacts in a more longitudinal vein whereby the long-term impacts of service-learning are investigated.
Sample size	The study findings were based on small sample sizes or on less generalizeable samples (e.g., students in parochial schools).	Service-learning studies should involve larger sample sizes and samples that are shown to be more representative of the total population.

Service-learning research will inevitably have naturally occurring conditions that will impose several unavoidable limitations on a study. For example, the structure of class schedules that operate in schools and the human subjects' protections that are afforded to young students may not allow education researchers to randomly assign subjects to particular groups. The researcher may also have little control over the way the program is organized and the degree to which students are involved. Nonetheless, making efforts to reduce limitations that have appeared in previous studies can result in more effective methodologies that can advance the field's understanding of the impacts of service-learning.

DEVELOPING A COMPREHENSIVE APPROACH

Although there are a number of ways in which these and other limitations of service-learning research can be addressed, one strategy is to develop a more comprehensive methodological approach for studying service-learning. The comprehensive approach should include mechanisms that allow for the full exploration of possible effects of service-learning, taking into account the variations in program definition and program diversity. Although a broad-based comprehensive approach is not always ideal for conducting deep investigations of particular outcomes, it does provide a means for capturing some of the primary, core impacts of service-learning. Given the relatively young age of the service-learning field, such an approach might prove useful at this stage to assist researchers in identifying which of the many purported effects service-learning produces most frequently and most strongly.

In developing this comprehensive approach, three fundamental questions need to be considered. The first question focuses on addressing the broad range of findings that have emerged across previous studies. If service-learning can potentially produce all of the outcomes reported in the literature, then how does a researcher determine which particular set of outcomes to investigate? The second question focuses on identifying the proper units of analysis for studying service-learning. If service-learning involves a complex interplay of various players, then which of those players should be included in the analysis? The third question focuses on developing findings that are generalizeable to other service-learning programs. If studies are inherently limited in their scope and scale because of the idiosyncratic and contextualized nature of service-learning, then how can researchers produce findings that can be generalized beyond the program studied? Answers to each of these questions are explored.

Addressing the Broad Range of Outcomes

As was mentioned previously, most studies of service-learning have focused on studying one or a few impact areas. This approach isolates an area of impact in order that the effect of service-learning on the impact area(s) can be measured.

Although this approach is extremely valuable in deepening understanding of the effects of service-learning, it can be problematic when conducting large-scale studies that include service-learning programs that are operationalized differently in different classrooms. For example, in their study of 35 service-learning partnerships in California, Ammon et al. (2002) found that the goals and intentions of the service-learning programs differed substantially from classroom to classroom, even among classrooms that engaged in the same type of service-learning activity (e.g., buddy reading).

Studies of service-learning need to incorporate designs that can more effectively capture the range of potential effects of service-learning. In particular, studies of service-learning should seek to paint a more comprehensive picture of the impacts of service-learning by investigating several outcomes simultaneously. Limiting the investigation to one or two expected outcomes, as most service-learning studies have done, might miss some of the likely outcomes that may result from a service-learning experience. As Berman (1990), Furco (2002), and Mainzer, Baltzley, and Heslin (1990) found, the outcomes of service programs often move beyond their intended purposes. For example, a service-learning program might be instituted to improve students' civic participation, but in actuality, the strongest outcomes are in the development of students' self-esteem and academic achievement. As a way to explore the manifestations of these unintended outcomes, studies of service-learning should incorporate more comprehensive methodologies that can measure a broad range of possible outcomes.

By utilizing more comprehensive methodologies that can assess multiple outcomes, researchers can begin to unearth the conditions that foster particular outcomes. For example, if future studies of service-learning were able to investigate impacts in the six domains (cognitive, civic, social, moral, personal, and academic development) identified by Root (1997), and then attempt to identify the programmatic features that might have contributed to outcomes in one or more of the areas, then service-learning researchers could gain a better understanding of which outcomes are fostered under which conditions and circumstances. This understanding would ultimately help researchers better predict outcomes that certain types of service-learning experiences might foster for particular students.

Determining the Appropriate Unit of Analysis

Most studies of service-learning have focused on studying groups of students engaged in one or more service-learning programs. The unit of analysis typically has been the service-learning classroom or program, with a measurement of outcomes on the whole student group. Although this design is plausible in most contexts, there has been a tendency in the field to over-generalize group findings without considering the differences in outcomes among individual participants.

As was mentioned earlier, previous studies by Conrad (1980) and Furco (2002) suggest that the most likely predictor of outcomes for students are the characteristics of individual students in the program rather than the service activities themselves. Even when a group of students engage in the same service-learning project, the outcome of that experience is likely to vary among the individual students. Thus, although a project might enhance one student's career and social development, it might impact another student's personal and academic development. For some students, a service-learning experience might impact them intensively in one domain, whereas for others, the impacts are less intensive and span across various domains (e.g., academic, social, career, etc.).

Therefore, the unit of analysis in service-learning studies needs to be considered carefully, with greater emphasis placed on studying the individual student rather than the overall service-learning program or classroom. Service-learning researchers must seek designs that are able to capture more fully the individual service-learning experiences of students and how those experiences (oftentimes the same or similar experiences) affect each student. However, because of the situational nature of service-learning, the analyses of students' individual and collective experiences must be considered within the broader programmatic context in which they are occurring. This means that researchers must assess how the particulars of the program (e.g., duration of the service activity, degree of student choice in selecting the service activity, amount and type of reflection, etc.) might shape the service-learning experience and how the nature of the service-learning experience ultimately affects individual students.

Researchers of service-learning must also collect data from a variety of sources (not only from the students) and they should include analyses of both disaggregated data (specific to individual students and programs) and aggregated data (combined across students and programs). Data collected from various sources will allow for data triangulation. Data that are analyzed in both the aggregate and disaggregate can help researchers see which outcomes are particular to specific types of service-learning activities and which outcomes are manifested across program types. Conducting such analyses has implications for the third and final issue.

Allowing for Broader Generalizations of Findings

Because of the idiosyncratic nature of service-learning, the generalizeability of previous findings has been minimal. Research findings from a service-learning program in which 12th-grade students in a social studies class study how and why people become homeless and then assist homeless persons in locating shelter cannot be generalized readily to a sixth-grade service-learning science class in which students are planting trees as part of an ecology unit. Although some of the high school findings might provide insights into potential impacts of service-learning, those findings cannot be used easily to justify the implementation of the elementary school program.

Although a few researchers, such as Conrad (1980), Newmann and Rutter (1983), and Melchior and Bailis (1997), have conducted multisite studies, the use of multiple sites aimed to increase the sample size of the study rather than to conduct an analysis of outcome differences among individual programs. Service-learning studies that utilize multiple sites or programs for comparative purposes can provide some important generalizeable information about the ways in which service outcomes are manifested across projects and classrooms. Miles and Huberman (1984) wrote:

> More and more [sic] researchers are using multisite, multicase designs, often with multiple methods. The aim is to increase generalizeability, reassuring oneself that the events and processes in one well described setting are not wholly idiosyncratic. Put another way, the problem is seeing processes and outcomes that occur across many cases or sites, and understanding how such processes are bent by specific local contextual variations. (p. 151)

By gathering the same or similar information from various sites, researchers may be better able to observe and analyze impact patterns across a wide range of situations and programs. However, as Bailis and Melchior (chapter 8, this volume) describe, researchers who conduct such studies face a variety of methodological challenges.

At this point in its development, service-learning research needs more multisite and multioutcome studies that incorporate multilevel analyses across a host of variables. Studying service-learning projects at different types of schools (large–small, public–private), in different communities (poor–wealthy, urban–rural), on varying issues (homelessness, the environment, public health, literacy), and in different courses (sixth-grade social studies, ninth-grade math, 12th-grade English) can provide much needed information about which outcomes manifest themselves in which situations. This is the first step in gaining a deeper understanding of what service-learning really means and how different types of service-learning experiences affect different students.

One approach for accomplishing this is to administer the same comprehensive battery of instruments to a variety of sites and then to analyze the data across a variety of strata and levels, using various combination of variables as controls (e.g., number of hours served, type of service activity, degree to which service and learning are integrated, etc.). The goal is to produce findings that can be generalized across students, service-learning activities, and school sites.

In order for the findings of service-learning studies to be useful to the field, the studies must be based on a common conceptual framework that builds on previous study findings. The three issues raised in this chapter can provide a first step for establishing a coordinated, systematic, and comprehensive approach to studying service-learning. If service-learning researchers consider these issues in their future investigations, the field can begin to produce studies that can take into account service-learning's amorphous, complex, and idiosyncratic nature. One conceptualization of how these issues can be applied to development of a more comprehensive approach for service-learning is through what is termed here as the *grand-design* approach.

THE GRAND-DESIGN APPROACH

The *grand-design approach* involves the coalescence of a selected set of constructs, instruments, and methodologies that have been utilized successfully in independent studies of service-learning and that, in turn, are streamlined and applied as a package to a new, larger study that includes a multisite cross section of service-learning programs. In the vein of meta-analysis and hierarchical linear modeling, the grand-design approach takes the best service-learning research designs, instruments, data collection strategies, and data analysis techniques and combines them strategically and purposefully into one large design that can comprehensively and simultaneously investigate a variety of issues within and across a set of program sites. The grand-design approach strives for comprehensiveness as well as for universality; that is, the system is applicable and relevant to any service-learning program.

Structure of the Grand-Design Approach

To study the impacts of service-learning on students, a number of service-learning researchers have attempted to use well-tested, valid, and reliable social and psychological attitudinal and behavioral survey instruments (e.g., those that measure alienation, resiliency, locus of control, empowerment, and personal attitudes). However, as Waterman (1997) noted, many well-tested psychosocial scales contain items that may not be applicable to service-learning participants (e.g., questions about students' personal behaviors at home or students' attitudes about love). In addition, because many these instruments are constructed for and validated on specific populations, their use on a broad range of subjects may not be appropriate.

To address this issue, some service-learning researchers have developed new instruments designed specifically for students in service-learning programs. Unfortunately, not all of these newly designed instruments maintain high reliability and validity, and relatively few of them have had much utility beyond the programs for which they were designed. In addition, many of these new instruments measure narrowly defined, program-specific constructs; they typically do not assess full range of program outcomes (e.g., social, personal, ethical, civic, career, and academic outcomes) associated with service-learning.

As a result, the grand-design approach seeks out well-designed instruments that are universal in their applicability to a broad range of service-learning programs and comprehensive enough to capture the multitude of potential service-learning outcomes. Through the grand-design approach, a battery of these instruments (well-tested and/or newly designed) are combined and applied as a package to measure various outcomes (intended and unintended) within and across a broad range of service-learning programs.

Supplementing this common set of instruments, which are applied to all of the participating sites, is a second set of protocols that allow the researcher to investigate each unique program site in fuller detail. These supplemental protocols are based on the same conceptual framework (e.g., set of outcomes measured) as the first set of instruments. However, unlike the first set of instruments, the supplemental protocols are adapted to meet the specific needs of each individual site. In particular, the protocols are designed to explore program depth, capturing the particular and unique characteristics of individual programs.

For example, a researcher may want to obtain data about students' understanding of academic content by administering a protocol that involves students responding to a set of journal essay questions. Typically, in multisite studies, the prompts are purposely kept broad and general, such as, "Describe what you have learned in class." This is done to allow the prompt to be applied to a variety of service-learning programs. Because the nomenclature used by individual programs is likely to vary, the actual questions asked about academic achievement for each program should be phrased differently, depending on each program's context. For example, students in a ninth-grade mathematics service-learning activity named, *Community Learning Experience*, might be asked to address the following journal entry: "Describe at least two math concepts you have learned and have practiced through your participation in the Community Learning Experience program." In contrast, students in a 12th-grade English service-learning class called *Writing for Your Community* would be asked to address the entry: "Describe at least two English writing skills and concepts you have learned and practiced through your participation in the Writing for Your Community project." These more focused prompts are likely to yield more useful data. The additional set of protocols in the grand-design approach allows for contextualized data to be captured at individual sites, which can, to a degree, be compared across sites. However, great caution should be taken in developing these protocols because minor changes in wording might trigger different responses from study participants.

In compiling the battery of instruments and protocols for the grand-design approach, both quantitative and qualitative measures should be considered. Quantitative approaches in the study of service-learning are important in that they facilitate the collection of data from larger samples and provide quantifiable data that can be analyzed through statistical procedures. Qualitative approaches, on the other hand, are able to capture the idiosyncratic, programmatic characteristics of individual service-learning experiences that often elude quantitative measures. According to Hicks and Hirsch (1991) and others, there is a limit to the depth of information one can gather about students simply through quantitative research. They wrote, "Personal interviews and/or focus groups with students could provide a credible base of qualitative information to back up and flesh out the quantitative data and substantiate the informal anecdotal evidence that currently exists" (pp. 10–11). Indeed, an increasing number of service-learning researchers have concluded that because of its complex nature, the study of service-learning must include indepth, qualitative information about the programs being studied (Shumer, 2000; Waterman, 1997).

Thus, in order for the grand-design approach to be effective, it must incorporate both quantitative and qualitative approaches. The combination of quantitative and qualitative methodologies in the grand-design approach makes it possible to capture simultaneously both the breadth and depth of the service-learning programs being studied. Using a comprehensive quantitative-qualitative system, the approach incorporates multiple measures that not only explore a broad range of outcomes, but also allow for the triangulation of data. For example, a finding observed on a quantitative measure can be affirmed or refuted by evidence from the qualitative data. Data triangulation can help researchers draw robust conclusions about the strength and nature of service-learning impacts.

Advantages of the Grand-Design Approach

As a strategy that can be used to study service-learning across a wide range of program sites, the grand-design approach addresses both the lack of a universally accepted program definition for service-learning as well as the idiosyncrasies and diversities among service-learning programs. The grand-design approach also facilitates the garnering of information from multiple data sources. For example, using the grand-design approach, a study that seeks to investigate the effects of service-learning on students would gather data not only from students, but also from teachers, community members, and other constituents who might influence the ways in which students are impacted by service-learning. This would help advance the study of service-learning since most studies that have explored the impacts of service-learning on students have used students as the sole data source.

Finally, the grand-design approach provides a comprehensive approach to collect data systematically from a large sample of subjects who represent various programs, allowing researchers to conduct a host of multilayered analyses that might include both within group and between group comparisons, based on different units of analysis. Because common and complete sets of data are collected from a variety of data sources and from all levels of the program, the collected data can be analyzed qualitatively and quantitatively at the subject level (e.g., individual students' impact), the classroom level (differences in impacts among the classrooms), and at the school level (differences in impacts among the schools). The results from an analysis such as this can help researchers better understand the degree to which program design, service activity, teachers' teaching style, student background, and many other variables affect the outcomes of service-learning activities for students. With these data, researchers can begin to gain a better understanding of the conditions under which certain outcomes of service-learning are manifested. However, as the next section describes, the use of the grand-design approach brings with it several methodological challenges.

Applying the Grand-Design Approach

The grand-design approach was used in a pilot study conducted by the University of California-Berkeley that investigated the impacts of service-learning on students in 19 classrooms at a California high school—11 classrooms that used service-learning and eight classrooms that had no service activities. The pilot study involved the implementation of the grand-design strategy as a means to assess student development in six educational domains: academic, social, personal, career, ethical, and civic.

Even though the 11 service-learning classrooms operated within the same school site, the nature of the service-learning activities varied greatly, from fully integrated service projects to service projects that were peripheral to the rest of the class' learning. As each classroom dynamic was being studied, it became evident that each class was unique, even when, in some cases, students were studying the same topics with the same teacher during a different class period. All the classes approached service-learning differently. These differences included the amount of time spent on service-learning, the number of projects students worked on during a semester, the nature of the student working groups, the way the teacher introduced and prepared students for the projects, the placement of the service activity in relation to the learning component, the intensity of the service project, the distance needed to travel to and from the service site, and a host of other issues. The idiosyncrasies of the service-learning experiences were especially evident in one classroom in which each student served at a different community service site. However, despite the variations in service-learning practice, several common themes began to emerge across the different service-learning classrooms; these themes were evident among the service-learning classrooms but were not found among the no-service classrooms.

Because an experimental design with random assignment of participants into control and experimental groups was not possible, the pilot study had a quasi-experimental, nonequivalent control group design that compared student outcomes at the start and end of the program. This approach allowed for the monitoring of the educational development of students (across the six aforementioned domains) as they progressed through their respective service-learning programs. Individual students' raw data were aggregated by classroom and were compared across classrooms to determine if there were particular outcome patterns between schools in each of the six educational domains.

In the search for reliable research instruments that could both capture students' educational development across six domains and be appropriate for administration to a large sample, it became evident that no single existing instrument could measure the six domains key to this study. At one point, a battery of eight well-tested attitudinal survey instruments that covered the six domains was considered for administration. However, given the ages of the students, this approach was deemed impractical because the entire battery would have taken each student several hours to complete. Also, each of the instruments in the battery contained several items that were inappropriate for students in service-learning programs, and each of the test-battery instruments utilized a different measurement scale, making any systematic data analysis quite complicated. Ultimately, a new quantitative survey instrument was developed for pilot testing. This new instrument pooled items from existing attitudinal surveys to form a comprehensive survey that could measure outcomes in six educational domains. This new instrument was then supplemented with a series of qualitative instruments and protocols that helped establish a comprehensive approach to assessing educational outcomes of students in these 19 classrooms.

What resulted was a grand-design tool called the Evaluation System for Experiential Education (ESEE). ESEE was designed as a compilation of a variety of measures that could capture students' educational development through a variety of measures. ESEE included 10 instruments and protocols used to collect information from various data sources over the course of a year.

- A researcher-designed student pre-test/post-test attitudinal survey;
- Eight student journals questions with specified prompts;
- Semistructured focus group interviews;
- A content analysis of samples of student produced work (papers, portfolios, and presentations);
- A student placement questionnaire;
- Teachers' program goals and objectives;
- Classroom site visits and observations;
- A teacher focus group interview;
- A community-based organization questionnaire; and
- Formal and informal meetings with site administrators.

These instruments were designed specifically to gather the full range of students' service experiences as they related to each of the six educational domains explored in the pilot study. Collectively, they provided a comprehensive and rich data set that allowed for a variety of quantitative and qualitative analyses to be conducted. These data captured the essence of individual programs while providing a mechanism to analyze different and distinct programs uniformly. In addition, they allowed the researcher to understand and interpret more fully the experiences of students within and across the various types of service programs, especially when these experiences were compared with the experiences of students in non-service-learning classrooms.

One of the major challenges in using the grand-design approach was managing the large volume of data that were collected. Given that 10 instruments and protocols were administered to a variety of data sources (students, teachers, community agency representatives) who were part of different service-learning programs at different sites, it was not long before the amount of data collected became difficult to manage. Another challenge in this approach was to collect data across sites within a sensitive time frame. Not every site was on the same service-learning calendar. Consequently, journal questions, surveys, and other measures were administered at various points of the semester, depending on the schedule of individual classes. Not only did this create logistical challenges for the researcher, but it also brought into question the impact the various time tables might have on the overall results.

Although it was often difficult to see any programmatic resemblance among the classrooms, the grand-design approach was able to shed light on common themes that appeared among the service-learning classrooms. The approach allowed the researcher to find evidence that in all the service-learning classrooms, regardless of their differences, (a) service-learning engaged students in learning activities when the service experiences were meaningful, (b) service-learning had a greater effect on students when students have strong beliefs regarding the community issue they are addressing, and (c) how a teacher presented service-learning to students (e.g., as an activity that is fun, challenging, expected, required, optional) made a difference as to how students perceive service in general. These and other themes were not evident in the classrooms that did not engage students in service experiences.

The Meta-Matrix Technique

Conducting the cross-site analyses, especially given the amount and variety of qualitative data included in the study, proved a bit difficult and cumbersome to manage. After reviewing several ways to organize the data, the meta-matrix sorting technique was selected as a viable means to order the data. Miles and Huberman (1984) described meta-matrices as follows:

> Cross-site (or cross-case) analysis multiplies the data set by as many single sites as are in a study. . . . Before this amount of data can be analyzed it has to be managed. Meta-matrices are master charts assembling descriptive data from each of several sites in a standard format. The basic principle is inclusion of all relevant data. . . . From there, the analyst usually moves to partition the data further (divide it in new ways) and cluster data that fall together so that contrasts between sets of sites on variables of interest can come clearer. (pp. 151–152)

Basically, the meta-matrix approach is a qualitative strategy for analysis that provides a framework for organizing information from all the data sources into recurring themes. Along with sorting out the data according to the hypotheses of the study, the meta-matrix is also helpful in identifying emerging or recurring themes among the data.

In the meta-matrix, the data are entered into cells that correspond to the specific constructs that are being measured (e.g., students' academic development, personal development, social development, etc.). For example, in the pilot study, all data from students' journal entries that referred to students' academic development were placed in one cell. Data about students' academic development from another measure (e.g., student interviews) were placed in an adjacent cell, and so on. Once all the data were sorted and organized into their various cells, comparisons across all the academic development cells, for example, were conducted. Through this comprehensive analytical process, the frequency and strength of the qualitative data within each cell could be quantified and various comparisons across the cells could be made. Because the qualitative data were collected ethnographically and longitudinally, the patterns and trends observed in the meta-matrix were able to strengthen the conclusions drawn from statistical analyses conducted for the study's quantitative data.

The meta-matrix allows a variety of analyses, such as within individual programs, between programs, across all or some programs, and within or among particular domains. Although the meta-matrix may be cumbersome, it does facilitate a researcher's ability to study the results in a systematic fashion. The cell structure forces the researcher to place each piece of data in a file. At the end of the data collection phase, the researcher is left with a set of files that was ordered by a set of predetermined constructs (e.g., academic development, personal development, etc.). These files could then be examined individually by construct or by program site, or in cross-construct or cross-site groupings. As a result, analyses of the interaction effects among variables can be conducted. Although the meta-matrix technique is not without its flaws, it can be a useful tool for managing large quantities of data across multiple sites. This technique, as well as other data analysis techniques, should be explored further to assist researchers who seek to incorporate a grand-design approach in their study of service-learning.

CONCLUSION

Studies of single service-learning programs, in and of themselves, have not been effective in producing generalizeable evidence about the impact of service-learning on students' educational development. The amorphous and idiosyncratic nature of service-learning poses serious challenges to service-learning researchers. The grand-design approach is one means to address the inherent methodological limitations of service-learning research. The types of analyses that its structure facilitates provide service-learning researchers with a useful tool for exploring new ways to study the outcomes of service-learning. However, in utilizing the grand-design approach, great care must be taken to maintain control over mounting volumes of data. In addition, efforts should be made to ensure that the grand-design approach does not overburden the teachers, students, school administrators, and community members involved in the study. If the constituents feel that the entire process is too cumbersome, it is less likely they will participate fully.

Although the grand-design approach may be a useful tool in helping researchers grapple with the methodological challenges of studying service-learning, it only addresses one piece of the puzzle. There are many other issues in addition to program definition and diversity that must be considered before assertions about the impacts of service-learning can be made. Although the chapter focused specifically on developing comprehensive methodologies for studying the impact of service-learning on students (service providers), the issues addressed in the chapter are applicable to broader investigations of service-learning's impact on communities, schools, and other program participants. Other comprehensive methodological approaches that take into account complex and idiosyncratic nature of service-learning should be explored as the field works to gain a deeper understanding of service-learning and its various impacts on students, teachers, institutions, and communities.

REFERENCES

Ammon, M. S., Furco, A., Chi, B., & Middaugh, E. (2002). *A profile of California's CalServe service-learning partnerships: 1997-2000.* Sacramento, CA: California Department of Education.

Andersen, S. M. (1998). Service-learning: A national strategy for youth development. New York: New York University.

Batchelder, T. H., & Root, S. (1994). Effects of an undergraduate program to integrate academic learning and service: Cognitive, prosocial cognitive, and identity outcomes. *Journal of Adolescence, 17*(4), 341–355.

Berman, S. (1990). Educating for social responsibility. *Educational Leadership, 48,* 71–80.

Billig, S. H. (2000, May). Research on K–12 school-based service-learning: The evidence builds. *Phi Delta Kappan, 81*(9), 658–664.

Bringle, R. G., & Hatcher, J. A. (1996). Implementing service-learning in higher education. *The Journal of Higher Education, 67,* 221–239.

Calabrese, R. L., & Schumer, H. (1986). The effects of service activities on adolescent alienation. *Adolescence, 21*(83), 675–687.

Conrad, D. E. (1980). Differential impact of experiential learning on secondary school students. Unpublished doctoral dissertation, University of Minnesota.

Conrad, D., & Hedin, D. (1989). *High school community service: A review of research and programs.* Madison, WI: University of Wisconsin, National Center on Effective Secondary Schools.

Eyler, J. S., & Giles, D. E., Jr. (1999). *Where's the learning in service-learning?* San Francisco: Jossey-Bass.

Furco, A. (1994). A conceptual framework for the institutionalization of service programs in primary and secondary education. *Journal of Adolescence, 17,* 395–409.

Furco, A. (1996). Service-learning: A balanced approach to experiential education. In *Expanding boundaries: Combining serving and learning* (pp. 2–6). Washington, DC: Corporation for National Service.

Furco, A. (2002). Is service-learning really better than community service? A study of high school service program outcomes. In A. Furco & S. H. Billig (Eds.), *Service-learning: The essence of the pedagogy* (Vol. 1, *Advances in service-learning research*, pp. 23–50). Greenwich, CT: Information Age.

Gray, M. J. (1996, Spring). Reflections on evaluation of service-learning programs. *NSEE Quarterly, 21*, 8–9, 30–31.

Hamilton, S. F. (1989). *Career pathways for youth.* Ithaca, NY: Cornell University.

Hicks, L., & Hirsch, D. (1991). Research needs: Focus on undergraduate student service: Campus Compact's preliminary assessment. Providence, RI: Campus Compact.

Jacoby, B., & Associates. (1996). *Service-learning in higher education: Concepts and practices.* San Francisco: Jossey-Bass.

Mainzer, K. L., Baltzley, P., & Heslin, K. (1990, November). Everybody can be great because everybody can serve. *Educational Leadership, 48*(3), 94–97.

McMillan, J. H., & Schumacher, S. (1984). *Research in education: A conceptual introduction.* Boston: Little, Brown, & Co.

Melchior, A., & Bailis, L. (1997, Spring). Evaluating service learning. Practical tips for teachers. *CRF Network.* Los Angeles: Constitutional Rights Foundation.

Miles, M. D., & Huberman, A. M. (1984). *Qualitative data analysis: A sourcebook of new methods.* Beverly Hills, CA: Sage.

Morton, K. (1997). Issues related to integrating service-learning into the curriculum. In B. Jacoby & Associates (Eds.), *Service-learning in higher education: Concepts and practices* (pp. 276–296). San Francisco: Jossey Bass.

Newmann, F. M., & Rutter, R. A. (1983). *The effects of high school community service programs on students' social development*: Final report to the National Institute of Education. Madison, WI: Wisconsin Center for Education Research.

Root, S. C. (1997). School-based service: A review of research for teacher educators. In J. A. Erickson & J. B. Anderson (Eds.), *Learning with the community: Concepts and models for service-learning in teacher education* (pp. 42–72). Washington, DC: American Association for Higher Education.

Scales, P., & Blyth, D. (Winter, 1997). Effects of service-learning on youth: What we know and what we need to know. *The Generator*, 6–9.

Schine, J. (Ed.). (1997). Service learning: Ninety-sixth yearbook of the National Society for the Study of Education. Chicago: University of Chicago Press.

Shumer, R. (2000, Fall). Science or storytelling: How should we conduct and report service-learning research. *Michigan Journal of Community Service Learning,* Special Issue, 76–83.

Wade, R. C. (1997). *Community service-learning.* Albany, NY: State University of New York Press.

Waterman, A. S. (1997). Service-learning: Applications from the research. Mahwah, NJ: Erlbaum Publishing Company.

Williams, R. (1991). The impact of field education on student development: Research findings. *Journal of Cooperative Education, 27*, 29–45.

Yates, M., & Youniss, J. (1996). A developmental perspective on community service in adolescence. *Social Development, 5*, 85–111.

Zlotkowski, E. (1999). Pedagogy and engagement. In R. Bringle & D. Duffy (Eds.), *Colleges and universities as citizens* (pp. 96–120). Boston: Allyn & Bacon.

3

Epistemology and Service-Learning Research

Fredric A. Waldstein
Wartburg College

INTRODUCTION

Evidence that service-learning as a pedagogy is maturing is found both in the growing body of research directed at service-learning and the increasing interest researchers and theoreticians are devoting to the nuances of research techniques and their implications within a broad epistemological context. As Richman (1996) pointed out, "A pedagogy must assume an epistemology. That is, a method of teaching, as a method of increasing knowledge, requires an account of what knowledge is and how it is acquired and tested" (p. 5). The purpose of this chapter is to identify some general themes and issues raised regarding research in service-learning, and place these within perhaps a more global context about how a better common understanding of the methodological vocabulary for research on service and experiential education might be developed. It is not the purpose to of this chapter to enter the philosophy of science debate represented by the exchange between Liu (1995) and Richman (1996), for example, except as it relates explicitly to research methods pertinent to service-learning.

The typology adopted here is to consider the language used to express one's understanding of service-learning research within two contexts. The first is defined as an *internal context* of which the focal point is on multidisciplinary research about service-learning. The second is described as an *external context* of which the focal point is disciplinary methodology that may be brought to bear on service-learning.

Even a cursory review of the literature indicates the existence of a significant amount of research on service and its relationship to patterns of behavior, mostly in young adults and adolescents. The extant research is generally unconstrained by a disciplinary convention that is both a strength and a weakness. It is a strength in that the research is enriched by the exchange of ideas from a broad range of disciplines that is the hallmark of interdisciplinary study. It is a weakness in that it lacks the formal conventions that help define research within the confines of the traditional academic disciplines. Thus, there are relatively few parameters to help guide the researcher in the quest to link his or her research to that of previous studies, which gives it a coherence and anchors it in the body of literature. It is somewhat analogous to gardening. Cross-pollination and fertilization enriches the environment, which creates an explosion of growth. But if left unchecked that growth itself can limit the garden's ability to bear fruit. The garden must be pruned back to maximize its productivity.

THE PUBLIC DEBATE

Demands for research are driven by political agendas that are diametrically opposed to one another. On the one hand, there are those who believe service has no place in the academic curriculum and that it detracts from the basic, traditional educational curriculum (the "3 Rs"), which society needs and from which it has strayed. On the other hand, those who support the service-learning and experiential education pedagogy believe it has the potential to offer a means to encourage students to take ownership of their education and connect them to civic life in a manner that enhances values that define a democratic society.

The research agenda seems quite straightforward. Either service-learning works to meet its objectives or it does not. Both camps expect evidence that will settle the issue in their favor. Indeed, a body of empirical evidence is being built as this volume demonstrates. But the lens through which that evidence is measured has too often been ground to fit the ideological orientation of those doing the looking. Both camps are guilty of this error, oftentimes with the best of intentions. Those committed to empirical research realize the evidence is unlikely to be so clear cut. Because the stakes are high and the focus of attention is on the results of research, those engaged in research must be especially diligent about how they conduct it and how they present it. Like it or not, the pedagogy of service in the curriculum has become politicized in a way that requires those engaged in research to be clear about the research methodologies employed and the results they deliver.

METHODOLOGICAL ISSUES AND
THE PUBLIC DEBATE

There are at least three points that may serve to aid one's understanding of the general problems associated with comparing the traditional academic pedagogy with that which incorporates service into the curriculum. First, what one is trying to measure may be very different. In the traditional pedagogy the researcher normally measures outcomes based on a given set of responses to questions. The SAT and ACT tests are archetypal examples. These tests place premium value on their capacity to capture an individual's aptitude for a given knowledge domain. How that aptitude is developed is of little consequence within the context of the test. There is virtually no value associated with the process of learning, only the outcomes.

There is a very long track record associated with these kinds of measurements that allow them to inherit the mantle of credibility by default: "It's the way we've always done it," mentality. Experiential education, on the other hand, places a great deal of value on the process of learning. However, because there are few accepted standards for how one measures the process of education, evaluation tends to fall back on instruments designed for an entirely different (and in some ways antithetical) set of criteria. They are different because what one is trying to measure is fundamentally different. They are antithetical in the sense that to the extent the process of learning is ignored, its value is discounted by default. There are plausible reasons for this. For instance, educators generally have less confidence in the ability to measure the effectiveness of the process for acquiring knowledge than in the ability to measure the knowledge acquired. Indeed, the means through which individuals acquire knowledge and the value of knowledge based on the means of acquisition is a debate as old as philosophy itself. It is certainly a debate with which social scientists are familiar (e.g., Brown, 1963; Levison, 1974).

Second, the demand that research prove or disprove the utility of service in the curriculum is misplaced and is counterintuitive to the principles of the scientific method, which is so misunderstood by friend and foe alike of service in the curriculum. The Falsifiability Principle, articulated by Karl Popper (1961), for example, helps one appreciate that, according to the rules of formal logic, definitive proof through empirical research is impossible. What is needed is to engage continually in research that is replicable within the limits of the social sciences so that over time confidence in expressed hypotheses is based on the accumulated preponderance of the evidence provided by research that tests the hypotheses.

Third, social scientific research in a democratic society, by its nature, is challenged by the problems associated with cause and effect and the ability to use instruments to disaggregate the two. Is the dependent variable really dependent? Can one control for sufficient variance to gauge the effect of the independent variables? Replication of previous studies is especially challenging in the social sciences where individuals with complex, ever-changing personalities are involved in the experimentation. Comparative methodology offers hope for addressing these questions.

METHODOLOGICAL ISSUES
WITHIN THE RESEARCH COMMUNITY

Many of the chapters in this volume identify certain methodological weaknesses within the research literature, and the contributors have offered their respective insights about how these might be addressed. However, before this is possible two issues must be addressed that, in many ways, are mirror opposites of one another, but which are equally frustrating. Both issues will be addressed throughout the chapter within the context of specific methodological concerns, but a general statement about each may help the reader better appreciate the need for balance between the two.

The first of these is the "splitting of hairs" phenomenon, one that is omnipresent in the broad arena that defines the service-learning literature. Here the dilemma is one of trying to be unnecessarily narrow in the definition of terms. Terms such as *research, evaluation*, and *assessment* are sometimes treated as if they should be mutually exclusive of one another. Although one must applaud the interest of scholars to make necessary distinctions among terms for the sake of clarity of meaning, it is also true that one ought not ignore or discount among terms the penumbra of ambiguity that is often present. For example, if researchers want to conduct an assessment of a given service-learning project, they may very well expect to engage in research toward that end, and continually evaluate whether the research meets the objectives of the assessment. Thus, research, evaluation, and assessment are all part of the same enterprise to enhance one's knowledge about a given set of activities. A number of other permutations could be offered to make the same point. The point is this: It is important not to choke the life out of terminology by putting it in such a confining straight jacket that either it is irrelevant or cadaverous. For language to be useful, it must exhibit properties of shared understanding and be adaptable enough to be useful in a variety of contexts. The apparently endless effort to distinguish among service-learning, community service, and experiential education is perhaps the best example of questionable hair splitting. Even if the scholarly literature could come to consensus about distinctions among the three, it is doubtful that it would translate very well to many of the practitioners in the field who, more often than not, are teachers at various levels simply trying to find ways to stimulate their students to learn more through a variety of pedagogical techniques. Teachers, for example, are less concerned about the conflicting definitions used by academics to describe specific patterns of behavior than they are about what stimulates their students to learn in the particular environments in which they find themselves. Indeed, some of the hair splitting can seem pedantic and be intimidating to those who might otherwise experiment with a pedagogy that employs resources beyond the traditional classroom. This is not to minimize the value of using terms precisely.

The second phenomenon is quite the opposite but in some ways more problematic and prevalent. Here it is referred to as the *undefined term* phenomenon. It is perhaps most often observed in reviews of the literature where various types of data analysis are compared. Examples that fall into this category include such terminology as *hard data* and *rigorous methods* as if these words had some self-evident, intrinsic meaning, which of course, they do not. Often implicit in the use of such terminology is that empirical information that is subject to statistical analysis is on its face more legitimate than information collected and analyzed by other means.

A corollary of this phenomenon is the overt use of terminology in highly idiosyncratic ways. For example, the term *empirical research* has been defined as research that is quantifiable and subject to statistical analysis. This is a gross misrepresentation of the concept of empirical research as commonly understood. This topic is addressed in more detail later in this chapter.

A second corollary is the use of language that is meaningless either because it is undefined, or because it is part of the jargon of a particular discipline, or both. Such language usage is confusing and trivializes accepted norms to the detriment of interdisciplinary collaboration in the building of a useful *corpus* of literature on which researchers and practitioners can build and use. The exhibition of these phenomena does not render valueless the analysis undertaken or the conclusions drawn, but they do compromise the utility of the value the studies may have.

A third corollary presents perhaps the greatest obstacle of all because it transcends the capacity of the individual researcher to address the problem. That is the evolution of different meaning for the same word across disciplines. For example, the term *normative* is used in the service-learning literature, but it is a term that has different meanings in different disciplines. Indeed, psychology and sociology have relied heavily on the descriptive mode of analysis and use the term *normative* in that context. But economists and political scientists have used the term in a different way, as a theoretical point of reference for understanding how people behave or should behave. The intent of the descriptive model used by psychologists is different than the intent of the normative model used by political scientists. The different intention has implications for the consequences of how each is used and understood (Bartos, 1967). This is not to say that psychologists use the term in a more appropriate manner than political scientists or vice versa. The point is simply that researchers cannot take for granted the language of discourse used in service-learning research.

The line between the splitting hairs phenomenon and the undefined term phenomenon can be rather thin. One person's splitting of hairs may be another person's attempt to define terminology adequately. The purpose here is not to determine where that line should be drawn in some categorical sense. Rather, the purpose is to remind the researcher to be conscious of the pitfalls inherent in each and take them into account.

EMPIRICISM, DATA SETS, AND COMPARATIVE METHODOLOGY

Empiricism as a modern epistemological reference has its roots in the philosophical work of John Locke and David Hume. It means, quite simply, that the sole source of human knowledge is derived from the senses. In the 20th century the Logical Positivists of the Wiener Kreis (Vienna Circle philosophers, *circa* 1924–1936) reformulated the empirical criterion of meaning to its logical conclusion: the method of verifying a proposition is the meaning of that proposition. Although this definition was not universally accepted, it gave broad latitude to the meaning of empiricism and did not limit the definition only to quantitative data, which lends itself to statistical analysis. Perhaps the greatest empiricist of the 19th century was Charles Darwin. His acute observations and analysis of life on the Galapagos Islands and elsewhere, which culminated in the publication of *On the Origin of Species* in 1859, led to the present understanding of the theory of evolution. It is not quantitative in the sense that it is readily subject to statistical analyses (or, at least, the original methodology did not assume it was necessary). Yet a more profound empirical work would be difficult to identify.

Empiricism is based on the existence of observable data. The nature of the data may take many different forms and is subject to manipulation depending on what information the empiricist is seeking. The organization of the data in a particular context or format constitutes a data set. The collection of archaeological artifacts in the British Museum constitutes a data set. Whether it is quantifiable or not, or subject to statistical analysis, is beside the point and says nothing about its legitimacy as a data set. It is no more or less legitimate than a data set that can be entered into a computer and interpreted through statistical analysis. It serves little apparent purpose to claim that one type of analyses is more empirical than another. Analyses are based on empirical evidence or they are not (e.g., logical evidence). One study is not more empirical than another because its analysis is based on data that is quantifiable and the other is not, and a data set is not defined by whether or not it can be analyzed using a given mathematical formula. Arguments to the contrary violate the language of science (semiotics) that is based, in part, on the need to find common understanding of language that has applicability to a broad range of individuals from a variety of disciplines. This is especially important with respect to experiential learning that draws scholars from so many different fields.

Understanding the method of accumulating empirical data, organizing them into data sets, and analyzing them is, of course, crucial to the evaluation of research. The comparative method is a methodology that has been used with effectiveness in the research on service-learning. Arend Lijphart (1971) wrote what many political scientists believe is one of the clearest and most succinct analyses of comparative methodology and its utility in the discipline. Much of his analysis applies to the use of comparative methodology in research on service-learning as well, and is worthy of some elaboration.

Lijphart compared and contrasted comparative methodology with experimental methodology, among others. The experimental method is a methodology favored by scientific researchers when it is appropriate to do so. "The experimental method, in its simplest form, uses two equivalent groups, one of which (the experimental group) is exposed to a stimulus while the other (the control group) is not. The two groups are then compared, and any difference can be attributed to the stimulus" (Lijphart, 1971, p. 683). But social norms limit the degree to which social scientific research that focuses on human behavior can place humans in a controlled setting for purposes of practicing the experimental method.

A much more frequently utilized methodology in research on service-learning is the comparative method, which, while not the equivalent of the experimental method, nevertheless is regarded as a method of discovering empirical relationships among variables. This is done most effectively, if four rules are adopted whenever possible. One of these rules is to increase the number of cases as much as possible, echoing the call for increased research on service-learning that is voiced throughout the book. A second rule is to reduce the property-space of the analysis. For example, if one were doing a comparative study on patterns of service projects it would be more feasible to divide the service activities into a relatively few, broad categories rather than to try to identify every specific activity. This gives the researcher more cases for every cell of the matrix, which increases the confidence she/he may have in the interpretation of the results. A third, related rule is to focus the comparative analysis on the key variables. "Comparative [analysis] should avoid the trap into which the decision making approach to the study of international politics fell, of specifying and calling for the analysis of an exhaustive list of all variables that have any possible influence on the decision-making process" (Lijphart, 1971, p. 690). The second and third rules speak to the need for uniformity and continuity in research methodology.

A final rule is to focus the comparison on comparable cases. "In this context, 'comparison' means similar in a large number of important characteristics (variables) which one wants to treat as constants, but dissimilar as far as those variables are concerned which one wants to relate to each other" (Lijphart, 1971, p. 687). One means for accomplishing this is by engaging in longitudinal analysis. Longitudinal studies allow the researcher to observe a given data set at Time $_T$ and compare it with observations of the same data set after a given interval, Time $_{T+1}$. One of the advantages of longitudinal studies is the opportunity to control for variability in the population if the same data set is observed over time. However, the greater the interval or intervals between observations, the less confident the researcher can be that observed differences or similarities are attributable to a given dependent variable.

SCIENTIFIC METHOD, THE QUESTION OF PROOF, AND THE NATURE OF EVIDENCE

The scientific method is a methodology for practicing empiricism. It is not the only methodology, but it is certainly one that was dominant in the 19th and 20th centuries, and it appears unlikely that it will give way to another methodology early in the 21st century. It is a methodology that is very powerful, in part because its rules are relatively simple to understand. It is based on the premise that empirical knowledge is connected with experience in such a way that it can be tested. A theory or hypothesis is empirical to the extent that it allows the possibility of a counter-instance to stand against it. That is, there is the possibility that it can be refuted through empirical evidence. Rigorous application of the scientific method is the Falsifiability Principle as articulated by Popper (1968):

> In other words: I shall not require of a scientific system that it shall be capable of being singled out, once and for all, in a positive sense; but I shall require that its logical form shall be such that it can be singled out, by means of empirical tests, in a negative sense; *it must be possible for an empirical scientific system to be refuted by experience.* (pp. 40–41)

> We say that a theory is "corroborated" [not "confirmed" or "verified"] so long as it stands up to these tests. The appraisal, which asserts corroboration (the corroborative appraisal), establishes certain fundamental relations, viz. compatibility and incompatibility. We regard incompatibility as falsification of the theory. But compatibility alone must not make us attribute to the theory a positive degree of corroboration: the mere fact that a theory has not yet been falsified can obviously not be regarded as sufficient. (p. 266)

What the Falsifiability Principle avoids is the assumption that confirmation alone constitutes proof. Inductive proof would mean that one could predict the consequences or stasis of all forms of observable behavior. In most instances involving empirical knowledge, this is not possible. For example, if one observed *x* number of a given species of animal and that animal was always the same color, one might be led to conclude that all species of that animal are a particular color. Proof would require that one observe every species of the animal to verify the color. But the demands of such verification are unrealistic. One cannot be certain that there is not at least one member of the species that does not exhibit symptoms of albinism, for example, and has no color.

Appreciation of the Falsifiability Principle can be useful when encountering those unfamiliar with the scientific method who have made erroneous assumptions about what it can and cannot do. For example, this writer has had to dampen expectations by his research sponsors and other interested parties that one can either prove or disprove the validity of service-learning as a pedagogy through quantitative analysis. One means to address this expectation is to explain the Falsifiability Principle within the context of the scientific method. It is a concept relatively easy to both explain to and be understood by the lay public.

But the Falsifiability Principal can create its own set of problems for the social scientist if it is accepted as the standard by which all social scientific research, including that which pertains to service-learning, is measured. As noted earlier in this chapter, social scientific research does not take place in the controlled environment that is characteristic of chemistry, for example. This has led to much debate about the degree to which social science is really a science. Those who are the intellectual progeny of the logical positivists would generally argue that it is not. In the words of Goodwin and Klingemann (1996): "The truths of political science, systematic though they may be, are and seem inevitably destined to remain essentially probabilistic in form. The 'always' and 'never' of the logical positivist's covering laws find no purchase in the political world, where things are only ever 'more or less likely' to happen" (p. 9). The same argument would seem to hold for almost all of the social sciences. Social scientists, including those who conduct research on service-learning, sometimes fail to understand this essential character of their work. It may be that this failed understanding is part of the reason why some social scientific research pertaining to service-learning lacks clarity and can leave the reader confused. The following examples serve to illustrate this point.

One of the commonly misspecified or, perhaps more accurately, unspecified concepts in the service-learning literature is *anecdotal evidence* which is often cast in a pejorative light. Exactly how one should define anecdotal evidence is unclear given its varied usage in the literature. Stripped to the core, it would seem to be evidence that is empirical but that is not subject to the rules of the scientific method. Although evidence that fails to meet these rules is of limited utility, it does not follow that anecdotal evidence is inherently useless as is sometimes implied in the literature. Indeed, the value of the evidence may be limited only by the absence of a research design capable of taking full advantage of what the evidence has to offer. Early observations contrary to the laws of classical or Newtonian mechanics could be described as anecdotal, but they were nevertheless taken seriously. Some of these observations helped lay the groundwork for quantum mechanics and the atomic era. Anecdotal evidence can offer rich insight into patterns of behavior that otherwise would not be perceived. Evidence that would be accurately defined as anecdotal has offered rich insight into this writer's understanding of patterns that emerged from quantitative analysis of survey data. A more egregious error in the literature is a tendency to identify any research that is not subject to quantitative analysis as anecdotal at which point it is dismissed out of hand. This is wrong for two reasons: (1) It demonstrates a misunderstanding of what anecdotal evidence is, and (2) it demonstrates a failure to appreciate what anecdotal evidence has to offer to the careful researcher.

Another area where the absence of clarity has caused confusion is the assumption that quantitative research that employs statistical models is *ipso facto* more objective than research that is defined as more qualitative. For example, one of the characteristics of the service-learning literature is the implicit (often explicit) assumption that the results of action research and other similar variants of ethnographic study are somehow less persuasive than survey data subjected to quantitative analysis. The use of terms such as *rigorous methods* and *hard research* are often associated with quantifiable data and analysis as if this made such research more objective. But all methodologies, those that employ quantifiable data or otherwise, are based on assumptions that

are ultimately subjective. Models that employ sophisticated mathematical
formulae are ultimately grounded in one's understanding of the world and how
that understanding is grounded in the model. Evidence for this understanding is
offered by formal theorists themselves.

Otomar Bartos (1967) wrote eloquently and simply about this matter in his
analysis of the difference between Markov chain models and game-theoretical
models of human behavior—two types of models that can be represented by
complex mathematical formulae. Bartos wrote that the "Markov chains models
represent the approach which aims at describing how men actually behave,
while the game-theoretical models exemplify how men should behave" (p. 298).
Which model is more appropriate depends on what it is the researcher wishes to
investigate. This leads to two points: (1) All models of human behavior and the
modes of analyzing data within the framework of any given model are
ultimately based on some subjective criteria about the researcher's
understanding of the world, and (2) the misspecification or misapplication of
formal mathematical models will surely lead to faulty analysis. The implications
for action research (indeed, for all research methodologies) are straightforward:
Understand and state clearly the strengths and weaknesses of the methodology
employed, and the means for mitigating the weaknesses to the extent that is
possible.

BROADENING THE THEORETICAL BASE
OF SERVICE-LEARNING

One final point about the research on service-learning pertains to the theoretical
underpinnings on which much of the literature rests. No one can doubt the
significant and central importance of John Dewey's (1944) philosophy,
particularly as it pertains to education. Service-learning advocates rely heavily
on Dewey for theoretical justification of the pedagogy. But it behooves scholars
interested in understanding the potential of service-learning and engaging in
research about it to look at a broad range of theory, which has the potential to
buttress and to suggest insights about how to approach research that a more
narrowly defined body of theory might not.

If more researchers were able to bring to bear the theoretical arguments in
their own disciplines and substantive areas of interest that are applicable to
service-learning, the field would be the richer for it. This is one of the great
strengths of interdisciplinary study and all researchers and theoreticians
interested in service-learning ought to be taking better advantage of it. Although
this is not the place for an exhaustive theoretical discussion, three examples of
well-known contemporary theorists help illustrate this point. One of these is the
work represented by Paulo Friere (1970) and his understanding of dialogical
education. His belief that the educational process is dependent on the extent to
which individuals commit to mutual co-inquiry and learning from one another

on an equal footing offers much potential insight into the way one thinks about service-learning.

A second theoretical framework for thinking about service-learning that is worthy of more attention is the idea of emancipatory learning represented by the work of Jürgen Habermas (1971) and Carroll Pateman (1970), among others. Within this framework, taking ownership of one's education is not only conducive to maximizing the possibility of one's ability to develop the skills of lifelong learning, it may also be a necessary condition for developing and sustaining a democratic society.

A somewhat different theoretical framework looks specifically at the role of the humanities and their ability to connect citizens to a sense of community. The contributors to *Standing with the Public: The Humanities and Democratic Practice* (Veninga & McAfee, 1997) are representative of this framework. Such work is important because it attempts to integrate learning associated with what are often perceived as the more esoteric disciplines with the real world; something that experiential education strives to achieve. Each of these three frameworks offers complimentary insight into the student-teacher-community triad, which comprises the service-learning core. They may help focus the attention of researchers more broadly than simply on the impact service has had on students, which has been the primary focus of attention.

SUMMARY

This chapter has identified several contexts and issues within those contexts that pertain to methodology and research in service-learning. These include methodological issues within the service-learning research community itself. Especially pertinent is a better understanding and clearer articulation of the meaning and interrelationships of empiricism, the scientific method and the nature and use of evidence. Always a challenge, the difficulty of this task is compounded by the political debate surrounding the merits of service-learning. Those who define both the advantages and limits of their research with care and integrity will conduct the most valuable research. This represents the best chance for researchers to provide a base of data that is not only independent of the prevailing political breezes but that may actually serve to affect them as good scholarship can. Properly conducted and reported, those committed to research in the field of service-learning may contribute to informed public dialogue on education that will constitute significant service to our civil society and democratic culture.

REFERENCES

Bartos, O. J. (1967). *Simple models of group behavior.* New York: Columbia University Press.

Brown, R. (1963). *Explanation in social science*. Chicago: Aldine.

Dewey, J. (1944). *Democracy and education*. New York: The Free Press.

Friere, P. (1970). *Pedagogy of the oppressed*. New York: Continuum Books.

Goodwin, R. E., & Klingemann, H-D. (Eds.). (1996). *A new handbook of political science*. New York: Oxford University Press.

Habermas, J. (1971). *Knowledge and human interest*. Translated by J. J. Shapiro. Boston: Beacon Press.

Levison, A. B. (1974). K*nowledge and society: An introduction to the philosophy of the social sciences*. New York: Bobbs-Merrill.

Lijphart, A. (1971). Comparative politics and the comparative method. *American Political Science Review, 65*, 682–693.

Liu, G. (1995). Knowledge, foundations, and discourse: philosophical support for service-learning. *Michigan Journal of Community Service Learning, 2*, 5–18.

Pateman, C. (1970). *Participation and democratic theory*. Cambridge, England: Cambridge University Press.

Popper, K. R. (1968). *The logic of scientific discovery*. New York: Harper & Row.

Richman, K. A. (1996). Epistemology, communities, and experts: A response to Goodwin Liu. *Michigan Journal of Community Service Learning, 3*, 5–12.

Veninga, J. F., & McAfee, N. (Eds.). (1997). *Standing with the public: The humanities and democratic practice*. Dayton, OH: Kettering Foundation.

4

Using Developmental and Learning Theory in the Design and Evaluation of K–16 Service-Learning Programs

L. Richard Bradley
Learn and Serve Ohio

Numerous studies point to the positive benefits of engaging students in service activities. Benson (1990) found that students who serve their communities are less likely to engage in risky behaviors. Cohen (1991) and Duckenfield and Swanson (1992) found that service-learning is an effective strategy for the prevention of substance abuse and dropping out of school. Conrad and Hedin (1982, 1987, 1989) found that students engaged in service gain in social and personal responsibility and in academic performance. Calabrese and Shumer (1986) reported that students engaged in fieldwork have few discipline problems and lower levels of alienation. Newmann and Rutter (1983) found an increase in problem solving skills and improved communication skills, particularly with adults. For a more complete review of the research, see Root (1997) and Billig (2000).

Despite these findings, establishing direct links between service-learning program objectives and outcomes for students has been difficult. One reason has been that service-learning practitioners have not always connected program design and evaluation to existing developmental and learning theory. This theme was echoed at the Service-Learning Summit, sponsored by the W. K. Kellogg Foundation (1995). Their *Wish List* for service-learning research included: (a) studies that go beyond the Conrad and Hedin scale; (b) longitudinal studies; and (c) the development of better tools for assessing civic attitudes, civic problem solving, critical thinking, and other key dimensions of personal development. The research questions might be put this way:

- Are there reasons, based on accepted developmental or learning theories, for asserting that service-learning will have positive impacts on K–16 students?

- If there are, what do developmental or learning theories suggest about the design and evaluation of service-learning programs?

47

- How would the use of developmental or learning theories help practitioners better understand the links between program design and program outcomes?

The last question is particularly important. Research suggests that experiential learning, such as the kind embodied in service-learning, may be one of the best ways to invite and encourage movement from one stage to the next (Hersh, Paolitto, & Reimer, 1979). However, whether movement through developmental stages occurs is dependent upon a number of factors, including the level of cognitive development (Gilligan, 1982; Kohlberg, 1981; Perry, 1970; Piaget, 1965) and the level of social perspective taking (Selman, 1980).

One way of accounting for the discrepancies between intent and action is offered by Person-Environment Interaction Theory (Lewin, 1936; Walsh, 1973). This theory suggests that an individual's behavior (B) is a function (f) of the person (P) and his or her interaction with the environment: $B = f \{P \times E\}$. The environment is made up of various internal variables, such as the level of cognitive and moral development, learning style, concern for others, commitment to prosocial values, self-esteem, and personality type; and external variables, such as opportunity to work with people from diverse backgrounds; quality of program design; cultural, school, and peer norms about helping others; and experiencing positive relationships with others. These variables interact in ways that complicate the relationship between program design and program outcomes. Theory-based research can help clarify these relationships and give practitioners more guidance in designing high-quality service-learning programs that have a high probability of achieving the desired outcomes for participants.

This chapter examines three theories of development and the two learning theories that could be used, either individually or in combination, to design and evaluate the effectiveness of service-learning programs: (1) psychosocial development Erikson (1963, 1964, 1968, 1982) and Chickering (1969); (2) cognitive development (Gilligan, 1982; Kohlberg, 1981; Perry, 1970); (3) personality type (Jung, 1971); and (4) multiple intelligences (Gardner, 1983, 1993). Table 4.1 illustrates how these two types of theory interact in the development of young people.

Using theories in the design and evaluation of service-learning programs can serve practitioners in two ways. First, theories can provide a rationale for designing particular service-learning activities. For example, research in the field of cognitive and moral development indicates that movement from one stage to the next requires repeated exposure to an issue over an extended period of time. Although a single visit to a homeless shelter may convey important information about homelessness, it is not likely to change student attitudes or behaviors toward the homeless. Multiple visits over an extended period of time are needed.

Second, theories can act as filters or lenses through which anticipated and actual program outcomes may be assessed. In the preceding example, a research question based on moral development might focus on whether the service activities were appropriate for participants in relation to their ages, the duration of the project, and learning styles. Research studies resulting from the use of development and/or learning theories would focus on program outcomes in relation to levels of psychosocial, cognitive, and moral development and /or the learning styles of participants.

TABLE 4.1
Comparison of Developmental and Learning Theories

School Level	Erikson/Chickering	Selman/Kohlberg/ Gilligan/Perry	Learning Theories Jung/Gardner
Elementary	Initiative vs. Guilt Industry vs. Inferiority	Kohlberg: Stage 2	T h
Middle	Identity vs. Identity Confusion	Kohlberg: Stages 2, 3	r o u
High	Identity vs. Identity Confusion Intimacy vs. Isolation	Kohlberg: 3 Perry-Position: 1, 2	g h o u
College	Intimacy vs. Isolation	Kohlberg: 3, 4 Perry-Positions: 3–5	t

THE PERSPECTIVE OF PSYCHOSOCIAL DEVELOPMENT

Psychosocial theory describes the content or issues with which individuals may be dealing during a given period in their lives. Two theories are examined here: Erik Erikson (1963, 1964, 1968, 1982) for K–12 youth and Arthur Chickering (1969) for college age youth.

Erikson: The Elementary School Years

According to Erikson (1963), children face two main tasks in elementary school. The first, occurring typically during Grades K–3, is for children to develop a sense that there are things they can do for themselves and be supported in the necessary exploration. Children's curiosity about how things work and what impact they can have on their world leads to seemingly endless questions about what, why, how, and when. If children are led to believe that their curiosity is pointless or that their questions are a bother, Erikson suggested they may emerge from this stage of life with an excess of guilt. Children who are encouraged to try a wide variety of activities and explore their inner and outer worlds are likely to emerge from this stage with a sense of initiative.

During Grades 4 and 5, the developmental task typically is to see how quickly abilities and skills in broad areas of life can be learned. If children's efforts to initiate and complete projects, to establish relationships, and to explore new interests on their own are perceived by adults as mischief or wasted effort, children may emerge from this stage with a sense of inferiority. If children are supported in their efforts, they are likely to emerge from this stage with a strong sense of industry.

Erikson: The Middle School Years

The main developmental task typically facing youth in Grades 6 through 8 is to begin putting together a coherent, unified idea of the self out of a bewildering array of possible identities: child, student, friend, and sexual being. Younger adolescents take their first hesitant steps to move away from the various identities given to them by parents, teachers, and others toward an identity they choose for themselves.

Identity confusion typically results when the tasks associated with the previous stages have not been adequately resolved or when the negative messages young teens receive from others, such as "You're no good! You can't do anything right!" outweigh positive messages. The result is often a heightened sense of isolation, an overall sense of shame, and a general sense of not knowing who they are or where they fit in. A positive sense of identity is most likely to develop when teens are surrounded by adults who affirm them and encourage them to discover their own identities.

Erikson: The High School and College Years

High school students must prepare themselves for transition into the adult world. Resolution of two psychosocial tasks predominates during this stage. The first task is finishing work on Identity versus Identity Confusion. The second focuses on issues related to intimacy and isolation. In this stage adolescents begin to develop a sense of their own unique identity. This makes it possible for them to begin to explore meaningful, healthy, and intimate relationships with those around them and to share with and care about others without undo fear of losing themselves in the process.

To assist children and youth in successfully resolving the developmental tasks associated with each of Erikson's stages, Duckenfield and Swanson (1992) suggested that curriculum-based service-learning programs be designed with very specific needs and opportunities in mind as shown in Table 4.2. These design criteria also suggest research questions relating to the appropriateness of service activities for each age group.

TABLE 4.2
Psychosocial Stages and Service-Learning Activities

Psychosocial Stage	Need	Appropriate Service-Learning Activities
Elementary School Initiative vs. Guilt Industry vs. Inferiority	• Develop a sense of personal competence and self-worth • Belong to and be approved by the group • Try out different roles • Be accepted for who they are by peers and adults alike • Develop responsibility and independence • Be involved in creative, intellectually satisfying activities	• Learning and performing skits and short plays for others (Language Arts) • Intergenerational projects of all types (Language Arts) • Making "care" packages for the homeless (Social Studies, Health) • Working with a local pet store to develop materials to educate other students on caring for animals (Math, Science, Language Arts) • Creating specialized planting areas in local parks (Science) • Environmental and recycling projects (Science) • Helping sort foodstuffs at local food pantries (Social Studies, Health)
Middle School Identity vs. Identity Confusion	• See that their efforts make a difference in their school/community • Participate in and be part of a group • Explore adult roles and careers • Interact with people from diverse backgrounds • Be accepted by peers and others who are important to them • Learn and practice decision making skills • Develop a sense of competence	• Working at a local homeless shelter or senior center (Social Studies, Language Arts) • Organizing and being involved in an "Empty Bowls" project (Social Studies, Language Arts, Art) • Intergenerational projects such as cross-age tutoring, reader's theater, and so on (Language Arts) • Almost any kind of environmental project (Science) • Serving at a facility for those with special needs (Health, Social Studies, Language Arts)

(continued on next page)

TABLE 4.2
Psychosocial Stages and Service-Learning Activities (Cont.)

Psychosocial Stage	Need	Appropriate Service-Learning Activities
		• Beautifying schools (by special needs students)
High School Identity vs. Identity Confusion Intimacy vs. Isolation	• Become more self-reliant and achieve psychological independence from parents • Expand peer relationships • Assume responsibility for career planning and its consequences • Achieve capacity for responsible, intimate relationships • Learn how to manage time and personal health • Develop citizenship skills necessary for responsible participation in society	• Assisting local civic groups with mailings (Business Education) • Cross-age tutoring projects (All Subject Areas) • Literacy awareness programs (Language Arts) • Intergenerational projects (Language Arts, Health, Science) • Planning and implementing an "Empty Bowls" project (Social Studies, Language Arts, Art) • Delivering "Meals-on-Wheels" (Social Studies, Health) • Making baby quilts (Life Skills) • Preparing community service directory (Language Arts) • Various environmental projects (Science) • Building a house with Habitat for Humanity (Social Studies, Practical Arts, Language Arts, Math, Science)

Chickering

Arthur Chickering (1969) divided Erikson's stages of Identity and Intimacy into seven vectors or developmental tasks associated with the college years. Each vector rises to prominence at a certain time during a person's life, taking from one to five years to resolve. Like Erikson, Chickering believed that resolution can be positive or negative, affecting future vectors. Successful resolution of each vector depends on offering opportunities to explore tasks associated with each vector. The seven vectors and possible curriculum-based service-learning activities are shown in Table 4.3.

TABLE 4.3
Chickering Vectors and Service-Learning Activities

Vector	Definition	Service-Learning Activities
Developing Competence	Intellectual, social-interpersonal, and physical-manual	Service in settings where students think they might have a vocational interest to see whether they have skills in this area
Managing Emotions	Dealing with sexual impulses and feelings, moving toward acceptance of emotions	Service among people who are "different," (such as serving meals at a shelter, followed by opportunities for structured reflection and personalized feedback)
Developing Autonomy	Learning to take initiative, solving one's own problems without continual need for outside reinforcement	Intergenerational activities that give students opportunities to try out new roles and develop a sense of independence
Establishing Identify	Using data from the first three vectors to come to terms with sexual orientation; body acceptance; and knowing the kinds, frequency, and levels of intensity of experience one prefers	Service activities, such as cross-age tutoring or serving at a shelter for battered women, that give students opportunities to explore what they like to do and how often
Freeing Interpersonal Relationships	Developing a depth of understanding and intimacy in their friend-ships, relationships with a significant other, and their relationships with persons culturally different from themselves	Service activities that give students opportunities to take the role of others, providing experiences that are likely to foster thought and reflection on issues relating to caring and community
Developing Purpose	Integrating vocational, avocational, lifestyle, and values into an initial commitment to a life structure	Service activities that give students indepth opportunities to sort out what they will do for a livelihood and what they will do to express other values that are important to them
Developing Integrity	Developing consistency between espoused values and actual behaviors	Service activities that give students opportunities to put their values and commitments "on the line" for the sake of others

Research by Chickering (1969) and others suggests that tasks associated with the first three vectors are typically addressed during the freshman and sophomore years of college; tasks associated with the fourth vector during the late-sophomore year or junior year of college; whereas tasks associated with the last three vectors are not typically resolved until the senior year of college or beyond.

THE PERSPECTIVE OF COGNITVE THEORY: PIAGET, SELMAN, KOHLBERG, GILLIGAN, AND PERRY

Stages of Cognitive Development

Stages of cognitive development follow a hierarchical, invariant sequence first identified by Piaget (1965), with each successive stage building on previous ones. Earlier ways of reasoning are not lost, but are integrated into the reasoning process of later stages. Movement from one stage to the next is not like learning how to do something faster (e.g., speed reading) but like learning how to read in another language. In designing service-learning programs appropriate for K–16 youth, two of Piaget's stages of are involved.

Concrete Operational Stage, which first appears at about the age of six in most children, involves the ability of the child to solve conservation problems. Logical operations are developed, thereby allowing the child to solve problems involving concrete situations or data by a process of serialization. Research suggests that 50% to 70% of adults never progress beyond this stage of thought.

Formal Operational Stage, which may appear at about the age of 10, represents a qualitative change in the approach to problem solving. The individual is no longer limited by concrete details and experiences. Abstractions are now possible, enabling the individual to reason out possible explanations and weigh their consequences.

An example of the difference between these two forms of thought and their implications can be seen in the story of two little girls who were playing with scissors. The first girl, Marie, wanted to give her mother a nice surprise by cutting out a piece of sewing; however, she did not know how to use the scissors properly and accidentally cut a big hole in her dress. Another girl, Margaret, took her mother's scissors and accidentally cut a little hole in her dress.

Marilene, age six, was asked which child should receive the greater punishment. "The one who made the big hole." When she was asked "Why?" she replied, "because she made a big hole." When Julie, age eleven was asked the same questions, she replied that neither child should be punished because "they made the holes accidentally and not on purpose." These comments illustrate the difference between concrete operational and formal operational thought.

Simons (1994) suggested that service-learning activities reinforce the following Piagetian concepts.

1. Learning, particularly for young children, needs to be experientially based, and is more effective when the classroom is expanded into the real world.

2. Cognitive development relies not only on physical and mental interactions with the environment, but also on social interactions, centered in relevant experiences with others, that help children gain a better understanding of others and recognize the shortcomings in their own thinking.

3. Children learn best through self-initiated activity, in which they have the freedom to explore, discover, choose their own tasks, construct knowledge, and direct their own behaviors and learning experiences.

4. Reflection enhances learning by bridging the gap between the abstract and the real, identifying common elements, and building new more mature understandings.

Levels of Social Development

Research by Rosen (1980) indicates that the transition from concrete operational thought to formal operational thought is influenced by the individual's ability to see things from another's point of view, that is, by the individual's level of social perspective-taking. Questions about why service-learning activities appeal to students of one age but not students of another may, therefore, be related to student levels of social perspective-taking (Selman, 1980). Selman outlined five sequential stages in the development of social awareness and understanding. Research into the implications of Selman's work for the design and evaluation of service-learning programs has been published by Woehrle (1993). Woehrle's results are shown in Table 4.4.

Stages of Moral Development

Research by Kohlberg (1981) and Lickona (1976) suggests that the development of moral reasoning passes through distinctive cognitive structures or stages that determine: (a) what a person sees, (b) how a person organizes information, and (c) the judgments a person makes about what someone should do under carefully prescribed circumstances. It is important to note here that Kohlberg's theory is not about what a person actually does.

Kohlberg's (1981) theory suggests fours stages of moral development encompassing the K–16 years. According to this theory, the underlying reasons for participating in school-based service-learning activities will vary according to the student's stage of moral development, as shown in Table 4.5.

TABLE 4.4
Stages of Social-Perspective-Taking and Possible Service-Learning Activities

Stage of Social Perspective Taking	Possible Service-Learning Activities
Stage 0 (about ages 4 to 6): Character-ized by the child's inability to make a distinction between a personal interpre-tation of social action (either by self of other) and what he or she considers the true or correct perspective.	
Stage 1 (about ages 6 to 8): Children at this age see themselves and others as actors with potentially different interpre-tations of the same social situation, determined largely by the data each has at hand. They assume that only one perspective is "right" or "true," the authority or their own, although they recognize the existence of different viewpoints.	Grades 1 to 2: Children enjoy making things for others, but also need experiences that help them learn that being a good neighbor means treating others as friends. Possible service activities could include having students make things, such as cards, artwork, home first aid kits, then personally deliver these items.
Stage 2 (about ages 8 to 10): Children are now aware that people think or feel differently, because each person has his or her own uniquely ordered set of values and purposes. They can now "get outside" the two-person situation and reflect on behaviors and motivations from a third-person perspective.	Grades 3 to 4: Students begin to understand that others have physical needs and that their actions can make a difference. They want personal contact with the people they are helping.
Stage 3 (about ages 10 to 12): Children develop the ability to differentiate and can consider each party's point of view simultaneously and mutually. They can put themselves in another's place and view themselves from that vantage point before deciding how to react (The Golden Rule).	Grades 5 through 8: Students see them-selves as the center of an increasingly complex world and want opportunities to experience this world through service to others.
Stage 4 (about ages 12 and up): Perspective taking is raised from the level of dyad to the level of a general social system involving a group. Individuals realize that each person considers a shared or generalized point of view in order to facilitate communication with and under-standing of others. Stage 4 may appear among high school students, but is more likely to be seen among college students.	Students are now capable of forming relationships with the people they encounter through their service-learning experiences. It is not uncommon for teachers to hear students refer to these people as "people who have feelings, ideas, and interests just like me," rather than as strangers who just need some-thing. Students at this stage tend to view their participation in service activities in terms of civic responsibility and duty. Students may also tend to dismiss the significance of their efforts, saying that they benefited as much or more from their service as the recipients did.

TABLE 4.5
Moral Development and Service-Learning

Stage	Reason to "do" the right thing	Reason to participate in service-learning activities
1	Grades 1 through 3. Children are motivated to do the right thing because they don't want to get into trouble with those in positions of authority.	Students participate because they do not want to get into trouble with their teachers or parents.
2	Grades 4 through 8. Students are motivated to do the right thing only when it is in their best interest to do so.	Participation hinges on a sense of reciprocity, that is, students need to have a sense that they will get something, such as extra credit or extra privileges in class, in return for their service.
3	Grades 9 through 12 and some adults. Individuals are motivated to do the right thing because they want to be liked and thought of as being "good people" in the eyes of those whose opinion of them matters.	Students participate in the expectation that they will be perceived of as being "good" young people in the eyes of those whose opinion matters to them.
4	College students and many adults. Individuals are motivated to do the right thing to preserve the social order.	Participation may hinge on two factors: (1) Is there a rule that requires them to do this? (2) Are they able to see their participation in the context of their responsibility to society?

Gilligan (1982) proposed an alternate model for moral development, based on her work with women facing real-life, rather than hypothetical, dilemmas involving moral issues. At Level 1 (girls, Grades 4 to 8), goodness is defined by a pragmatic focus on the self. There is a feeling of powerlessness that often makes relationships painful. The transition from Level 1 to Level 2 is characterized by moving from selfishness to a sense of responsibility for others. There is an increasing ability to see one's limitations and oneself realistically that makes relationships with others less painful.

At Level 2, characteristic of many young women of high school and college age, society's values are adopted and goodness is defined as sacrificing self for others. Fear of abandonment makes acceptance by others increasingly important, often resulting in an avoidance of self-assertion. The transition from Level 2 to Level 3 involves shifting the focus from goodness to truth, with an increasing tendency to question the logic of self-sacrifice. At Level 3 goodness is defined in terms of nonviolence and caring for others.

From Gilligan's (1982) perspective, motivation for participating in service-learning activities would be: Level 1, pragmatic self-interest; Level 2, desire to protect the less fortunate; and Level 3, a sense of caring for others (while caring for self).

William Perry's (1970) model of intellectual development is based on his work with college students but can be extrapolated backward to include high school students. His model includes three broad positions—dualism, relativism, and commitment—that tend to guide the individual's perception, organization, and evaluation of knowledge and values.

The position of dualism, which would include almost all high school students and most college freshmen, is characterized by a belief that all information is either right or wrong. Where uncertainty seems to exist, there are only three possible explanations: (1) the authorities are playing games with me, (2) the authorities have made a mistake, or (3) the authorities do not have all the answers yet, but someday they will. The position of relativism, which would include most college sophomores and juniors, is characterized by a belief that knowledge and questions of personal identity are either uncertain or valid only within the context of non-absolute criteria for making judgments. The position of commitment, not achieved by most college students until their senior year or later, is characterized by attempts to reflect on and define one's identity in terms of commitments made and lived out, with actions and beliefs being fully integrated.

Key Issues in the Design and Evaluation of Service-Learning Programs

Erikson's theory of psychosocial development contributes to the design and evaluation of service-learning programs by describing the predictable developmental challenges children and young people feel and have during their years in school. Knowledge of these challenges can be used to guide decisions about the kinds of service activities that are most appropriate for each age group and also to frame research questions regarding observed student outcomes.

Unfortunately, assessing the relationship between program design and student needs from the perspective of psychosocial development is not straightforward. One instrument, *Measures of Psychosocial Development* (MDP, Hawley, 1988), is available to assess positive and negative resolution of tasks associated with Erikson's stages. However, there is no similar instrument for assessing resolution of Chickering's vectors. Instead, a combination of instruments is needed, including: (a) the *Erwin Identity Scale* (EIS, Erwin, 1978); (b) the *Interpersonal Relationship Inventory* (IRI, Mines, 1978); (c) the Omnibus Personality Inventory (OPI, Heist & Yonge, 1968); and (d) the *Developing Purposes Inventory-2* (DPI, Barrett, 1978).

The developmental theories of Kohlberg (1981), Gilligan (1982), and Perry (1970) contribute significantly to the design of service-learning programs by describing the process people use to perceive and make meaning out of what they experience. Kohlberg provided service-learning practitioners with a model for understanding how students view what is right and their reasons for then doing it. Gilligan raised important gender issues and reminded program designers of the importance of caring.

Perry's (1970) unique contribution may be his description of the alternatives to moral development: temporizing, escape, and retreat. These alternatives may result when there is either an overload or a prolonged absence of challenge within the environment. In addition to the original Perry oral interview, one written tool exists to assess development along Perry's model, *Measures of Epistemological Reflection* (MER, Magolda & Porterfield, 1988).

Problems exist in assessing the actual relationship between program design and impact from the perspective of moral development. The first relates to the tools used to assess levels of moral development. The original assessment tool, Kohlberg's (1958, 1981) *Moral Judgment Inventory*, requires subjects to be interviewed using a set of standardized moral dilemmas. Responses are tape-recorded, transcribed, and then scored by a trained rater, a process that is both time consuming and expensive. Two alternatives exist, both using Kohlberg's dilemmas. One is Rest's (1979) *"Defining Issues Test"* (DIT). Subjects are offered multiple responses to each question and are asked to select the response that is closest to their current way of thinking. The second, the *Measure of Sociomoral-Moral Reflection* (SMRM, Gibbs & Widaman, 1982), is a paper-and-pencil instrument that requires subjects to generate their own responses to each question.

Research on moral development indicates that individuals can recognize a response before they can spontaneously produce it on their own (Rest, 1979). This means that scores on the DIT are typically about one stage higher than an individual's true level of moral development. Related to this is the fact that the DIT does not really measure moral development, but rather levels of what Rest called "principled reasoning."

A second problem is that research in moral development indicates that movement from one stage to the next can take anywhere from six months to three years (Rest, 1979). Given the fact that most school-based service-learning programs last less than nine months, detecting significant pre-to-post changes in stages of moral development may be problematic at best. The third issue has to do with the fact that both the DIT and the SMRM require at least a middle school reading level, thus making assessments of middle school and at risk students difficult.

Additional factors influencing development, and therefore, student outcomes, include:

- The degree to which the individual cares about the issue related to the service activity. There are two issues to consider in this regard:

  1. When students are personally involved in selecting the service activity, they are far more likely to buy into the program and care about what happens; and

  2. When there are clear connections between the classroom and the service activity, students are far more likely to see the importance of what they are doing and more likely to invest themselves in the program.

- Opportunities for reflection are included throughout the service activity, enhancing the likelihood of positive impacts from the service. Without reflection, they are likely to view their service experience negatively.

- How often the challenge is repeated. Service experiences need to be repeated many times and in many different ways to maximize potential positive learning impacts.

- Whether the level and kind of challenge associated with the service activity is balanced by an appropriate level of support from teachers and other adults who care about what the student may be experiencing.

In simple terms, if students are involved in a service activity, such as working with the homeless, they may perceive their experience to be extremely challenging to their world view and sense of how things are. If no adults are present to encourage them to continue their involvement in this service activity and to help them reflect on the meaning of their experiences, the students may feel overwhelmed and quit. On the other hand, if students are involved in service activities only with people like themselves, they may find their experiences to be too supportive. There is no challenge and hence, no reason to examine their current world views. Well-designed service-learning programs seek to balance developmentally appropriate challenge with appropriate levels of personal support in order to invite and encourage student risk-taking and growth.

Possible strategies for balancing challenge and support in K–16 students, based on Kohlberg's theory are shown in Table 4.6.

TABLE 4.6
Balancing Challenge and Support in Service-Learning Activities

Stage of Moral Development	Challenge	Service-Learning Support Mechanisms
2	• Experiences that elicit empathy or caring, involving persons likely to show appreciation, such as children, senior citizens, or handicapped persons • Cross-age tutoring from highly structured curriculum, spelling out what is to done, how it is to be done, and by when • Volunteer work in nursing home or day-care center with specific, clearly defined tasks and responsibilities • Peer counseling	• Close supervision in the field • Simple, clear tasks • Grade based on quantity of service performed (e.g., the number of hours) • Journal writing, based on responses to questions provided by the teacher, coupled with timely teacher responses • Work in teams to develop loyalty and responsibility to others

Continued on next page

TABLE 4.6
Balancing Challenge and Support in Service-Learning Activities (Cont.)

Stage of Moral Development	Challenge	Service-Learning Support Mechanisms
3	• Work in social and human service agencies, involving moderately complex tasks • Self-inventories, processed by teacher • Cross-age tutoring, with appropriate freedom to select activities, methods, and materials within curriculum guidelines • Individual projects, based on areas where growth is desired • Peer counseling about sensitive, controversial issues, such as sexual activity or substance abuse • Role-playing, structured discussions, fields trips, structured discussions, interviews, and group experiences	• Approval and recognition from teacher and/or site supervisor • Grade based on quantity and quality of service performed (e.g., number of hours plus feedback from supervisor) • Team or group work to consolidate this stage • Journal writing, responding to a choice of questions related to multiple explanations, causes, and the conflict between pleasing others and upholding rules • Timely responses from teachers and/or site supervisors to any written work
4	• Indepth, extended opportunities for students to confront stereotypes through service with people from backgrounds that differ from their own • Cross-age tutoring programs, especially those that involve students with students from other economic and cultural groups • Encouraging students to become advocates for causes associated with their service activities • Self-inventories, processed with the teacher	• Journal writing, responding to a choice of questions related to causes and issues underlying their service activity • Timely responses from teachers and/or site supervisors to any written work • Regular meetings with other students involved in the activity to process and plan

Design and Evaluation Questions Based on Stages of Development

The following is a list of design and evaluation questions resulting from use of these theories that can be used to guide service-learning research and practice.

   • Were service activities designed from the perspective of one or more developmental theories? If so, what assessments were made? In what ways were these assessments or assumptions reflected in program design?

- What assumptions were made about participants' levels of cognitive/moral development? What assessments were made to check these assumptions? What evidence supports the validity of these assumptions? In what ways were these assessments or assumptions reflected in program design?

- In planning service-learning activities, was sufficient attention paid to the motivations arising from the students' stages of moral development? If so, in what ways? If not, why not?

- In what ways did service-learning activities allow and encourage students to be physically active? Were activities appropriate for any special needs participants may have had?

- In what ways did service-learning activities help counter student feelings of inferiority and inadequacy and enhance their self-esteem?

- In what ways did service-learning activities give students opportunities to explore the kind of person they wanted to become?

- In what ways did service-learning activities help students learn to use critical-thinking and problem solving skills?

- In what ways did service-learning activities help students see and experience connections between personal decision making and personal responsibility?

- In what ways were students involved in deciding group guidelines? In planning their service activities? In helping to evaluate program impacts?

- In what ways did service-learning activities provide opportunities for youth to develop social skills through interactions with peers and adults, especially those from different backgrounds?

- In what ways did service-learning activities provide youth with opportunities to interact physically, mentally, and socially with their environment?

- In what ways did service-learning activities enable students to develop deeper understandings of people from diverse cultural, ethnic, and/or religious backgrounds?

- In what ways did service-learning activities engage students in real-life problem solving situations that allowed them to explore options, make decisions, and reflect on outcomes?

- In what ways were students given the freedom to explore, discover, choose their own tasks, construct knowledge, and direct their own behaviors and learning experiences?

- In what ways did service-learning activities enable indepth exploration of possible career options and related identities to see which ones might fit?

- In what ways was peer pressure used to influence the participation of other students in service-learning activities?

- What kinds of challenges did students experience in their service-learning activities? Was the level of challenge appropriate for the students' levels of moral development?

- What kinds of support (training, personal feedback, etc.) were available to students? In what ways was the level of support appropriate to the challenges students experienced?

- What evidence is there that levels of challenge associated with service-learning activities were balanced by appropriate levels of support?

- If the service-learning activities were judged to be too challenging, what could be done the next time to increase the level of support?

- If the service-learning activities were judged to be too simple, what could be done the next time to increase the level of challenge?

THE PERSPECTIVE OF LEARNING STYLES: PERSONALITY TYPE (MBTI) AND MULTIPLE INTELLIGENCES

Personality Type: The Myers-Briggs Type Indicator

Another way of approaching the design and evaluation of service-learning activities is through the use of learning styles. Two approaches are considered in this section: Jung's (1971) theory of psychological types and Gardner's (1983, 1997) theory of multiple intelligences.

According to Jung, there are four basic mental processes—sensing, intuition, thinking, and feeling—used by everyone but not equally preferred and developed (McCaulley, 1988, 1997). Individuals tend to use the processes they prefer most and, through repeated use, develop expertise in the kinds of activities associated with these preferences, resulting in characteristic habits, attitudes, and behaviors associated with that type. Jung suggested that, as individuals move into mid-life and beyond, they are increasingly challenged to appreciate and make appropriate use of their less preferred learning styles (Staude, 1981).

Jung's theory was operationalized by Myers (1980) in the Myers-Briggs Type Indicator (the *MBTI*) and by Meisgeier and Murphy (1987) on the Murphy-Meisgeier Type Indicator for children (the *MMTIC*). The MBTI, which assumes a high school reading level, identifies four basic personality dimensions: (1) extraversion–introversion, (2) sensing–intuition, (3) thinking–feeling, and (4) judging–perceiving.

The MMTIC, which has a reading level appropriate for Grades 3 through 6, adds an additional scoring category; classifying children who do not demonstrate clear preference for one side of the E-I, S-N, T-F, or J-P scales as *undetermined*, based on the assumption that psychological type is a developmental phenomenon and that some children may not be fully developed in terms of their type.

The extraversion–introversion preference indicates a person's preferred way of interacting with the world. Extraverted individuals, designated by the letter E, prefer to spend most of their time and energy interacting with the world of people, events, and things. Introverted individuals, designated by the letter I, prefer to spend most of their time and energy being alone with their thoughts. Extraverts typically need to experience something before they can understand it, whereas introverts usually need to understand something before they will risk doing it.

The sensing–intuition preference has to do with basic differences in how people become aware of what is going on in their world. Sensing individuals, designated by the letter S, are primarily interested in facts and details and in what is going on here and now. They focus their time and energy on collecting information with their five senses. Intuitive individuals, designated by the letter N, use this information to speculate on meanings and future possibilities.

The thinking–feeling preference has to do with how people make decisions and commitments. Thinking individuals, designated by the letter T, prefer to make decisions and commitments logically and impersonally, based on a careful analysis on the potential consequences of various courses of action. *Fairness* is defined as impersonal adherence to rules and principles; treating everyone the same. Feeling individuals, designated by the letter F, prefer to make decisions and commitments based on a prioritized set of personal values, including how they feel about the issue in question. Because consideration for the needs of others is important to them, they define *fairness* as standing up for the rights of the individual, regardless of what the rules say.

The judging–perceiving preference has to do with the kind of world in which people prefer to live. Judging individuals, designated by the letter J, prefer to live in a decisive, orderly, planned way and are oriented more towards controlling life than experiencing it. In contrast, perceiving individuals, designated by the letter P, take a more flexible, adaptable, tolerant approach to life, preferring to experience life rather than control it. The relative frequency of each preference is shown in Table 4.7.

TABLE 4.7
Relative Frequency of Preferences in the General Population

Extraversion	46%	Introversion	54%
Sensing	68%	Intuition	32%
Thinking	53%	Feeling	47%
Judging	58%	Perceiving	42%

Differences related to gender and ethnic background have also been observed (Hammer & Mitchell, 1995).

The existence of four different preferences, resulting in 16 different personality types (no one type better than another), is supported by a growing body of empirical evidence. There is also a growing body of research supporting the hypothesis that these preferences are linked to visible and measurable differences in preferred learning styles (Lawrence, 1982; McCaulley & Nutter, 1974; Zeisset, 1985). These preferences would also result in potentially different learning experiences and outcomes for participants. Some possibilities are shown in Table 4.8.

Multiple Intelligences

Howard Gardner (1983) suggested that intelligence has more to do with the capacity for solving problems and fashioning products in a context-rich and naturalistic setting than with looking at how a student does when taken out of his or her natural learning environment and asked to do tasks he or she will probably never have to do again (e.g., taking a standardized test such as the SAT or ACT). The eight intelligences identified by Gardner (1983, 1997) and curriculum-based service-learning and reflective activities that might be related to them are shown in Table 4.9.

Research by Armstrong (1994) and Campbell (1997) indicated that teachers can use the theory of multiple intelligences in a variety of ways.

- As an instructional process that provides numerous entry points into lesson content;

- As a reason to develop each student's talents early in life;

- To organize classroom learning stations;

- To teach students self-directed learning skills; or

- To establish apprenticeship programs with community experts to teach students real-world skills.

TABLE 4.8
Myers-Briggs Personality Type and Service-Learning/Reflection

Preference	Possible Curriculum-Based Service-Learning Activities	Possible Reflective Activities
Extraversion: Action oriented—doing comes before understanding; prefers to work with others; variety in service projects is more important than depth	Direct group hands on service projects such as cross-age tutoring, intergenerational projects, working with people from other economic, cultural groups	• Oral reports (view as draft of final report) • Role-plays, skits • Make a model of what was learned • Journaling (for growth)
Introversion: Thoughtful—understanding comes before doing; prefers to work alone or in small groups; prefers fewer service projects in more depth	Indirect, individual or small group service projects such as recycling, air/water quality monitoring, or behind-the-scenes planning	• Journaling, writing prompts based on service theme • Creating instructions for future students • Compile a scrapbook or final report based on service theme • Oral report based on final report (for growth)
Sensing: Focus on details; dislike working on new problems unless they can use existing skills; need to know what is expected of them	Direct or indirect hands on service projects such as cross-age tutoring, environmental service	• Role-plays, skits • Make a model of what was learned • Writing prompts or other written work based on service theme • Journaling, using *what, so what, now what* (for growth, focus on *now what*)
Intuition: Bored with details, prefer service activities that allow them to add new skills/do it their way; need to understand the issue involved	Direct, indirect, or advocacy service projects that allow them to identify a need and brain-storm strategies for addressing it and then implement it their own way	• Create a poster or banner showing what they learned • Express service theme through fine arts • Writing prompts, using open-ended what if questions based on service theme • Journaling, using *what, so what, now what* (for growth, focus on *what*)

Preference	Possible Curriculum-Based Service-Learning Activities	Possible Reflective Activities
Thinking: Make decisions and commitments logically and impersonally, based on careful analysis on consequences; *fairness* is defined as treating everyone the same	Direct, indirect, or advocacy service projects that speak to the head and involve intellectual challenge around issues of justice and fairness	• Expert paper outlining issues behind service theme, possible solutions and con-sequences • Advocacy papers, articles, presentations • Journaling, using *what, so what, now what* (for growth, focus on *so what* and the human dimension of the issue)
Feeling: Focus is on interpersonal relationships; caring for others; *fairness* is defined as standing up for the individual, regardless of the rules	Direct, indirect, or advocacy service projects that speak to the heart such as cross-age tutoring; visits to nursing homes; work with people who are different by virtue of race, age, economic status	• Role plays, skits • Advocacy papers, articles, presentations focusing on human dimension of service theme • Journaling, using *what so what, now what* (for growth, focus on *so what* and logical analysis on the issue)
Judging: Prefer to live in a decisive, orderly, planned way; oriented towards control rather than understanding	Group or individual service projects that allow them to be in control of what happens and how and when it happens; projects that remind them of values they ought to hold and things they ought to be doing	• Reflective strategies need to be highly structured, with clear and unambiguous instructions and due dates • Spontaneous class discussions (for growth)
Perceiving: Prefer to live in a spontaneous, flexible, adaptable way; oriented towards experience rather than control	Group or individual service projects offering a variety of options; reminding them of things they are already doing and values they already hold	• Reflective strategies need to be open-ended and flexible, allowing students more latitude in choosing both what they do and how they do it • Written questions for ref-lections (for growth)

TABLE 4.9
Multiple Intelligences and Service-Learning/Reflection

Type of Intelligence	Possible Curriculum-Based Service-Learning Activities	Possible Reflective Activities
Verbal/Linguistic: Capacity to use words effectively, to express what is on your mind	• Interview senior citizens to gather firsthand infor-mation about an issue	• Journal • Essay, expert paper • Guide for future volunteers

(continued on next page)

Type of Intelligence	Possible Curriculum-Based Service-Learning Activities	Possible Reflective Activities
and to understand other people.	• Write letters to gather information • Write brochures about service theme	• Press releases, public speaking
Logical-Mathematical: Capacity to reason well, the way a scientist or logician does; or to manipulate numbers the way a mathematician does.	• Gather and graph data related to service project • Cross-age tutoring in math	• Compile and present statistics and other data • Gather information needed to understand project impacts • Surveys, field-based research
Spatial: Ability to represent the spatial world internally in your mind—the way a pilot or chess player does.	• Monitor air/water quality and graph results • Prepare/read directions related to service project	• Photo, slide, video essays, scrap-books, drawings, collages, drawings, paintings based on ser-vice theme
Bodily-Kinesthetic: Expertise in using one's whole body to express ideas and feelings, for example, through athletics, the performing arts, dancing, and acting.	• Perform a skit based on service theme • Learn and use sign language to involve hearing impaired people in service project • Build a nature trail in a local park	• Build something that reflects what was learned • Develop and implement an exercise program for seniors • Dance or theater presentation based on service theme
Musical: Capacity to perceive, discriminate, transform, and express musical forms.	• Develop rap songs that reflect service theme • Tape music for the visually impaired	• Assemble songs based on service theme • Write a rap or other song based on service theme
Interpersonal: Ability to perceive and make distinctions in the moods, intentions, motivations, and feelings of others.	• Work in groups • Cross-age tutoring in any content area	• Letters to and from senior citizens, veterans, and the like • Write a role-play or simulation activity based on service theme • Train other students for service
Intrapersonal: Ability to understand yourself, to know who you are, what you can do, what you want to do, how you react to things, which things to avoid, and which things to gravitate towards.	• Design a web page for service project • Individualized service project	• Keep a personal reflection journal • Complete project activity/checklists
Naturalist: Ability to discriminate among living things and non-living things.	• Plant a garden of local plants to provide produce to a shelter • Cross-age tutoring in science	• Expert papers, essays, videos • Public speaking on service theme

Design and Evaluation Questions Related to Personality Type and Multiple Intelligences

The following lists design and evaluation questions that may be investigated based on theories related to personality types and multiple intelligences.

- What assumptions were made about participants' personality types? What assessments were made to check these assumptions? In what ways were these assessments–assumptions reflected in program design?

- What assumptions were made about participants' preferred learning styles? What assessments were made to check these assumptions? In what ways were these assessments–assumptions reflected in program design?

- In what ways did service-learning activities take into account and support the personality types, and related preferred learning styles, of the students involved?

- In what ways did service-learning activities take into account and challenge the personality types, and related preferred learning styles, of the students involved?

- If assessments of personality type were not done, what assumptions about type were made in planning service-learning activities? Looking back at program outcomes, were these assumptions valid or not?

- In what ways does an understanding of personality type theory help account for some of the student outcomes (levels of satisfaction, dissatisfaction) you may have observed?

- In planning service-learning activities which of the eight intelligences are used most often? Which ones are used least often? For example, which of the following activities are typically included or avoided in planning and implementing service-learning activities?

  - Brainstorming (Linguistic and Interpersonal Intelligence)
  - Word games with body movements (Linguistic and Bodily-Kinesthetic Intelligence)
  - Classifying using Venn diagrams (Logical-Mathematical and Spatial Intelligence)
  - 3-Dimensional models or constructions (Spatial and Logical-Mathematical Intelligence)
  - Rap and poetry (Linguistic and Musical Intelligence)

- Journals (Linguistic and Intrapersonal Intelligence)
- Cooperative Learning (Bodily-Kinesthetic and Interpersonal Intelligence)
- Dissecting or taking things apart (Spatial, Bodily-Kinesthetic and Naturalistic Intelligences)
- Graphs and charts (Logical-Mathematical and Spatial Intelligence)
- Hands-on learning (Bodily-Kinesthetic and Spatial Intelligence)
- Math concepts set to music (Logical-Mathematical and Musical Intelligence)

- If assessments of multiple intelligences were not done, what assumptions were made in planning service-learning activities? Looking back at program outcomes, were these assumptions valid?

- In what ways does an understanding of multiple intelligence theory help account for some of the student outcomes (levels of satisfaction, dissatisfaction) you may have observed?

Concluding Comments

The purpose of this chapter has been to show how developmental and learning theory may be used, alone or in combination, in the design and evaluation of age-appropriate, curriculum-based service-learning activities. It is hoped that this theory-based approach will contribute to a better understanding of the connections between service-learning programs and resulting student outcomes. As these connections become clearer, service-learning programs can be designed to maximize the probability of achieving positive academic, personal, interpersonal, ethical, and vocational impacts for each and every student who participates in service-learning.

REFERENCES

Armstrong, T. (1994). *Multiple intelligences in the classroom.* Alexandria, VA: Association for Supervision and Curriculum Development.
Barrett, W. (1978). Construction and validation of the Developing Purposes Inventory. *Technical Report on Studies* Nos. 12, 15, 26. Iowa City, IA: Iowa Student Development Project.
Benson, P. (1990). *The troubled journey: A portrait of 6th–12th grade youth.* Minneapolis, MN: Lutheran Brotherhood and the Search Institute.
Billig, S. H. (2000). Research on K–12 school-based service-learning: The evidence builds. *Phi Delta Kappan, 81*(9), 658–664.
Calabrese, R. L., & Schumer, H. (1986). The effects of service activities on adolescent alienation. *Adolescence, 21*(83), 675–87.

Campbell, L. (1997, September). Variations on a theme: How teachers interpret MI theory. *Educational Leadership, 55*(1), 14–19.

Chickering, A. (1969). *Education and identity.* San Francisco: Jossey-Bass.

Cohen, E. (1986). *Designing group work: Strategies for the heterogeneous classroom.* New York: Teachers College Press.

Conrad, D., & Hedin, D. (1982). The impact of experiential education on adolescent development. *Child and Youth Services, 4*(3/4), 57–76.

Conrad, D., & Hedin, D. (1987). *Youth service: A guidebook for developing and operating effective programs.* Washington, DC: Independent Sector.

Conrad, D., & Hedin, D. (1989). *High school community service: A review of research and programs.* Madison, WI: University of Wisconsin, National Center on Effective Secondary Schools.

Duckenfield, L., & Swanson, L. (1992). *Service learning: Meeting the needs of youth at risk.* Clemson, SC: National Dropout Prevention Center.

Erikson, E. (1963). *Childhood and Society* (2nd ed.). New York: Norton.

Erikson, E. (1964). *Insight and responsibility: Lectures on the ethical implications of psychoanalytic insight.* New York: Norton.

Erikson, E. (1968). *Identity: Youth and crisis.* New York: Norton.

Erikson, E. (1982). *The life cycle completed: A review.* New York: Norton.

Erwin, T. (1978). *Validation of the Erwin Identity Scale.* Iowa City, IA: University of Iowa. Unpublished doctoral dissertation.

Gardner, H. (1983). *Frames of mind: The theory of multiple intelligences.* New York: Basic Books.

Gardner, H. (1997). The first seven . . . and the eighth. *Educational Leadership, 55*(1), 8–13.

Gibbs, J., & Widaman, K. (1982). *Social intelligence: Measuring the development of sociomoral reflection.* Englewood Cliffs, NJ: Prentice-Hall.

Gilligan, C. (1982). *In a different voice.* Cambridge, MA: Harvard University Press.

Hammer, A., & Mitchell, W. (1995). The distribution of MBTI types in the U. S. by gender and ethnic group. *Journal of Psychological Type, 7,* 2–15.

Hawley, G. (1988). *Measures of psychosocial development.* Odessa, FL: PAR.

Heist, R., & Yonge, G. (1968). *Omnibus Personality Inventory: A technical manual.* New York: The Psychological Corporation.

Hersh, R., Paolitto, D., & Reimer, J. (1979). *Promoting moral growth: From Piaget to Kohlberg.* New York: Longman.

Jung, C. (1971). *Psychological types.* Princeton, NJ: Princeton University Press.

Kohlberg, L. (1958). *The development of modes of moral thinking choice in the years 10 to 16.* Chicago: University of Chicago. Unpublished doctoral dissertation.

Kohlberg, L. (1981). The meaning and measurement of moral development. The Heinz Werner Lecture Series, Vol. XIII (1979). Worcester, MA: Clark University Press.

Kohlberg, L. (1981). *The philosophy of moral development.* New York: Harper & Row.

Kohlberg, L., Colby, A., Gibbs, J., & Speicher-Dubin, B. (1976). *Moral stage scoring manual.* Cambridge, MA: Harvard University, Center for Moral Education.

Lawrence, G. (1982). *People types and tiger stripers.* Gainesville, FL: Center for Applications of Psychological Type.

Lewin, C. (1936). *Principles of topological psychology.* New York: McGraw-Hill.

Lickona, T. (1976). *Moral development and behavior.* New York: Holt, Rinehart and Winston.

Magolda, M., & Porterfield, W. (1968). *Assessing intellectual development: The link between theory and practice.* Alexandria, VA: American College Personnel Association.

McCaulley, L. (1977, 1988). *Introduction to the MBTI for researchers.* Palo Alto, CA: Consulting Psychologists Press.

McCaulley, M., & Nutter, F. (1974). *Psychological (Myers-Briggs) type differences in education.* Gainesville, FL: Center for the Application of Psychological Type.

Mines, R. (1978). Change in college students along Chickering's Vector of Freeing Interpersonal Relationships. *Technical Report on Studies,* Nos. 12, 15, 26. Iowa City, IA: Iowa Student Development Project.

Murphy, E., & Meisgeier, C. (1987). *Murphy-Meisgeier Type Indicator for Children.* Palo Alto, CA: Consulting Psychologists Press.

Myers, I. (1962). *Manual: The Myers-Briggs Type Indicator.* Princeton, NJ: Educational Testing Service.

Newmann, F. M., & Rutter, R. A. (1983). *The effects of high school community service programs on students' social development.* Final report to the National Institute of Education. Madison, WI: Wisconsin Center for Education Research.

Perry, W. (1970). *Intellectual and ethical development in college students.* New York: Holt, Rinehart and Winston.

Piaget, J. (1965). *The moral judgment of the child.* Translated by M. Gabain. New York: Free Press.

Rest, J. (1979). *Development in judging moral issues.* Minneapolis, MN: University of Minnesota Press.

Root, S. (1997). School-based service: A review of research for teacher educators. In J. Erickson & J. Anderson (Eds.), *Learning with the community: Concepts and models for service-learning in teacher education* (pp. 42–72). Washington, DC: American Association of Higher Education.

Rosen, H. (1980). *The development of sociomoral reflection.* New York: Columbia University Press.

Selman, R. (1980). *The growth of interpersonal understanding: Development and clinical analysis.* New York: Academic Press.

Simons, P. (1994). A call to service: Merging the hearts and minds of America's young children elementary school service-learning. In R. Kraft & M. Swadener (Eds.), *Building community: Service-learning in the academic community* (pp. 215–232). Denver, CO: Colorado Campus Compact.

Staude, J. (1981). *The adult development of C. G. Jung.* Boston: Rutledge and Kegan Paul.

Walsh, B. (1973). *Theories of person-environment interaction: Implications for the college student.* Iowa City, IA: The American College Testing Program.

Woehrle, T. (1993, November). Growing up responsible. *Educational Leadership,* 40–43.

Zeisset, C. (1985). Three ways to look at your students. *Type Reporter, 2,* 1–13.

5

Issues Regarding the Selection of Variables for Study in the Context of the Diversity of Possible Student Outcomes of Service-Learning

Alan S. Waterman
The College of New Jersey

There is a wealth of testimonial data endorsing the value of service-learning programs. These endorsements have been provided by students participating in service projects, by teachers conducting the programs, by administrators overseeing the programs, and by community representatives and those who have benefited from the students' efforts (Bell, Sharp, McDaniel, & Stowell, 1999; Hamilton, 1979). But testimonials have limited standing in the education research community or with policy planners because the individuals providing the endorsements may be seen as having a vested interest in the continuation of the programs. Also, cognitive dissonance theory suggests that when people invest extensive time, money, and other resources in an undertaking, it would be psychologically unacceptable to acknowledge that all their efforts, and those resources, were wasted. So it has been concluded that however extensive and eloquent the praise students and educators express concerning a project or program, the reports of participants cannot necessarily be taken as an accurate portrayal of what has occurred or the benefits that have accrued from it.

Qualitative research studies have provided more extensive accounts of the nature of the benefits to be derived from service-learning programs and these reports have been generally consistent with claims made in the testimonials (Shumer, 1997). Although qualitative research can provide information on whether service-learning or other experiential education programs are having an impact, and the types of benefits to be derived, by its nature qualitative research lacks precision regarding the parameters and magnitudes of those impacts. Further, the value of qualitative research is dependent on the researcher's ability to be objective in the assessment of a program's costs and benefits, its strengths and limitations.

The desire for greater precision and objectivity is the basis for the development of quantitative research methods for the assessment of service-learning and other experiential education programs. Quantitative methods are valued not only for their actual strengths but because they carry the mantle of being "scientific," science having produced such dramatic gains in our culture's knowledge base. But the record of quantitative investigations of the outcomes of experiential education programs, including service-learning, is marked by extensive inconsistency. There are many quantitative studies that document the benefits of service experiences across a wide variety of domains including academic performance, problem solving, and skill development (Cohen & Kinsey, 1994; Follman, 1998; Morgan, 2000; Santmire, Girard, & Grosskopf, 1999; Shumer, 1990), citizenship (Giles & Eyler, 1994; Hamilton & Zeldin, 1987; Kahne & Westheimer, 2001; Miller, 1997), self-esteem (Conrad & Hedin, 1982; Giles & Eyler, 1998; Luchs, 1987; Yates & Youniss, 1996), social attitudes (Eyler & Giles, 1995; Metz, McLellan, & Youniss, 2000; Myers-Lipton, 1994; Newmann & Rutter, 1982), and personality functioning (Batchelder & Root, 1994; Calabrese & Schumer, 1986; Switzer, Simmons, Dew, Regalski, & Wang, 1995).

But there are also a large number of studies in which statistical tests have failed to detect such outcomes. It is difficult to assess the size of this literature because studies with nonsignificant findings are less likely to be accepted for publication and may never be submitted for publication (i.e., the file-drawer problem). A review of the research entries in *Dissertation Abstracts Internationale* (Waterman, 2001), in which findings are reported independent of statistical significance, provides evidence for the difficulties in documenting significant effects of service-learning. It should also be noted that the research designs developed by doctoral candidates are often methodologically less sophisticated than studies conducted by more experienced researchers. However, even large-scale, well-designed studies carried out by established researchers have yielded results that have been less consistent and less impressive than had been hoped for by those conducting the studies (Blyth, Saito, & Berkas, 1997; Melchior, 1999). Are the difficulties encountered in trying to establish the nature and extent of the benefits of service-learning and experiential education through quantitative research a result of the benefits being relatively thin and inconsistent in their appearance? Or are such difficulties due to the possibility that the quantitative methods employed in such research endeavors are relatively insensitive in identifying the presence of benefits that are, according to the endorsements and qualitative research, manifestly there?

Three principal sets of problems with quantitative research on service-learning are addressed in this chapter. Taken together, these problems provide a basis for concluding that, due to the anticipated diversity of possible outcomes of such programs, existing methodologies are relatively insensitive assessment techniques. These sets of problems are: (a) problems associated with the selection of outcome variables for study, (b) problems associated with the selection of research instruments to measure the variables selected, and (c) problems associated with confounding life events that make it difficult to attribute observed impacts to the program under study. An alternative methodological approach using the individual student as the unit of analysis will be proposed as a means to address many of the problems raised here.

PROBLEMS ASSOCIATED WITH THE SELECTION
OF OUTCOME VARIABLES FOR STUDY

One of the greatest difficulties in documenting the effectiveness of service-learning programs (and other forms of experiential education), as compared to more traditional modes of instruction, pertains to the range of likely program impacts. Whereas for traditional instruction, the range of impact is viewed as relatively narrow, for service-learning this range is considerably broader.

With regard to traditional forms of instruction, there is a presumption that the principal area of impact will involve the content of material presented in the classes and the readings, related problem solving, or other cognitive skills. The outcome measures appropriate for such instruction are generally considered to be tests on the course material. In traditional classrooms, teachers know the type of material they will be placing on the tests, or that is included on standardized tests, and consciously teach to the material on which students will be tested. There is nothing wrong with this, indeed it is expected by school administrators, students, and their parents. From a research perspective, these circumstances represent a narrow range of anticipated outcomes that is comparatively easy to assess.

It is also true that a traditional program of instruction may affect students' future plans and goals, attitudes and values, as well as aspects of their psychosocial functioning. For example, students who are doing well in a particular subject may be expected to show gains in feelings of competence or self-confidence, particularly when the success comes in a new area of study. This in turn can lead to consideration of new career choice possibilities. However, it can be anticipated that, on average, such gains will be balanced out by losses in feelings of competence or self-confidence on the part of students who did not do well in the content area. Such losses will be particularly evident for students whose prior record in a subject had been good, but whose performance has deteriorated. This can result in the student dropping a career plan that had previously been adopted. For such reasons, the impact of traditional educational programs, aside from content-related measures, is generally not seen as systematic and is seldom assessed.

With regard to service-learning and other forms of experiential education, the range of anticipated, systematic outcomes is considerably broader. Advocates of such curricula prefer this choice on academic, developmental, and psychosocial grounds. However, a careful analysis of their reasoning suggests that classroom tests may not be the best measures for use in program evaluations. The usual academic claim for service-learning is that through involvement in real-world projects, students will be able to appreciate the relevance of the material being presented and will therefore care more about mastering it. The project experiences are also expected to make more vivid impressions on the students such that the material will stay with the students more effectively than the same material presented in a more traditional manner. But appreciation of relevance, motivation to learn specific material, and maintenance of learning over time are not the content of typical academic outcome assessments during or at the time of completion of a particular course. Under these circumstances, it would not be surprising to find no differences between service-learning and traditional instruction with respect to content-based, classroom tests on the same material. A fairer evaluation of the academic claims for service-learning would involve follow up evaluation of students with regard to their mastery of the material after a period of one to two years. Due to practical difficulties in conducting research of this type, such assessments are not typically undertaken.

Unlike traditional approaches to instruction, service-learning and other forms of experiential education are expected to promote systematic gains in such areas as feelings of competence and self-confidence, psychosocial development, and reflective attitude and values changes. Such changes are expected to occur for most participating students, not just those who are doing well academically. It might therefore be expected that there would be extensive documentation of personal development benefits from service-learning programs relative to those derived from traditional classroom instruction. Although the research record does indeed point in that direction, the record in not as consistent as the proponents of service-learning might wish. The explanation probably lies in the range of possible outcomes from involvement in service-learning projects and the likelihood that students differ in the areas in which they experience benefits from their participation.

There are three primary sources of variability in the types of outcomes that may result from participation in service-learning programs: (a) *between program differences* in the service-learning programs offered, (b) *within program differences* in the nature of the service and learning experiences afforded to participating students, and (c) *between student differences* within programs regarding what students bring to the service experiences they are having.

Between Program Differences

One source of the diversity in the outcomes of service-learning programs is a very wide range of program characteristics. Programs differ in the grade level at which they are directed, the nature of the service experiences provided, the duration of the programs, their intensity (in terms of the number of hours of service), the extent and nature of the reflective activities employed, and the extent and nature of the program's integration with in-class curriculum. Given this diversity of program characteristics, it is unreasonable to expect that they would affect students in similar ways.

Within Program Differences in Student Experiences

Not only do programs in service-learning differ with respect to between-program characteristics, but also inevitably, within every program each participating student will have a different set of experiences. For example, in a tutoring program or a program that involves working with senior citizens, or residents in a homeless shelter, each student will likely work with his or her own set of clients. Some clients are more responsive, cooperative, and interesting to work with than are others. In programs that involve students in environmental clean-up projects, some students will have tasks that are more (or less) palatable than others. In contrast to traditional classroom instruction, in experiential education, it is almost impossible to standardize the experiences students will be having because those experiences are occurring in naturalistic settings.

Between Student Differences Within Programs

The diversity of the students participating in a service-learning program includes differences in gender; cultural background; cognitive capability; prior school record; developmental readiness; the child-rearing practices with which students were raised; the extent and quality of peer relationships; and personality traits, goals, values, beliefs, and motivations for participation, among other factors. Given such differences, it is not plausible to expect that students in any educational program will be affected by it in similar ways. Rather, it can be anticipated that what a student brings to a program will materially affect what that student derives from it. The same program may benefit different students in quite different ways (Waterman, 1997).

Given the diversity of what students bring to a program and the diversity of experiences students actually have during their program participation, how can appropriate outcome measures be selected for the evaluation of the effectiveness of service-learning? In response to the dilemma contained in the question, most evaluators choose measures that they anticipate will be ones on which the largest segment of the participating sample will show gains. That this strategy works is evident in the number of studies yielding findings attesting to the success of particular service-learning programs. However, the presence of students in a sample who may well be benefiting from the same program, but benefited in ways not tapped by the measures used, will tend to suppress the strength of the relationships under investigation and, across studies, may contribute to the inconsistencies in outcomes reported. As important, the failure to identify and assess gains made by students in areas not measured by the scales chosen for the evaluation means that program effectiveness is being underestimated. One conclusion that follows from this is that the reported outcomes of service-learning, and other forms of experiential education, represent baseline estimates of program effectiveness. There is likely to be a range of undocumented benefits that accompany those that are documented in a particular assessment, although those benefits may be more idiosyncratic and may occur for different students than those contributing to the documented outcomes. It is also possible that there will be a range of undocumented costs as well. However, it seems more plausible that in programs that have been shown to be effective in specific ways, the undocumented effects are more likely to be benefits than costs.

Although it is always the case in educational program evaluations that there will be undocumented outcomes, the implications of the failure to identify the ways in which individual students benefit are more serious for experiential education programs than for traditional forms of instruction. Because the almost exclusive focus of assessment for traditional education programs is on academic outcomes, evaluators need only look at this one area to determine the effectiveness of a particular curriculum or to compare curricula designed for the teaching of the same material. Undocumented effects occurring outside the area of student learning would not materially change the results of the evaluation. In contrast, for service-learning programs and for other form of experiential education, the benefits claimed go beyond academic learning to include gains in psychosocial development, personality variables such as self-confidence, self-efficacy, and leadership, civic engagement and citizenship values, and a variety of attitude variables such as appreciation of diversity, social acceptance, and tolerance. A standardized assessment battery tapping several of these variables may document the gains made by some students on the particular measures under investigation. However, if more idiosyncratic, undocumented benefits had also been identified, a better picture of a program's impact would be obtained. Whereas as the standardized assessment battery may yield effects that appear thin, because only some students are benefiting in those particular ways, if undocumented gains made by other students had been identified, the overall assessment of the program might have been considerably more favorable.

This discussion of problems associated with the selection of outcome variables for study given student diversity, and both between and within program diversity, leads to a recommendation to supplement standardized assessment batteries with techniques designed to individualize assessment. A procedure for conducting individualized assessments as part of larger standardized assessments will be presented later in this chapter.

PROBLEMS ASSOCIATED WITH THE SELECTION OF RESEARCH INSTRUMENTS

Once a set of particular outcome variables is selected as the object of study in the evaluation of the effectiveness of a service-learning program, attention shifts to the selection of instruments by which to obtain data on those variables. At this point, there are two strategies by which a researcher or evaluator can proceed: A choice may be made from among existing (*off the shelf*) instruments, or new (*homegrown*) instruments will need to be developed for the evaluation to be undertaken. The advantage of *off the shelf* instruments is that they almost always have previously established norms and psychometric properties (e.g., reliability and validity estimates). By their nature, *homegrown* instruments have neither norms nor known psychometric properties outside those identified in the research study being conducted. The choice of existing instruments is typically a more convenient process in comparison to the efforts involved in creating new assess variables of interest, they are not necessarily sufficient to outweigh all other considerations.

The most important consideration in the selection of research instruments should be the likelihood that the measures employed will provide an assessment of the particular ways students are expected to develop during the course of the program under evaluation. The choice of instruments because of pre-established psychometric properties or convenience, but measuring variables different from those tapping expected impacts, is very likely to be counterproductive. Given the diversity of service-learning programs in existence, and the range of possible outcomes of those programs, serious consideration should be given to tailoring each outcomes assessment to the particular program being evaluated.

Typically, *off the shelf* research instruments assessing psychosocial development, attitudes and values, and personality functioning have been developed for studies unrelated to the outcomes of educational programs. The constructs tapped are likely to be relatively broad. Further, they may be more appropriate for some age groups rather than for others.

For example, one type of service-learning program often used with high school science courses involves River Watch activities (Hill & Pope, 1997). The academic requirements may include measuring the quality of water; assessing biodiversity; analyzing the health and functioning of plants, insects, and fish; and studying the effects of runoffs and sewage treatment on water quality. The service elements may include planning water clean up projects, developing monitoring programs to be carried out over time, and teaching elementary school students about the environment. It is reasonable to expect that programs of this type will increase awareness of environmental issues and concerns about environmental protection. However, using an established instrument to assess environmental attitudes, such as the New Environmental Paradigm Scale (Dunlap & Van Liere, 1978) or the recent revision, the New Ecological Paradigm Scale (Dunlap, Van Liere, Mertig, & Emmet-Jones, 2000) may not be best suited to determining the impact of River Watch programs. The items on such scales pertain to a relatively wide range of environmental issues unrelated to water resources. Although there are grounds to expect some generalization of environmental information and concerns from the topic of clean water to topics related to clear air, littering, solid waste disposal, and nuclear hazards, the extent of such generalization may be limited or time-delayed. A multitopic measure will almost certainly be less sensitive to immediate program impacts than an instrument focusing on those aspects of the environment specifically related to streams and rivers. Evidence of the impact of such a program may be more likely to be generated by devising an instrument specific to the content of the program being evaluated.

Similarly, the use of global measures of self-esteem may not be particularly sensitive to the nature of the impact a service-learning program has on a student's self-evaluation. Participation in a River Watch program will not likely have any direct or notable effects on performance on the baseball or field hockey teams, relationships with friends or with parents, or dating popularity. Because these are likely far more important contributors to global self-esteem than a time-limited, likely far more important contributors to global self-esteem than a time-limited, school-related, service project, the likelihood that the impact of program participation on self-concept will be documented with a general self-esteem instrument is limited. But self-evaluations with respect to community concern and civic responsibility may well be affected by involvement in the service-learning activity. Even here, however, some of the impacts may be specific and some time-delayed. For example, increased concerns for the physical environment will not necessarily translate into recognition of the importance of each person's vote in an election. Again, the development of a *homegrown* instrument, specific to expected benefits, may be more sensitive to the actual impacts of a program than will use of an established measure developed for other purposes.

When developing and using *homegrown* instruments in assessing service-learning programs, an effort should be made to determine the psychometric properties of the scales developed. Both internal consistency and test-retest reliability can be determined either with data collected from students participating in the program or from other classes at the school. Determining the validity of *homegrown* measures represents a greater challenge and entails a greater investment in effort. If a *homegrown* instrument yields the expected results, this can be interpreted as support for the instrument's validity. If it does not, the failure to document the effectiveness of the service-learning program may be due either to weaknesses of the instrument, or the outcome may be an accurate reflection of an unsuccessful program.

PROBLEMS ASSOCIATED
WITH CONFOUNDING LIFE EVENTS

From the standpoint of the scientific evaluation of the effectiveness of service-learning programs, it would be ideal if all students involved in the educational program being studied, and all students in any comparison sample, had reasonably comparable life events throughout the time-frame of the evaluation. But this, of course, does not occur. Life events of the students will vary greatly both within and between classrooms. The sources of noncurricular variation will include developmental maturation, collateral events arising within the school, and collateral events arising outside of school, for example with respect to physical health, family circumstances, and social relationships. The challenge becomes trying to identify whether observed changes in educational performance, or psychological functioning, or other outcomes are due to the program under study or to confounding life events. It is also possible that the failure to observe positive changes may be a consequence of confounding life events actively interfering with the outcomes an educational program is designed to promote.

Because maturational timetables throughout childhood and adolescence are variable among students, what the students initially bring to a service-learning program may be quite different. For a service-learning program designed to promote particular forms of student development, minimal impacts may be observed among students who are maturationally advanced at the time the service program is initiated. Because they will have already made the advances anticipated to be an outcome of the education program, pre-/post-test assessments can reveal little change. Such students will look as good at the start of a program as they are expected to look at the end. Similarly, minimal impacts may be found among students who are maturationally delayed, and therefore, not optimally ready to take advantage of the particular challenges posed by the educational program. If these students are not yet ready to make the kind of advances under study, they will tend to score poorly at both the time of the pre- and the post-assessment. Maximal impacts of effective programs will only be found among those students for whom a program is well-timed to provide developmentally appropriate challenges.

There is another problem associated with maturational development. Given the span of a school semester or a school year, it can be anticipated that some observable maturational changes will occur irrespective of the educational programs in which the students are engaged. In the absence of a comparison group of students not engaged in the educational program under evaluation, the findings of *normative* developmental changes could easily be interpreted as a consequence of the program under study. Even when one or more comparison groups are included in a research design, it is possible to misinterpret normative maturational changes as program impacts if the groups under study were not equivalent at the start of the assessment. Because participation in service-learning programs is often self-selected, it is not unusual for various groups within a study to vary extensively at the time of pre-testing. Analysis of covariance is a commonly used procedure is to render groups equivalent for statistical purposes. However, this technique is based on the assumption that the assessment measures constitute an interval scale, whereas for many instruments the scale is no more than ordinal. Particularly when the service-learning participants are more advanced developmentally than the comparison groups at the start of the assessment period, the possibility of ceiling effects could work against documenting program effectiveness.

In research involving the use of comparison groups it is assumed that confounding life events will be equivalent across groups leaving the educational program under study as the principal difference between groups. Although differences between groups may exist in any given study, across a large number of evaluations this assumption is generally sound. For this reason, research information about events in student lives outside of the context of the study is seldom collected in conjunction with program evaluation. However, collateral life events can be thought of as noise within a signal-detection paradigm. The greater the number of important collateral life events occurring with family, friends, or school unrelated to program participation, the more influences there will be on the dependent measures used in the evaluation, whether those measures pertain to academic, psychosocial, or attitudinal variables.

Documentation of the effectiveness of a service-learning or other experiential educational program will occur only if the program's effects are sufficiently strong enough to outweigh the noise created by other sources of variation. By collecting information about collateral life events, it becomes possible to assess the level of noise present for individual students and to better determine whether any changes observed, whether positive or negative, are due to the students' educational experiences or to other events in their lives.

A METHODOLOGY FOR INTEGRATIVE COMPARISONS WHEN EACH STUDENT IS THE UNIT OF ANALYSIS

If each student in a service-learning class is starting from a different place with respect to academic, psychosocial, attitudinal, and personal development variables, and if the actual service-learning experiences of each student are different both on the site and in the classroom reflection activities, and if the outcome impacts of those experiences can be expected to vary widely among the students, then it is plausible to consider the evaluation of a service-learning project as a simultaneous series of $N = 1$ research design assessments (Davidson & Costello, 1969). In a pre-/post-test, $N = 1$ design, each participant is assessed at two points in time, with the analyses involving individualized sets of assessment variables. In psychology, $N = 1$ designs are most frequently employed in research on psychotherapy (Howard, Moras, Brill, Martinovich, & Lutz, 1996), an area with many parallels to the study of the effectiveness of experiential learning programs.

   $N = 1$ designs allow for the descriptive analysis of patterns of change over time under specifiable conditions, on a participant by participant basis. Although variations in the nature of what is changing can be expected from participant to participant, across $N = 1$ comparisons, it is still possible to identify regularities in the patterns of change. What is proposed here is the possibility of quantitative statistical analyses across multiple, simultaneous pre-/post-test $N = 1$ assessments. Whereas research designs employing traditional analysis of variance and regression techniques rely on use of a common set of outcome measures for all participants, a simultaneous pre-/post-test $N = 1$ research design allows for the use of individualized outcome measures for each participant.

   For educational program evaluations, there are logically a minimum of five student groups that can be formed with respect to the outcomes of a given program: (1) Students who have had an established record of high levels of success prior to involvement in the program and who are successful in the program (*high maintainers*); (2) Students who had an established record of moderate levels of success prior to involvement in the program and who are moderately successful in the program (*average maintainers*); (3) Students who have established a record of poor performance prior to involvement in the program and who are consistent in showing low levels of performance while in the program (*low maintainers*); (4) Students whose level of performance while in the program is greater than their established prior record (*gainers*); and (5) Students whose level of performance while in the program is poorer than their established prior record (*decliners*). In the context of a multiple, simultaneous $N = 1$ design, where each student is the unit of analysis, the areas in which students can demonstrate gains or declines, success or failure, can be allowed to vary from participant to participant. This is possible as long as there is a basis for establishing each student's record of performance prior to the start of an educational experience through the use of relevant pre-test measures. Because a multiple, simultaneous $N = 1$ research design can be used for any set of educational experiences, it is possible to conduct comparisons between students participating in experiential education programs with those enrolled in traditional curricula courses.

Establishing the Student's Prior Record of Performance

Each student's record of performance prior to the start of an educational experience can be established by a variety of means including:

1. Grade point average from prior coursework;
2. Teachers' evaluations of notable academic and personal qualities from previous semesters;
3. Previous attendance record;
4. Student self-perceptions of prior academic success, level of aspiration, and clarity of future goals;
5. Pre-test scores on tests of academic material related to the service-learning program;
6. Pre-test measures of self-esteem, feelings of efficacy, and psychosocial variables; and
7. Pre-test measures of any attitudinal variables considered as potentially relevant to the educational experiences the student is to have.

Because service-learning and other forms of experiential education may be expected to yield widely differing outcomes with respect to the benefits derived, and because there is unlikely to be an a priori basis on which to anticipate who will show which types of changes, it is necessary that the initial assessment be as broad-based as possible, so that it can provide the foundation for identifying a substantial portion of the range of possible changes. For this reason, the initial assessment should include descriptive teacher profiles of each student and similar self-descriptive profiles written by the students. Both types of profiles can be developed from a standardized format covering salient aspects of the student's academic record, conduct, academic motivation, goals, attitudes in relevant areas, and personal qualities. Because teachers in the service-learning program may not have had prior experiences with students in their classes, these profiles may incorporate material provided by other teachers familiar with a student's performance in prior semesters. If sufficient support for a research project is available, independent assessments could be prepared by trained personnel not otherwise involved with either the service-learning or traditional curriculum. Further, although it is possible that the initial assessment might be prepared without a knowledge of the educational condition a student would be experiencing, it is unlikely, although not impossible, that a blind procedure could be carried out during the post experience phase of the research as well.

In addition to these initial profile descriptions, quantitative data should be collected with respect to (a) knowledge of subject matter and related skills prior to exposure to course material, (b) attitude variables likely to be affected by the service experiences, and (c) a limited number of personal variables such as self-esteem, feelings of self-efficacy, and psychosocial maturity.

ASSESSING STUDENT GAINS, DECLINES, AND MAINTENANCE AFTER PARTICIPATION IN AN EDUCATIONAL EXPERIENCE

The post-test assessment of the students involved in service-learning programs and traditional curricula should mirror as much as possible the initial assessment. The teachers should again prepare descriptive profiles of each student at the end of the experience and students should each prepare a self-assessment. The same quantitative measures should again be administered.

In the teacher-prepared descriptive profiles and in the student self-assessment, particular emphasis should be placed on the ways in which the student is seen as functioning differently at the end of the program than she or he was at the beginning. Encouragement should be given to speculate on the basis of any changes observed, both gains and declines in performance or behavior. Because the assessments are being collected in the context of a particular educational experience, it is possible that any changes observed may be attributed to that experience. But this should be true both for service-learning and traditional curricula. Also, because assessments are being collected from both teacher and student, the correspondence of the attributions can be assessed.

The teacher profiles generated prior to and following participation in the educational programs can be used to determine whether there is general comparability over time or whether the student has shown notable gains or losses between the two points of assessment. Not only can an overall determination of stability or change be generated, but specific areas of change can be noted. The procedure should be sufficiently sensitive to detect instances in which gains were made in some areas while declines were experienced in others. Similar comparisons can be made for the self-assessments generated by each student. In addition, relative stability, gains, or declines can be identified on each of the quantitative academic, personality, psychosocial, and attitudinal variables on which data were collected. The product for each participant is a rich descriptive statement regarding the extent and nature of any changes over the time during which program participation was occurring, along with both the teacher's and student's attributions as to the basis for such changes. These statements can then be used by an evaluator to place each respondent into one of the five categories previously described. Although the particular aspects of performance or behavior focused on each descriptive statement are individualized in terms of what was taking place for each student, the product of the evaluative process involves the use of a set of standardized categories in terms of maintenance, gains, and declines applicable across participants.

In addition to the establishing of categories based on patterns of student changes during program participation, it is also possible to create a continuous measure of student change despite the individual nature of such changes. Using the descriptive statements regarding the extent and nature of changes over time during program participation, independent assessors can report the overall magnitude of change on a numerical rating scale. For example, a 9-point rating scale might take the following form:

9 = dramatic gains during program participation

8 = substantial gains during program participation

7 = moderate gains during program participation

6 = slight gains during program participation

5 = neither gains nor declines during program participation

4 = slight declines during program participation

3 = moderate declines during program participation

2 = substantial declines during program participation

1 = dramatic declines during program participation

By using judgments of overall gains or declines, the particular manner in which the gains or declines occurred can be allowed to vary from student to student, thus individualizing the assessment. Extensive training of the raters would need to be undertaken regarding how to apply a common rating scale across gains and declines occurring across differing aspects of academic, psychosocial, attitudinal, and personal functioning. The criteria for success in such training would be the establishment of a high degree of interjudge agreement in use of the rating scale.

One advantage of the use of a continuous rating scale for student change during program participation is the ability to employ the measure in parametric statistical analyses, such as analyses of variance or regression analyses. It should also be recognized, however, that the scale may be heavily skewed in the positive direction because the frequency of gains should be substantially greater than the frequency of declines. Another drawback to the use of such a scale is that high, average, and low maintainers would all be given the same rating in the middle of the scale.

SOME HYPOTHESES AND RESEARCH QUESTIONS IN THE ASSESSMENT OF SERVICE-LEARNING PROGRAMS THAT CAN BE STUDIED THROUGH MULTIPLE, SIMULTANEOUS, $N = 1$ DESIGNS

Comparisons of the Proportion of Students Maintaining, Gaining, and Declining During Participation in Service-Learning and Traditional Curricula

If service-learning and other forms of experiential education programs are effective in yielding the types of benefits claimed for them, and if the nature of the benefits vary from student to student, then the proportion of students characterized as gainers and high maintainers should be significantly greater than the proportion characterized as decliners or low maintainers (and perhaps average maintainers as well). Because the range of benefits generally claimed for traditional curricula fall within a narrower range, and may be expected to be more strongly related to previous academic performance, the proportion of students characterized as maintainers, whether high, average, or low, should be greater than the proportion characterized as either gainers or decliners. Further, in comparisons of gainers and decliners in traditional curricula, the latter should be greater than the former because it is more likely students will reach the limit of their abilities in dealing with new material within a given domain than it is that they will surge ahead in a domain in which they have already experienced difficulties in connection with traditional teaching methods. If a numerical, overall rating scale is employed, the scores of participants in the service-learning program should be significantly higher than those obtained by students participating in the traditional curriculum. These are testable propositions that provide a basis for determining whether or not service-learning programs are more effective, as effective, or less effective than the traditional forms of instructions.

Identifying the Nature of Benefits of Service-Learning and Traditional Curricula

An examination of the areas of gains can yield a description of the particular benefits to be derived from participation in service-learning programs and in traditionally run courses within the same domains. Since the nature of the changes resulting from courses with service-learning components may vary widely within the same class, the numbers of students showing a particular form of benefit may be relatively small. At this level, the research design proposed here approaches a qualitative analysis. However, the design proposed here can eventually lend itself to secondary analyses in which numbers derived from a series of studies, across programs, can be combined to yield meaningful statistical comparisons regarding the relative frequency of various types of gains. Similarly, this research design can be used to identify the nature and relative frequency of declines among participating students in both service-learning and traditionally run courses.

Attributions of the Origins of the Benefits of Service-Learning and Traditional Curricula

It is possible that gains and declines in student performance occurring while students are enrolled in particular service-learning programs or traditional courses may be due to either to their educational experiences or to collateral events occurring at the same time but unrelated to their education. In most studies of educational impacts, such collateral events are treated as error variance. With the design proposed here, attributions of changes in performance by the students and their teachers can be used as a means to further evaluate the comparative effectiveness of educational programs. If service-learning as an educational technique has the merits claimed for it, then students showing gains will be likely to identify the basis of those gains in the service-learning curriculum, whereas students showing declines will be likely to identify the basis for the declines in life circumstances arising outside of school. In contrast, in traditionally run classes, the students will more frequently attribute gains to improved life circumstances outside of school, while attributing declines to difficulties with the course material itself. For both types of courses, it would also be expected that teacher attributions of the students' changes in performance will parallel those of the students' self-attributions.

IMPLICATIONS OF THE USE OF $N = 1$ DESIGNS FOR RESOLVING METHODOLOGICAL PROBLEMS

At the beginning of this chapter, three sets of problems were discussed that are associated with the diversity of anticipated outcomes of service-learning programs; problems that render traditional quantitative methodologies relatively insensitive to identifying the impacts of such programs. The use of pre-/post-tests, $N = 1$ research designs provide a mechanism for overcoming those problems.

First, rather than select a relatively narrow range of possible outcomes to be assessed for all students participating in a program, placing the focus on each individual student makes it possible to identify the varied and particular ways in which any given participant has been affected by his or her experiences. Each student, having unique experiences within a program may have outcomes that are comparatively specific. Use of multiple, simultaneous $N = 1$ designs provides a mechanism for recognizing and recording the unique gains made by individual students. And they also provide a mechanism for recording unique declines students' experience, should they occur.

Second, the use of $N = 1$ designs circumvents the problems associated with exclusive reliance on either *off the shelf* or *homegrown* measures. By relying on narratives provided by both the student and the teacher, supplemented by the use of either *off the shelf* and/or *homegrown* instruments, a much broader range of possible impacts can be identified. Here, a common set of academic tests and psychological questionnaires serve as only one source of information about gains or declines, rather constituting the exclusive bases for the documentation of program impacts. Because qualitative teacher profiles and student self-assessments can be used to generate either category placements for the students or a numerical rating of student change, it becomes possible to conduct statistical analyses with individualized student evaluations.

Third, the proposed research methodology provides a mechanism for attributing observed changes either to the service-learning programs being studied or to collateral events occurring in the student's life. When both the student and teacher make comparable attributions regarding the basis of change, there are grounds for greater confidence in the conclusions reached than when discrepant attributions are offered.

Research techniques in which each student serves as the unit of analysis have the potential to be sensitive to the breadth of impacts service-learning programs can have. Although they share elements of qualitative and quantitative research methodologies, they should be viewed as a complement to the other approaches. The information about experiential education programs generated by the use of multiple, simultaneous $N = 1$ designs is different from that generated by other techniques. A more complete understanding of the educational and personal contributions afforded by the integration of service and education experiences will result from the use of multiple methods, both within and across assessment studies.

REFERENCES

Batchelder, T. H., & Root, S. (1994). Effects of an undergraduate program to integrate academic learning and service: Cognitive, prosocial cognitive, and identity outcomes. *Journal of Adolescence, 17*, 341–356.

Bell, R., Sharp, G., McDaniel, J., & Stowell, L. (1999, October). Learning together about service-learning. Paper presented at the meetings of the National Society for Experiential Education, San Diego, CA.

Blyth, D. A., Saito, R., & Berkas, T. (1997). A quantitative study of the impact of service-learning programs. In A. S. Waterman (Ed.), *Service-learning: Applications from the research* (pp. 39–56). Mahwah, NJ: Lawrence Erlbaum Associates.

Calabrese, R. L., & Schumer, H. (1986). The effects of service activities on adolescent alienation. *Adolescence, 21*, 675–687.

Cohen, J., & Kinsey, D. (1994). Doing good and scholarship: A service-learning study. *Journalism Educator, 48*(4), 4–14.

Conrad, D., & Hedin, D. (1982). The impact of experiential education on adolescent development. *Child and Youth Services, 4*(3/4), 57–76.

Davidson, P. O., & Costello, C. G. (Eds.). (1969). *N = 1: Experimental studies of single cases.* New York: Van Nostrand Reinhold.

Dunlap, R. E., & Van Liere, K. D. (1978). Commitment to the dominant social paradigm and concern for environmental quality: An empirical analysis. *Society for the Study of Social Problems.*

Dunlap, R. E., Van Liere, K. D., Mertig, A. G., & Emmet-Jones, R. (2000). Measuring endorsement of the new ecological paradigm: A revised NEP scale. *Journal of Social Issues, 56,* 425–442.

Eyler, J., & Giles, D. E., Jr. (1995, April). *The impact of service-learning on citizenship development.* Paper presented at the meetings of the American Educational Research Association, San Francisco, CA.

Follman, J. (1998). *Florida Learn and Serve: 1996–1997 Outcomes and correlations with 1994–1995 and 1995–1996.* Tallahassee, FL: Center for Civic Education and Service, Florida State University.

Giles, D. E., Jr., & Eyler, J. (1994). The impact of a college community service laboratory on students' personal, social, and cognitive outcomes. *Journal of Adolescence, 17,* 327–339.

Hamilton, S. F. (1979, April). Evaluating experiential learning programs. Paper presented at the meetings of the American Educational Research Association, San Francisco, CA.

Hamilton, S. F., & Zeldin, R. (1987). Learning civics in community. *Community Inquiry, 17,* 407–420.

Hill, D., & Pope, D. C. (1997). High school programs. In R. C. Wade (Ed.), *Community service-learning: A guide to including service in the public school curriculum* (pp. 180–196). Albany, NY: State University of New York Press.

Howard, K. I., Moras, K., Brill, P. L., Martinovich, Z., & Lutz, W. (1996). Evaluation of psychotherapy: Efficacy, effectiveness, and patient progress. *American Psychologist, 51,* 1059–1064.

Kahne, J., & Westheimer, J. (2001, April). *The limits of efficacy: Active citizens in a democratic society.* Paper presented at the meetings of the American Educational Research Association, Minneapolis, MN.

Luchs, K. P. (1981). *Selected changes in urban high school students after participation in community-based learning and service activities.* Unpublished doctoral dissertation, University of Maryland, Baltimore.

Melchior, A. (1999). *Summary report: National evaluation of Learn and Serve America.* Waltham, MA: Center for Human Resources, Brandeis University.

Metz, E., McLellan, J., & Youniss, J. (2000). *Types of voluntary service and the civic development of adolescents.* Unpublished manuscript, Catholic University, Washington, DC.

Miller, B. A. (1997). Service-learning in support of rural community development. In A. S. Waterman (Ed.), *Service-learning: Applications from the research* (pp. 107–126). Mahwah, NJ: Lawrence Erlbaum Associates.

Morgan, W. (2000, February). *Standardized test scores improve with service-learning.* Bloomington, IN: Civic Literacy Project.

Myers-Lipton, S. (1994). *The effects of service-learning on college students' attitudes toward civic responsibility, international understanding, and racial prejudice.* Unpublished doctoral dissertation, University of Colorado, Boulder.

Newmann, F. M., & Rutter, R. A. (1983). *The effects of high school community service programs on students' social development. Final report.* Madison, WI: University of Wisconsin, Wisconsin Center for Educational Research.

Santmire, T., Giraud, G., & Grosskopf, K. (1999, April). *Furthering attainment of academic standards through service-learning.* Paper presented at the National Service-Learning Conference, San Jose, CA.

Shumer, R. D. (1990). *Community-based learning: An evaluation of a drop-out prevention program.* Report submitted to the City of Los Angeles Community Development Department, Field Studies Development, University of California, Los Angeles.

Shumer, R. D. (1997). Learning from qualitative research. In A. S. Waterman (Ed.), *Service-learning: Applications from the research* (pp. 25–38). Mahwah, NJ: Lawrence Erlbaum Associates.

Switzer, G. E., Simmons, R. G., Dew, M. A., Regalski, J. M., & Wang, C. (1995). The effect of a school-based helper program on adolescent self-image, attitudes, and behavior. *Journal of Early Adolescence, 15,* 429–455.

Waterman, A. S. (1997). The role of student characteristics in service-learning. In A. S. Waterman (Ed.), *Service-learning: Applications from the research* (pp. 95–105). Mahwah, NJ: Lawrence Erlbaum Associates.

Waterman, A. S. (2001). *A survey of recent dissertations on service-learning abstracted in PsycINFO.* Unpublished manuscript.

Yates, M., & Youniss, J. (1996). A developmental perspective on community service in adolescence. *Social Development, 5,* 85–111.

6

Creating and Utilizing Databases on Service-Learning

Carl I. Fertman
University of Pittsburgh

Yolanda Yugar
Allegheny Intermediate Unit

This is a story of Student 11234. He lives with his grandparents. He rides a bus to school and qualifies for free lunches. His race is "White/Other." Last year he took the state educational assessment test and scored in the bottom quartile. Student 11234 has been absent twice since the beginning of this school year and has received no *poor work* notices in any class as of March. His grades, usually Ds and Cs, have improved to As and Bs except in math where he is still laboring to get a C. Last year he missed 16 days of school (2 unexcused) and was tardy 6 times. He also received poor work notices in two classes (science and English).

Student 11234 attends School 309, which has 589 students in Grades 6 through 8. Students in School 309 provided 1,000 hours of direct service per year as part of their school's service-learning program. Student #11234, along with his peers in his English class, spends 30 minutes twice a week with a second grade reading partner, reading and discussing stories.

Since the inception of the cross-grade service-learning program, the English teacher noticed that his students' grades improved each grading period and that the students' attendance was up, especially on days when they worked with the second grade. He also noticed an improvement in the comprehension of material on in-class projects and improvement of capitalization, punctuation, and grammar in writing assignments. As his students prepare to take the state writing assessment and a standardized test, he wonders if the student gains he saw in the classroom will transfer to the formal assessments. He is also interested in finding out if his students are doing better in other classes.

Similarly, the second grade teacher, whose classroom was selected based on the end-of-the-year reading scores from last year's first grade cohort, saw an improvement from the fall to winter reading assessment. She also noticed that attendance was better on days that the seventh grade class visits. She wonders if more of her students will be at grade level or closer to grade level on the spring assessment than they were the prior year. Both teachers think that participation in the cross-grade service-learning project made the difference and want the program to continue. They want to be able to show the impact of the program in terms of student grades and performance on standardized, district, or state assessments. They also would like to know if participation is really affecting attendance, and perhaps disciplinary referrals as well.

Student 11234 does not really exist in any school district, but millions of similar students do, and a story can be told about each one. There are thousands of schools and community organizations, each collecting various types of data. There are thousands of cross-grade reading programs and many other types of service-learning programs operating in schools and communities across the country that are collecting data as well. This information is often used to fill out forms or write reports. In many cases the data remain untouched, sitting in file cabinets or in computer files. However, when the information from the thousands of service-learning programs is organized and presented, it can tell stories to willing ears and serve an ally and guide for teachers, students, parents, youth workers, administrators, funders, and community members. Examining how to create and utilize such databases for the purpose of service-learning evaluation and research is the focus of this chapter.

Databases are organized collections of stored information on a defined subject area and are of importance in carrying out a mission or running a program. The database may contain information on single subject or discipline or can be multidisciplinary, problem oriented, mission oriented, or oriented toward certain types of transactions (Fortier, 1997). Large databases bring together data from many programs, projects, schools, and community-based organizations.

Advancements in information sciences and computer technology have enhanced the means to create, access, and share large databases that were not available only a few years ago. Database software packages such as Microsoft®Access 2002, FoxPro®, and Paradox® provide new capacity to individuals to engage in evaluation and research activities through personal and professional computer use. Many database books, training, and resources are available and readily accessible in stores and on the Internet. Larger database packages, such as Oracle and Microsoft® SQL Server™ have increased institutional and organizational capacity to use the data generated from their activities and programs to make decisions.

This chapter focuses on creating and utilizing large databases for the purpose of service-learning program evaluation and research. It is drawn from Pennsylvania service-learning evaluations from which large databases were created and used to evaluate the effectiveness of K–12 service-learning programs. The functions, design, and characteristics of large effective databases are investigated, along with the types of skills necessary for individuals to build their own local, large database using existing information (data) from their schools and communities. Finally, the chapter considers ways in which national databases can be used by researchers to enhance service-learning evaluation and research.

FOUR FUNCTIONS OF A
SERVICE-LEARNING DATABASE

Databases perform many functions within the educational system and during educational evaluations and research (Gall, Borg, & Ball, 1996). Four functions of databases that are critical for service-learning research and evaluation and are important when constructing large databases are presented here. Any large database one might design would need to perform these functions.

First, databases provide a consistent and standardized format for data across program types, approaches, and models. The standard format provides a recognizable picture of the data. This allows the user to consistently compile, organize, preserve, and analyze large amounts of data. A uniform style of record keeping lets the user look back at the data to obtain a historical perspective. With a standardized format, there is a framework to inform decisions. With a standardized format comes the ability to test hypotheses and pose questions about service-learning activities and programs.

Second, databases serve as the basis for timely and accessible report generation. One frequently encountered challenge in educational evaluation and research is the task of efficiently distributing information to everyone who might need it. With databases at hand, information that teachers and school administrators might find useful to strengthen their service-learning programs can be distributed to all interested parties and stakeholders. Such data may include academic content areas, service foci (e.g., human needs, environment, public safety, and education), grade levels, and student demographic data (e.g., gender and age). Once a database is in operation, it can supply countless reports of various kinds to professionals, parents, community members, and students in school districts and counties who have a need for the information offered. Table 6.1 shows a sample description of a school district service-learning program generated from a database.

TABLE 6.1
General Service-Learning Program Description

Morris Area School District Service-Learning Program: Santiago County		
Schools: Columbus Elementary Concord Elementary West Elementary	Maria Elementary King Elementary	Morris Area Middle School Morris Area High School
Contact: Shula Kelly, Director Service-Learning Program Morris Area High School	Phone: 804-555-6564 Cell 804-555-6565 Email skelly@Morris.org	Fax: 804-555-0722
Description: The Morris Area School District focuses on curriculum-based service-learning in grades K–12. Service-learning is used as a teaching and learning method to teach science and writing. Students are active in planning, implementing, and assessing service-learning. The program works with over three dozen community agencies. Seventy-five percent of all students in the district participate in at least one of the ten service-learning projects completed during the year. Ninety seven staff and faculty members also participate in the program.		

Reports can be tailored to match the unique needs of specific stakeholders. A major contribution of the current database software packages is their emphasis on reporting. For example, specific software packages such as Crystal Report focus exclusively on reporting. Mixes of data types (e.g., numbers, photographs, hyperlinks, calculations, and descriptions) from a database are easily shared. For example, the Service Star Report shown in Table 6.2 is a sophisticated report generated from the Pennsylvania service-learning database for school district administrators to show a number of program variables. Each school district can receive an individualized report. Such reports can be compiled into a statewide report along with an executive summary and aggregate statistics for the entire state.

TABLE 6.2
Service Star Report

King Elementary School		
Participants: 48	Grading Period: 02-2	
Classroom Hours: 80	Reflection Hours: 26	Project Hours: 121
Advisory Board: 2 meetings, 7 members plus 2 service-learning corps members	**Curriculum Infusion:** 3 teachers Ms Roberta Michael—Section 206 Ms. Paula Giles—Section 204 Mr. Neil James—Section 504 **Content Areas:** Reading and Math	
Training: 3 staff participants, 9-hour training Topic: Facilitating Reflection	**Student Outcome Measures:** Student participation levels Number of mediations (Mediation) Number of student conflicts (Meditation) Reading interest (Book Buddy) State reading assessment Grades 2 and 5 State math assessment Grades 2 and 5	
Agencies: 4 Carnegie Library—Brookline Branch Brashear High School Children's Homeless Initiative Slippery Rock University	**Parental Involvement Strategies:** Transportation and Advisory Board members Home reading program	
Products: Math Game Video Service-Learning Parent Brochure Math Game Program Booklet Book Buddy Reflection Collection Student Mediation Guide	**Service Activities:** Student mediators Book Buddy Club Math games Homeless children: In-class Penny and clothing drives	

Third, queries can be made in a database to answer specific questions. A query searches the database for specific fields, or sets of fields with specific features that have been selected. It provides access to specific pieces of information. For example, the user could query a large state service-learning database to identify: (a) middle schools (b) that provide cross-grade service-learning reading programs (c) for more than four hours of direct service per week. Such a query would provide a quick list of schools meeting all three criteria. Queries can be simple, identifying one or two fields of data, or more complex, identifying several fields of data. Queried data can be taken a step further and imported into a report format for quick and easy report generation.

Fourth, databases serve as the basis for data analysis and management. Databases allow for easy record keeping, report generation, and queries, but their great strength lies in the user's ability to complete complex analyses of data quickly and easily. One of the challenges today in developing such information systems is in building the expertise of a data analyst into the systems so that the benefits of accurate and efficient analyses are available to those who require them. Database developers can try to anticipate the types of analyses that might benefit these people and make the results available to users.

DATABASE DESIGN

Databases hold the raw data for an evaluation or research project that will eventually be used for one of the database functions. Database design is contingent on the particular information needs of the user. Databases are only as good as the information they hold, so the design of the database is critical. When designing a database, large or small, three key elements need to be considered:

1.   The data themselves

2.   The relationships among the data, and

3.   The database schema.

It is important to hire an information specialist to design the database since only the user can identify the information that will need to be collected and determine how that information will be used. Some knowledge of the particular software program to be used to implement and operate the database is necessary. Although similar in many aspects, each software program has unique characteristics and attributes that may influence the database design and use. In essence, the data that are collected and stored in a database are the sum total of all the information that has been collected to document program implementation and to answer evaluation or research questions. They are the raw material for all calculations and reports that are then used to lead to discussions and guide decision making.

If clarity of purpose or use of the data are uncertain, there is an increased danger in collecting too little data or the wrong kind of data to answer the questions of the stakeholders. Conversely, collecting large amounts of extra information with the hope that the data might be needed or useful is problematic as well. Collecting too little data is often the product of not sufficiently canvassing and involving stakeholders in defining the purpose of the database. Collecting excessive data is also an indicator of poor planning. In most instances, collecting too many data adds confusion and, if left unexamined and unused, raises questions and frustrations that can detract from the program or the evaluation being conducted. Once a database is operating it can be modified over time; however, the time and energy to make changes to the database can be considerable and costly. Being clear about how data will be used to answer specific questions lessens anxiety and resistance to participation.

As part of the design process, experts recommend working backwards. It often helps to think the content of the report. Preparing mock tables, charts, and a report framework with section headings and explanations of how the data will need to be analyzed helps ensure that all the necessary data are identified.

Another suggestion to help identify data that need to be collected is to take time to talk to all the stakeholders and assess their areas of interest. In most cases program implementation and impact is shared with a variety of stakeholders, each having their own idea of what is important and what they would like to know about the program. Their ideas about what is important and what they want to know also provide guidelines for identifying which data to collect.

Once all the data are identified, the relationships among the data become important. Relationships refer to a correspondence among data items. It is important to remember that within the database, each data item has its own field. Fields are organized into tables. Individual fields within a table can be selected to run a query, or individual fields between tables can be selected (linked) to run a query. Knowing the relationships among data is essential when identifying what fields go into what tables. Clarity of the relationship between data items is critical so that the user will be able to query and manipulate the data in whatever fashion is necessary. When each data item is identified, in their own field and organized logically in tables, data items can be selected and linked in any combination. When each data item is not given its own field, or is not organized correctly by table, data analysis is more problematic.

A schema describes the organization and the relationships among data within the database (Fortier, 1997). Another term for schema is *point of view*. In the Pennsylvania database the organizing schema was the school. Data were reported at the school level. These data helped users keep consistent records of what was happening across the state. Without this agreed-upon schema the data can become unclear. A schema provides a unit of measure or analysis.

A database in a school district related to a program might include data on student demographics, family information, grades, attendance, participation levels, teacher notes, and standardized district and state assessment scores. Each data item would be related to a student and placed together in the student's record. Student records could be organized into classes and then grades (schema). Teachers and principals could then use the database to answer the questions posed in the opening scenario.

A larger statewide service-learning database presents the opportunity to expand the schema from the individual student, classroom, and school to many students, classrooms, and schools. By adding information about the school, community, and service-learning project, the database user has the ability to compare and contrast projects and programs. Interested stakeholders can move from questions about individual service-learning project implementation to examine questions related to service-learning best practices, program effectiveness and outcomes, cost and benefit analysis, and policy.

There are other factors that need to be considered as the database is being designed. They include accessing the database and security issues. A database may be shared among several users. The database design should allow people to access and use the data, while providing protection of the data. Determining who and to what degree individuals will have access to the database is also critical in its design. For example, some users may only have access to input or update data; others may have access to run queries, analyze data, and produce reports; whereas others may only be able to view data, queries, or reports. Protecting data from unauthorized disclosure, alteration, or destruction is a security issue that needs to be addressed early by a database administrator. This decision is usually based on the usefulness and sensitivity of the data with respect to the needs of the person wishing to have access privileges.

Once the database is established, a user's guide is developed. A user's guide typically includes descriptions of the research for which the database is prepared, data collection instruments and sources, sample design and implementation, data collection, management, and processing. The final section is information on the data files, codebook, and analyses. In the guide's appendices are copies of the instrumentation. If scores from statewide educational assessments are a data item, the assessment probably would also be included. Figure 6.1 shows the table of contents from a user's guide. A user's guide is critical for large database operation. It sets the database parameters and concretely sets the expectations and outcomes for the database.

Users' guides are written detailed descriptions of the database that can be shared. Although they have the potential to be quite overwhelming, they do not have to be. User's guides simply describe the database and help users navigate the database. The guides detail the relationships among the data. Ideally, for each report, table, and chart, a description of the data items and any calculations or manipulations of the data are included. Presentation options may be considered; for example, whether to use pie or bar charts.

Such information would be included in the user's guide section on data files
documentation (e.g., Section VI in Figure 6.1).

I.	**Introduction**
1.1	Overview statewide service-learning cross-grade reading program
1.2	Cross-grade reading program objectives
1.3	Study design and evaluation questions
II.	**Data Collection Instrumentation Descriptions**
2.1	State Reading Assessment
2.2	Teacher questionnaire
2.3	Service-Learning school profile
III.	**Sample Design and Implementation**
3.1	Evaluation design
IV.	**Data Collection**
4.1	Participating school
4.2	Participating community organizations
V.	**Data Management**
5.1	Data monitoring
5.2	Data preparation
5.3	Data processing
VI.	**Guide to Data Files and Documentation**
6.1	Identification codes
6.2	Data record file layout
6.3	Data analyses
6.4	Reports, tables and charts
Appendices	
Appendix A	State Reading Assessment
Appendix B	Teacher questionnaire
Appendix C	Service-Learning school profile
Appendix D	Sample correspondence with schools

Figure 6.1: Sample Table of Contents, Service-Learning Database User's Guide

EFFECTIVE DATABASES =
CURRENT AND ACCURATE DATA

Ensuring that data are current and accurate is another critical task (Stufflebeam,
2001). The Pennsylvania database developers learned how time consuming and
difficult this task can be. The process was dynamic, influenced by the
stakeholders, reporting requirements, funding requirements, and questions being
asked. Over time, with changes in the field of information management, the data
available changed in both quantity and quality.

In the beginning the task was simply to document what was happening in terms of service-learning across the state of Pennsylvania. The task required collecting service-learning program data that was beneficial and useful to individual programs in schools while being able to use the information for statewide evaluation reporting. Database developers began by collecting general program and school demographic information such as participating schools, program contacts, telephone numbers, e-mail addresses, fax numbers, and brief program descriptions of services being provided.

With this information developers created a program directory for the state. This directory report format was easy to formulate and proved to be very useful to the state service-learning coordinator, the evaluators, and even the individual districts. It provided a snapshot of what was going on in the state and served as an excellent resource and reference for participating districts. In addition to the individual district entries, it also provided a listing of districts by several topics including region of the state, county, and even type of service being provided. Districts used the guide to network and find support and resources as they built their service-learning programs.

The database also organized program implementation information. Early on the interest focused on what was actually occurring, who was participating, and to what degree. Data collected included the number of classrooms, projects, and reflection hours students accrued; how well integrated the service was into the curriculum; the types of service that were occurring; the number and type of collaborating agencies; the ways in which parents were involved; the amount and types of training teachers received; how active the advisory board was; and if any products were produced. The database could be queried to produce individual district reports, or queried by topic, to provide a local, county, or statewide snapshot of that topic.

Data were also collected as part of the evaluation process. Each school received at least one onsite visit during the grant cycle. During the visit the evaluator had a chance to observe or participate in one or more of the components of service-learning and had the opportunity to interview administrators, program coordinators, teachers, students, and sometimes parents and advisory board members.

School and program demographic information, program implementation data, and information collected during site visits all became a part of the statewide evaluation database, and the data were used to produce several types of brief reports as well as the yearly evaluation report.

In an attempt to collect consistent data across the state, instruments were created. These instruments were completed by hand by service-learning site coordinators. The information was then entered into the central evaluation database and various directories. Brief reports and evaluator reports were produced from the queried data. A hard copy of the reports was sent to the district. If the district personnel wanted the report distributed to interested parties, they had to photocopy it. The data belonged to the state. Districts received the final results. Although district personnel could use the information provided to them for decision making, they did not have direct access to the raw data; however, they showed little interest in using the data for any purpose than what was required for evaluation.

By providing the data collection instruments and reviewing them at meetings and during onsite visits, database administrators hoped to increase the chances of receiving accurate data. But, service-learning coordinators, like other school personnel, are busy and often wore more than one hat. To reduce their workload and increase the accuracy of the data received, the data collection instruments were placed on diskettes. This allowed districts to update their data electronically, saving them much time. However, it was very time consuming for the database administrators because every district had different computers (Mac vs. PCs), software packages, and the like, and data still needed to be entered into the database once the diskettes were received. There still could be errors in the data, it was still time consuming , and districts still received only completed district data.

By the mid 1990s all districts were required to have Internet access in order to submit certain data to the state Department of Education in Pennsylvania. This factor alone changed the way evaluation data could be collected and the accuracy of those data. The evaluator could now house the database on a website, and districts could access the website through whatever Internet access they had within the district, thus eliminating different computer or software difficulties. All security access issues could be addressed and built into the database system. Additionally, each data field parameter could be explicitly defined, almost eliminating errors in data entry, assuring increased accuracy in the data submitted. Service-learning coordinators, instead of providing data on the diskettes, would now enter them directly into the database via the Internet. Individual spreadsheets or filing systems were no longer needed to track individual program data.

BUILDING YOUR OWN LOCAL, LARGE DATABASE

The advancements in technology have provided service-learning practitioners, evaluators, and researchers with a major tool for managing their own data (Bennington, Gay, & Jones, 2000; Van Horn, 2002; Watt, 1999). Although the statewide evaluator can still run queries and produce whatever type of report necessary, districts can now be trained to query their own data and produce their own individual reports. Having access to their own data enables districts to go beyond documenting and reporting program implementation to addressing program impacts. To illustrate this power, consider the scenario presented at the beginning of the chapter. Locally, the coordinator knows the students who participate in the cross-age service-learning program. He or she may decide to answer questions related to attendance, grades, disciplinary action, standardized tests, and state assessments. At first, the coordinator might think all this information would need to be added to the service-learning database that was created to evaluate the program. This would be a huge task, and far beyond the scope or job description of any service-learning coordinator or even state evaluator. However, after doing a little research, exploring a few database packages and their capabilities, and speaking with an information development specialist, the coordinator would learn that it is not necessary to develop a new database, or even update an existing one, but rather the coordinator can import or export data, run queries and conduct data analysis using the data that are currently maintained by the district, teachers, or buildings.

Regardless of how narrow or vast the scope of the data analysis or the linking of data fields between databases, the same simple principles of identifying the data fields and the queries apply. Although this can be an expensive endeavor, the results can go far beyond the impact of service-learning especially when one remembers that one can link, sort, and generate data reports using data from any or all of the existing databases.

This is not to say that districts need to write large technology grants; buy expensive database packages with its accompanying training, technical assistance, or reports outputs; or hire expensive information development consultants to integrate the databases and create the designated queries or data analysis. Districts can be creative and can partner with companies that provide this service. Many companies have community service as part of the organization and may want to forge some type of exchange, for example, interns for services. The district develops the database it needs (and perhaps also provides a site for a senior project or service-learning project for an advanced computer programming course or interested student), and the company gets free interns. A partnership may also be developed with a college course or professor. Often a real-life project for college students, especially for upper-level students preparing for an internship, is preferred. The purpose here is not to offer a way to undertake this task, but to let the reader know that the technology and knowledge is available to perform such a task.

This district level example can be extrapolated to the statewide level. A person conducting a statewide evaluation could work with each of the state's participating districts to develop the same type of database system that would import district data to be queried with data in the service-learning database.

When developing a comprehensive information management system as described previously, the database developer may seek existing reports that highlight the data or review existing databases to see how similar or related indicators are identified, collected, and reported. This is necessary if the database user wants to compare and contrast these data with other local, state, or national data. Furthermore, with a database reflective of existing educational and service-learning evaluations and research data, the potential to contribute to broader service-learning theory and knowledge is possible.

UTILIZING NATIONAL DATABASES

Large national databases exist that can be accessed and utilized in local service-learning evaluations and research. With little effort, it is possible to access and link to national and regional databases to compare and contrast district, state, and national data. Exploration of these databases has the additional advantage of providing models for evaluation and research.

A number of databases at the national level can assist in locating potential linkages for service-learning data sources. There are two national clearinghouses that serve as central locations for collection and dissemination of information about education and service-learning programs, resources, events, participants, and organizations involved in the field. They are the National Service-Learning Clearinghouse located online at www.servicelearning.org and the Education Research and Improvement Clearinghouse (ERIC) located online at www.eric.ed.gov. The two clearinghouses, while not providing data on service-learning implementation, research, and evaluation, are excellent sources in which to locate and link to appropriate databases. A third source of educational databases is the Washington, DC- based nonprofit The Education Trust. They publish "Education Watch: The Education Trust Community Data Guide," available from their website at www.edtrust.org (click on "Reports and Publications").

In addition to these sites for information, there are many databases available at the national level that are applicable directly to the field of education and to service-learning. It is important to note that there are also a large number of national topical databases available in such fields as health, human services, agriculture, and criminal justice that are appropriate to utilize with service-learning projects focused in these areas. One excellent national database for service-learning evaluators and researchers to access is the National Center for Educational Statistics (NCES), which is a part of the U.S. Department of Education. The NCES conducts surveys, maintains data, and publishes reports intended to inform educational policymakers, teachers, researchers, those in the media who write about education, and the general public. There are 15 available NCES databases. NCES information is available on the Internet at http://nces.ed.gov/. Each database with its surveys has its own homepage that can be accessed through the Survey and Programs Area listed on the NCES homepage.

Four of the NCES databases most relevant to service-learning are: the Common Core of Data (CCD), the National Education Longitudinal Study (NELS:88), the National Household Education Survey (NHES), and the National Assessment of Educational Progress (NAEP).

1. **Common Core of Data.** The CCD is a set of five surveys sent to State Departments of Education as a means of gathering information about all United States public elementary and secondary schools, local education agencies, and state education agencies. The CCD contains three categories of information: general descriptive information on schools and school districts, data on students and staff, and fiscal data. The descriptive information includes names, addresses, telephone numbers,

and types of locale; the data on students and staff include demographic characteristics; and the fiscal data cover revenues and current expenditures.

2. **The National Education Longitudinal Study.** Beginning with an eighth-grade cohort in 1988, NELS began to explore trends in data concerning critical transitions experienced by young people as they develop, attend school, and embark on their careers. Data were collected from students, parents, teachers, high school principals, and existing school records (such as high school transcripts). Cognitive tests (in math, science, reading, and history) were administered during the base year of 1988, with follow up data collection in 1990, 1992, 1994, and 2000. The fourth follow up collected in 2000 is scheduled to be published in 2002.

3. **National Household Education Survey.** The NHES is a data collection system of the National Center for Educational Statistics (NCES), and is designed to address a wide range of education issues, such as early childhood education, participation in adult school safety and discipline, school readiness, and school safety and discipline. In 1996 data collection focused on civic involvement and participation among adults and children in Grades 6–12. The 1999 survey added more questions about youth service activities. The NHES will be repeated in 2003.

4. **National Assessment of Educational Progress.** This survey is designed to continually monitor the knowledge, skills, and performance level of the nation's children and youth. NAEP provides objective data on student performance at the national and regional levels in reading, mathematics, science, writing, civics, U.S. history, geography, social studies, art, music, literature, computer competence, and career and occupational development.

The NCES produces many different types of information from the databases it maintains. A report from each survey citing major findings, analysis reports, and methodological/technical reports are some of the publications that NCES produces. *Learning About Education Through* Statistics (1999) is an NCES publication that provides information about NCES surveys and how to access information from NCES. The *Mini-Digest of Educational Statistics* (2001) and *The Condition of Education* (1999) are produced from survey data.

Programs and Plans of the National Center for Education Statistics (2001) is a publication that summarizes NCES's existing statistical programs, publications, and plans for future work. Included are descriptions, timelines, and plans for all of NCES data collection programs. Also included are descriptions of NCES center-wide programs and services: customer service, technology, and training.

While these NCES databases are friendly, and will walk users through the steps they need to take to conduct their studies, they are primarily used by the experienced researcher. Exploring them, however, can give the novice a comprehensive view of how data are identified, collected, analyzed, and reported. It is equally helpful that all of the computerized databases presented have user guides that explain all aspects of data collection and analysis, and include copies of the instruments used for data collection. Although assistance is provided and user's guides are available, negotiating through large databases and becoming familiar with them does take time and practice.

The greatest asset in learning how to use these large national databases is not just being able to identify, compile, analyze, and report data or use existing data to conduct additional studies, but to gain the ability to integrate exiting databases into one's own work, and thus be able to compare and contrast data.

CONCLUSION

Service-learning evaluators and researchers have the opportunity to design and implement comprehensive information—management systems (databases) and make use of an extensive quantity of current data readily available locally and nationally. The capacity exists to utilize in our evaluations and research a range of data and data analyses. These are powerful tools in advancing service-learning and positive student outcomes.

REFERENCES

Bennington, T. L., Gay, G., & Jones, M. L. W. (2000). Using multimedia records to support mixed-method evaluation. In G. Gay & T. L. Bennington (Eds.), *Information technologies in evaluation: Social, moral, epistemological, and practical implications: New Directions for Evaluation #84* (pp. 59–72). San Francisco: Jossey-Bass.

Fortier, P. J. (Ed.). (1997). *Database systems handbook*. New York: McGraw-Hill.

Gall, M. D., Borg, W .R., & Gall, J. P. (1996). *Educational research: An introduction* (6th Ed.). New York: Longman.

National Center for Education Statistics. (1999). *Coalition of education*. NCES 1999-022. Washington, DC: U. S. Department of Education. [Online]. Available: http://nces.ed.gov/pubsearch/pubsinfo.asp?pubid=1999022

National Center for Education Statistics. (1999). *Learning about education through statistics*. NCES 1999-028. Washington, DC, U. S. Department of Education. [Online]. Available: http://nces.ed.gov/pubsearch/pubsinfo.asp?pubid=1999028

National Center for Education Statistics. (2001). *Programs and plans of the National Center for Education Statistics*. NCES 2001-038. Washington, DC, U. S. Department of Education. [Online]. Available: http://nces.ed.gov/pubsearch/pubsinfo.asp?pubid=2001038

National Center for Education Statistics. (2002). *Mini-digest of education statistics*. NCES 2002-026. Washington, DC, U. S. Department of Education. [Online]. Available:

http://nces.ed.gov/pubsearch/pubsinfo.asp?pubid=2002026
Stufflebeam, D. L. (2001, Winter). Evaluation checklists: Practical tools for guiding and judging evaluations. *American Journal of Evaluation, 22*(1), 71–79.
Van Horn, R. (2002, February). Internet2 and the K20 initiative. *Phi Delta Kappan, 83*(6), 481–482.
Watt, J. H. (1999). Internet systems for evaluation research. In G. Gay & T. L. Bennington (Eds.), *Information technologies in evaluation: Social, moral, epistemological, and practical implications: New Directions for Evaluation #84* (pp. 23–43). San Francisco, CA: Jossey-Bass.

7

Issues of Research Design and Statistical Analysis

Deborah Hecht
The City University of New York.

This chapter examines issues that often arise when empirical approaches are used to study the impact on students participating in service-learning. The focus is on methodology rather than results and on student outcomes rather than school, site, or community outcomes. Studying an educational program such as service-learning is difficult, especially when one tries to apply traditional methodologies. Unlike many educational innovations or reform programs, service-learning is not a specific program with identifiable characteristics. Rather, service-learning is an approach to teaching and learning that is given meaning by the school or organization where it is based. It is this challenge that faces researchers: to develop studies that account for the tremendous variability across and even within programs.

As is noted elsewhere in this volume, there is great diversity among service-learning programs. A student's service experience can include a wide range of activities, and even within a given activity, a wide variety of tasks can be performed. Visits to service-learning placement sites can be daily, weekly, or only occasionally, and preparation and reflection can occur in a large number of ways. In fact, it is often difficult to determine what actually constitutes service-learning. For example, some consider a one-time volunteer experience at a soup kitchen service-learning, whereas others believe service-learning must occur over an extended period of time. The Alliance for Service-Learning in Education Reform (ASLER, 1993) developed a list of essential elements or requirements for service-learning, but even these are not presented in terms that are easily operationalized.

This chapter assumes the researcher has established a definition of service-learning and clearly communicates this definition when discussing the research. Even with the definition problem addressed, researchers face a multitude of meaningful and extraneous variance that can complicate the study and affect the results. The chapter begins with an overview of how empirical studies of service-learning have been conducted, followed by a brief discussion of their limitations. It then presents some recommendations for further development of this work.

CHARACTERISTICS OF EMPIRICAL STUDIES

Most studies of service-learning attempt to identify areas where students experience growth, development, change, and so forth. After participating in service-learning (e.g., Andersen, 1998; Billig, 2000; Melchior, 1999). Pre-test and post-test designs are often used, with the data consisting of quantitative and qualitative responses from and about students. For the purposes of this discussion, it is assumed that all qualitative responses are converted into quantitative indicators. The length of time between pre- and post-administrations varies depending on the service-learning programs being studied. Analyses usually consist of measuring change from pre-test to post-test, and attributing that change, hopefully an improvement of some kind, to participation in a service-learning program.

Comparison data are frequently obtained from students who did not participate in service-learning. They are often selected based on their similarity to the service-learning students on select demographic variables, such as age, race and ethnicity, gender, or socioeconomic status. Using comparison data allows the researcher to explore whether group differences are most likely due to initial differences, maturation, or participation in the program. Although the use of a pre- and post-design with a comparison group assessed at the same points in time is considered a strong methodological design, the strength of this design is somewhat weakened when students are not matched or are not randomly assigned to groups (e.g. Campbell & Stanley, 1963; Cook & Campbell, 1979). Studies of service-learning are usually conducted with existing programs and rarely use random assignment for both financial and educational reasons.

One alternative to using a nonrandom comparison group would be to compare service-learning students to national norms on standardized tests and attitude measures.[1]. Saying that service-learning students of a given community perform better than the national average on given tests after participating in a program can be a powerful statement, but unless the measure is appropriate for a given program, this strategy becomes problematic as well.

Types of Programs Studied

Because service-learning programs vary widely, it is difficult to assess the effectiveness of service-learning as a whole. Some researchers have examined the effectiveness of specific types of programs. For example, Switzer, Simmons, Dew, Regalski, and Wang (1995) assessed the effects participation in the Helper Program had on self-image, attitudes, and behaviors of junior high school students. Youniss, McLellan, and Yates (1997) studied a particular type of high school class. Because the within-sample variability is reduced, the results of these types

---

[1] Standardized tests measuring academic achievement (e.g., Iowa) are norm referenced. There are also several databases of national academic and attitudinal norms (e.g., National Assessment of Educational Progress [NAEP]).

of studies can be powerful in determining the effects of a certain type of program. However, the results are often not generalizable to other types of programs.

Another approach has been to study exemplary service-learning programs (e.g. Conrad & Hedin, 1981; Newmann & Rutter, 1983; Scales, Blyth, Berkas, & Kielsmeier, 2000) or as Conrad and Hedin (1982) described, programs that have a "reputation for excellence and as representative of the major variables" (p. 59) of interest in the research. Thus, only programs that "presumably maximize their impact on students" (Newmann & Rutter, 1983, p. 3) are included. In the tradition of case study research, this is commonly called "information rich sampling" (Schunk, 2000). With this approach some of the variability among programs is eliminated and the differences with comparison students are maximized. One drawback of this type of study, again, is that the results may not generalize to programs in which the implementation is less than exemplary. Moreover, problems can arise in operationalizing exemplary programs and assuring they meet these criteria.

Still other studies attempt to evaluate service-learning as a whole, including a wide range of program types in their analyses. Nationally or state commissioned studies and meta-analyses (e.g., Follman, 1998; Melchior, 1999) fall within this category. Significant findings are considered meaningful since they emerge in spite of program and student differences. However, when a diversity of service-learning programs are aggregated for data analyses, less successful programs may increase the variance within the service-learning group and limit the overall effects of participating in service-learning. Real differences that are related to specific program features may not be identified. Furthermore, by not controlling for variables like program type, these large-scale studies may not have direct relevance for individual programs.

Most studies of service-learning select a sample based on data about the program. Information is usually reported concerning at least some student demographics and some program and site characteristics such as program length, frequency of service, and method of reflection. Although these variables are not usually fully included in the quantitative analyses, they do allow for some comparison of variables across studies.

Constructs and Statistics

Studies that assess the impact of participating in service-learning usually focus on one or more student characteristics or constructs, such as, self-efficacy, self-confidence, academic achievement, and academic involvement. These constructs are often assessed using some form of scaled scores or by collecting data from student records. In most cases, assessment tools have been reported to have adequate reliability coefficients. The actual measures are often included in the research reports allowing the reader to evaluate the appropriateness of the items (e.g., Conrad & Hedin, 1981).

Studies of service-learning generally look for student level differences using a variety of descriptive and inferential statistical procedures, with statistical significance established at the .05 level. Pre- and post-differences are typically examined using paired t-tests or analyses of covariance (e.g. Conrad & Hedin, 1981; Melchior, 1999). Some researchers have developed innovative methods. For example, Newmann and Rutter (1983) created a ranking procedure to identify program or student characteristics from distinguished schools that appear to have a greater impact from lower ranking schools. Although newer methodologies like Hierarchical Linear Modeling (Bryk & Raudenbush, 1992) are available to study multilevel data, most studies have relied on more traditional approaches which are often more interpretable to the general reader.

LIMITATIONS WITH CURRENT EMPIRICAL APPROACHES

Researchers of service-learning have struggled to find ways to document the unique characteristics of the service-learning experience. One problem that tends to limit the generalizability of studies is that the criteria for selecting programs to be studied are often unclear. In some cases it appears programs were selected based on convenience or a willingness to participate in all the required activities. Although a program's willingness to participate is an important concern, most researchers select a sample based in part on information about the service-learning program. A single school staff member, without additional confirmation and documentation, often provides information about the program. However, these reports are frequently inaccurate (Hecht, 1997). Even when schools are carefully selected, it is possible that the types of schools that support service-learning, especially an exemplary example, may be different from schools that do not. An exemplary service-learning program may be one component of an exemplary school. Thus, the findings are more about the school than service-learning as a separate program.

Another important issue when studying service-learning is choosing the proper construct to measure and the proper tool with which to measure it. Often, researchers attempt to make strong statements about service-learning by measuring its effect on a construct such as academic achievement or self-efficacy, using standardized measures. One problem with this kind of study, of course, is that such constructs may be fairly stable over a short period of time. It might be questioned whether an intervention such as service-learning, without additional support, even should be expected to produce measurable change in such broad areas. When service-learning is embedded within a larger program designed to produce change, these confounding factors may be responsible for any observed changes in students. Furthermore, the effect of service-learning is sometimes more subtle, or does not appear in students until some time after participation in a program.

Selecting or developing appropriate assessment tools is one of the greatest challenges to service-learning researchers. Most studies of service-learning have relied on paper and pencil measures, which are very different from the experiential approach of service-learning. During service-learning students are expected to reflect on their actions, consider different options, and learn from their choices. Students are often confronted with situations that do not have one right or best solution. In contrast, most surveys require students to provide a single answer. Even when students are encouraged to write about their experiences, responses are often categorized into discrete categories for purposes of analysis. It may be speculated that many students who would thrive with experiential, hands-on learning, such as service-learning, would find traditional paper and pencil surveys difficult to complete. Although the reported reliability coefficients for most assessments are generally adequate, few measures have been validated with service-learning students.

With pre-test and post-test designs, a problem that sometimes arises is that pre-test scores are assumed to reliably represent what students were like before they had any exposure to service-learning. However, pre-tests are subject to bias, particularly in cases where students have high expectations for the service-learning experience. Teachers often present service-learning to students as a powerful, life changing activity (Hecht, 1997; Hecht & Fusco, 1996), creating high expectations for the program. The experience itself, although enjoyable and educational, is often a great deal of work. Because students learn through real-world activities, the experiences can be frustrating and students do not always see that they have had a positive impact at the site. When post-tests are administered immediately after the last site visit, students may focus more on the struggles than the positive learning that occurred.

For example, if a pre-test asks students about their level of civic engagement, students who have participated in an orientation may portray themselves as more enthusiastic about civic involvement than students who have not participated in an orientation or who have never heard of service-learning. The result, of course, would be that the service-learning students statistically exhibit less or no growth in civic engagement than comparison students, evidenced by smaller pre/post differences. Furthermore, if the service experience was an intense activity, and students complete the surveys immediately following a great deal of hard work, their responses may be confounded by students being tired. Even if data from the service-learning and comparison groups were statistically equated, the service-learning group would show less growth.

A student's previous history can also be problematic for the researcher. Students who have prior volunteer experience or come from a family that values volunteerism, for example, are likely to have different outcomes than other students. And although age is usually controlled for investigations of service-learning, maturity is not. Even when a study includes children of the same age or grade-level, there are apt to be differences in effectiveness of program that are related to maturity or readiness for the service-learning experience. Another concern with the sample is that few studies have focused on service-learning with young children, particularly kindergarten through fifth grade. Studies of this age would most likely require new methodologies and different assessment tools.

Finally, service-learning programs are continually changing, and data collected about a program today may not be accurate in two months. Staff changes, schedule changes, the addition or elimination of sites, funding shifts, and so on can have a tremendous impact or very little impact, yet studies rarely account for these changes. Particularly exemplary programs may be adept at adjusting to the changing needs of the school and program.

Data Analyses

Data from studies of service-learning are usually analyzed using traditional statistical tests such as t-tests and analysis of covariance. Frequently multiple analyses are preformed, and all statistically significant results at the .05 level are reported. Although such an approach is useful for exploratory analyses, its general use can lead to erroneous conclusions since chance differences may be considered significant. The general rule, to divide the acceptable level of significance, such as .05, by the number of comparisons performed to obtain the level of statistical significance that differences need to exceed to be considered significant, is rarely followed. (See references to Bonferroni t statistic in texts, e.g., Pedhauzar & Schmelkin, 1991, or Stevens, 2000, for further discussions of this topic.) Furthermore, if the sample size is large, very small differences can reach statistical significance, despite small effect sizes. For example, a three-point difference might be statistically significant, but if the scale ranges from 0 to 200, it may not be a meaningful difference. The statistical significance of the result needs to be considered in the context of the meaningfulness of the findings. For a discussion of effect size, see Cohen (1988).

Finally, a word of caution needs to be made about the general way statistics have been used in service-learning research. Many studies have reported gain scores (post-score minus pre-score) as evidence of student change. Yet, there is a great deal of literature that addresses the problems with using gain scores. (See, e.g., Campbell & Boruch, 1975; Cronbach & Furby, 1970; Pedhazur & Schmelkin, 1991; or Reichardt, 1979.) Unreliability of the pre-scores, variance of post-test scores that are smaller than the variance of pre-test scores, ceiling and floor effects, and regression toward the mean are but a few of the problems that can bias the results.

Although data from studies of service-learning could be considered hierarchical, and statistical methods are available to handle these types of data, most studies rely on traditional methodologies such as t-tests and analyses of covariance. These analyses may be more easily understood, but the meaningfulness of their findings is often questionable given the large number of analyses that are typically performed and small effect sizes. Furthermore the assumptions which underlie these analyses are rarely met. Among these assumptions are that the covariate (typically the pre-test score) is free of measurement error and that subjects have been randomly assigned to groups.

(See Huitema, 1980, for a description of analysis of covariance.) Violation of these assumptions may result in an over, under, or correct estimation of group differences. Although the dependent measure is also usually fallible, this measurement error rarely biases estimated group differences, although it may reduce the power of the statistical test and lead to failure to detect statistically significant group differences.

RECOMMENDATIONS

Throughout this chapter, the need to carefully document school, program, and site characteristics has been stressed. Not only does this help anyone who wants to use the findings clearly understand who participated in the study, but it also provides a framework for interpreting statistically significant student change and findings that fail to reach significant levels.

Selecting the Service-Learning Programs to Study

Whether studying exemplary service-learning programs, a specific type of service-learning, or a broad range of programs, the researcher must carefully define what is and is not service-learning and these definitions should guide the sample selection. If comparison data will be collected, the definition should indicate what student or school characteristics are considered important for selecting the comparison group. If data will be combined from several service-learning programs, it is important to assure that each program is actually doing service-learning as defined by the researcher. When the study focuses on exemplary programs, the factors that make the program or programs exemplary need to be clearly described. Even if judges are used to rate programs, care must be taken that the judges work from the same definition, and interrater reliability should be established.

The process of sample selection should involve the collection and evaluation of information about potential programs for study. Too often, data about service-learning programs are collected using a simple multiple-choice survey or brief interview asking administrators or teachers about the presence of key features of service-learning at the school. These kinds of probes rarely allow researchers to see what is really happening at a school. The individuals providing information about the program, moreover, should be those individuals who are actively involved in service-learning and who are likely to know the details of a given program. Administrators who are not actively involved with students are likely to know what should be happening in the school, but not what actually is happening. For example, suppose that an elementary school requires 15-minutes of reflection about service each week, but in reality, only five minutes per week are spent on the activity. An administrator would be likely to report the 15-minute rule, but by speaking to a teacher or observing a class, one would establish a more accurate understanding of the program. Researchers need to know what occurs, not simply what is supposed to occur before selecting a program for inclusion in a study.

Program implementation should be monitored throughout the duration of the study. A single survey at the outset is hardly enough. It is advisable to collect data often, and from multiple sources, including observations, interviews, and reviews of school materials such as press releases, course listings, and awards. This type of information can provide important information about the maintenance of the program over the duration of the study. It can also be quantified and included as background information (covariates) during the analyses.

Furthermore, if several programs from within a school or school district are selected for participation in a study, it should not be assumed all have similar service-learning programs. As Sanders (1994) noted, "failure to check the accuracy of the obtained description of the program through direct examination or observation, or by confirmation by program personnel" is a common error. He continues by warning that one should not fall into the trap of "assuming that the program was uniformly implemented as intended" (p. 128). Service-learning is especially likely to be subject to variability across programs. Even when schools have participated in the same service-learning training programs, the implementation is likely to vary as service-learning is incorporated into that particular school's culture and classroom.

Collection of ongoing program data will help the researcher remain alert to the types of changes that can impact a study and affect the results. Observational and survey data from and about sites, student activities, reflection, and planning activities will to help assure the program is operating as expected. Development of systematic recording procedures can be used to help quantify the service experience. For example, researchers might record students' preparation activities, such as research, interviews, or group discussion, and whether these activities are teacher or student directed, done alone or in a group, involve outside participants or just the class, and so on. The specific characteristics that are examined will depend on the researcher's design and study goals.

Knowledge of the school's mission and curriculum are important for understanding a program, helping assure the results are generalizable, and putting the data into context, especially when making comparisons across schools. For example, suppose as part of two service-learning programs, students keep journals during reflection. Students in Program A also study poetry, although it is not part of service-learning. Students in Program B have an empirical writing class. Even if the same instructions are given for journal writing, it is likely that student journal entries will reflect these different curriculum experiences. Unless the researcher is aware of the different writing programs, differences in the journals might mistakenly be attributed to the service-learning experience.

Teachers also bring their own differences to service-learning that can have an impact on students' experiences and on the research results. Teachers who report service-learning is "how they always teach" are likely to have a different level of engagement to the task than teachers who found they "were assigned to service-learning." Teachers vary in their experience and comfort working as a facilitator with service-learning. Knowledge of these differences can provide important information for both sample selection and data interpretation and can highlight differences among service-learning programs or even classes within the same school.

As previously discussed, it is important to continually assess how a program is being implemented if the program is included in a study. Occasionally, a program will experience changes that have a profound impact on how service-learning is implemented. For example, if statewide test scores drop, the school may focus more on other pedagogies for master of standards rather than service-learning. There are several ways to handle data that indicate there have been significant changes within the sample. Minimally, this information should be included in the research report to help the reader evaluate the sample. If a program no longer includes all the key elements of service-learning as defined in the study, the program might be dropped from the study. Alternatively, the researcher may decide to use this information as another type of comparison group. Finally, examination of how the program changed might suggest key variables for further study. For example, if the amount of administrator support decreased at the program that was dropped, amount of administrative involvement might be a variable to include in a follow up study.

Finally, besides collecting information from the sample, it is often informative to examine characteristics of programs not selected or not willing to participate. This might involve interviewing teachers, administrators, or other key personnel, and reviewing the school's mission statement and class curriculum. These data can provide insights for understanding service-learning. Programs may decline to participate for reasons ranging from the time burden to reluctance to be evaluated. Knowledge of the reasons can help guide future sampler recruitment efforts and may help the researcher rethink aspects of the design.

The Design

The pre-test and post-test design provides a way to examine change on the variables of interest and to assess whether there are initial differences between the service-learning and comparison students. Pre-test scores are assumed to be indicators of what students are like before they have any exposure to a treatment (i.e., service-learning in this case). However, in studies of service-learning, this is rarely the case, and student expectations may have an impact on the findings. Student responses on the pre-test can be confounded by knowledge about the program, what is discussed during the service-learning orientation, or prior experiences participating in service-learning. Furthermore, as previously noted, a school that supports service-learning may have a culture that is different from a school that does not. Hecht (1998) found that teachers often present service-learning very positively and suggest that the experience will be life changing. If these experiences result in more positive pre-scores, the post- minus pre-differences will be reduced, suggesting service-learning had minimal impact. Therefore, the timing of administration of pre-tests, whether during the first class meeting, after or before the orientation, and so on, may be an important question to consider.

One possible solution is to collect data throughout the service experience. For example, if the service experience will last 15 weeks, students could complete brief surveys four times: at the beginning, twice in the middle, and again at the end. Student journals can provide another method to track changes over time.

Constructs and Assessment

Research about service-learning needs to begin with a strong theory about the areas in which student change might be expected. As noted earlier, studies often focus on traits that may be fairly stable over a short period of time. Even if one assumes that constructs could exhibit change within a short period, the theoretical framework must suggest that it is reasonable to see the hypothesized changes given the program characteristics. The areas in which student change is expected should reflect the study schools' objectives for service-learning.

Service-learning can be introduced for many different reasons, such as creating a safe environment, providing career skills, or creating real world links to the curriculum. The goals may be to address a specific problem, such as an increase in school violence, or a very broad one, such as to enrich and expand the school's mission. Researchers should look for student outcomes in areas where change would be expected given the program goals and activities. For example, to expect positive growth in literacy skills when students have been engaged in environmental testing of water or park clean-up may not make sense. However, simply knowing the goals for a service-learning program is not enough information.

Programs with very different goals may provide similar experiences for students, whereas programs with similar goals may provide very different experiences. Student outcomes depend on the activities and experiences at the site, during reflection and during planning, as well as how service-learning is infused into the curriculum. For example it might be hypothesized that students will have increased literacy skills, if as part of the water testing, students prepare reports about the findings for the community, write press releases, teach other students about water testing, and develop a booklet that will be distributed through City Hall. In another program, the focus might be on developing a scientific understanding of the characteristics of the water, chemicals that are present, and being able to create a graphic presentation of the findings. Accurate knowledge of what students are doing would help a researcher identify constructs to be investigated and to understand the results.

Talking with the students and teachers as well as reviewing school materials such as the mission statement, curriculum, and lesson plans can help researchers develop program specific hypotheses. A grid can be developed that identifies service-learning program goals and activities and links these with expected student outcomes. It often helps to have individuals not connected with the service-learning programs or the research review these grids and rate the likelihood that the expected student outcomes will be found given the design of the program. These ratings could be as simple as a five-point scale, with 1 indicating *very unlikely* to 5 indicating *very likely.* When a study includes numerous programs with different learning goals, ratings for different student outcomes are likely to vary across the different programs in the study. Data analyses could examine student outcomes aggregated across all programs, for individual programs and using the ratings as a variable in the analyses. For example, schools might differ in their rating of *improved academic achievement* as a student outcome variable. Rather than look for global improvement in academic achievement, a researcher could explore student achievement only among programs where it is likely and compare these students with the comparison students.

Studies of service-learning need to use multiple modes of assessing student outcomes. As discussed previously, use of paper and pencil surveys may not be the most appropriate approach. If the researcher uses an established assessment tool, it is important to assure the assessment is appropriate for the given population being studied. For discussion of this topic, see texts such as Nunnally (1994) or Thorndike, Cunningham, Thorndike, and Hagen (1991). An assessment that is highly reliable with urban high school students may not be as reliable with rural middle school students. Asking a small representative group of students to discuss the questions before administering it to the entire sample can be very informative. It is also important that the terminology of the assessment be understandable to students. For example, although the study is about service-learning, it is possible students in a given school call "service-learning" by a different name, such as home and careers, community service, community action, or simply mathematics or science. Although reflection may be a critical part of the program, it might not be identified as a separate component. Instead it may be necessary to prompt students when they talk about what they do in the community or when they write in their journals. Often it is valuable to adapt assessment tools to reflect these changes.

Methods for examining student change after participating in service-learning might explore how the assessment can be made more realistic. Students, who have successfully worked cooperatively on a service-learning project, may find answering a survey without consulting with peers at odds with the design of the service experience itself. Furthermore, it might be questioned whether some students for whom service-learning is a meaningful experience, and where the greatest change might be observed, are the same students who have a difficult time completing a survey that requires reading and writing proficiency.

For areas such as career awareness, students could be asked to demonstrate their learning through a self-developed project. This type of approach would focus the assessment on the program goals and emphasize tasks that are related to a student's service experience. A public presentation of what is learned through service-learning could take many forms. If service-learning occurs as part of an academic class, and the academic goals are clearly defined, students could be asked to share what they learned with another class, the community, parents, and the like. When researchers study a small number of classroom-based service-learning programs, they can help teachers develop assessments that directly link the assessment with the content and performance knowledge students are expected to gain. If the sample is too large to allow this type of individualized assessment, development of a service-learning rubric that is reviewed by teachers, could be used to collect similar data across classes, while allowing teachers to rate students relative to their individual lessons. A rubric can be developed and used to assess student learning in numerous dimensions, such as academic knowledge, understanding of others as reflected in choice of presentation materials, preparation, alignment with other knowledge, or real world applications. For a discussion on development of rubrics see Arter and McTighe, (2001) or Schrock (1995-2002).

Student portfolios that include student work related to the service experience are another method used to assess student change. Students or teachers could select work that demonstrates growth in the areas of interest. For example, the instructions could ask for inclusion of a piece of work that shows how the student demonstrated problem solving skills or how academics were enriched. The types of work that students select would provide another indicator of what students feel they have learned and what they value from service-learning. If student portfolios can be maintained over several years, this data could provide the basis for a longitudinal study of the impact of service-learning. The use of portfolio assessment in education can be found in De Fina (1994) or Grace and Shores (1998).

Student records can provide data concerning attendance, disciplinary incidents, awards, and choice of courses or extra-curricular activities. Examined over time these data can provide information about how service-learning has impacted a student in specific areas. Report cards, especially with younger children, frequently include narrative sections that can be analyzed. Finally, third party reports from other participants such as teachers and site coordinators can provide additional valuable behavioral indicators.

Data Analyses

Whether a researcher relies on a traditional paper and pencil survey or creates scores from other forms of assessment, data analysis must begin with a careful review of student responses. Missing data must be examined and a decision made whether to eliminate the student from the entire study, drop the student from some analyses, or estimate the missing responses. When a large number of students leave particular questions blank, it may suggest a problem with the assessment question or task; for example, students did not have enough time, the reading or task was too difficult, or the instructions were confusing.

Item analysis for questions with a specific percentage of missing responses (e.g., items that more than 20% of the students do not answer) can be performed to determine whether a specific subgroup of the sample found the question or task difficult. Breakdowns could compare the number of students who did and did not answer the question on variables such as type of site, program, type of reflection, dates the survey was completed, gender, age, or grade. To accomplish this, a dichotomous variable is created for each question (answered: 1; not answered: 0), and the number of students with a -1 or 0 falling into each category is compared using Chi Squares. If significant and meaningful differences are found, follow up interviews can provide insight into why questions were not answered. A decision must then be made concerning whether to retain the question or drop it from further analyses. This type of analysis may suggest groups that should be analyzed separately for particular constructs, such as looking at responses from males and females individually. The results can be used in later studies to help revise the assessment questions.

If the number of missing responses is small and appears to be randomly missing, researchers may decide to estimate the missing responses using one of several options. The missing response can be replaced with the overall mean for that item. However, if site, program, or other differences are suspected, a more appropriate choice may be to substitute the mean for that group. For example, the mean of students at a given site on an item can be substituted for the missing response rather than the overall mean. Another option is to estimate the scale using responses, given by the student, to other items on the same scale. A criterion, such as 90% of the scale items are answered, is established, and a scale score is estimated by averaging the other items. It is important that scale scores for all students be calculated as averages or that the average be converted to the same scale as other students. There are excellent resources for directing the researcher in ways to handle missing data, such as Allison (2001), Cohen and Cohen (1983), or Little and Rubin (1987).

Another issue related to data analysis is that many variables function as both independent and dependent variables. For example, student achievement might be an outcome variable for some analyses and a control variable in others. This suggests a modeling design, such as path analysis or structural equation modeling, is appropriate. It is important however to remember that these approaches require a strong theoretical model about the causal relations among the variables before testing the data. Although different hypotheses can be tested, these analyses are not used for exploratory purposes. For information about these approaches, see texts such as Pedhazaur and Schmelkin (1991).

Another option is to treat the data as multilevel data; that is, students are thought of as nested within sites and sites are nested within schools. A statistical technique called Hierarchical Linear Models (HLM) can be used to examine multilevel data of this type and will allow for the examination of both site and student characteristics (e.g., Bryk & Raudenbush, 1992; Raudenbush, 1988). Although HLM builds on a linear model, it extends the analyses far beyond the traditional analysis of variance, analysis of covariance, and regression designs. Using this approach, it is possible to explore "relations occurring at each level and across levels and also assess the amount of variance at each level" (Bryk &

Raudenbush, p. 3). HLM also allows for control variables, similar to the control variables in an ANCOVA design. However, an advantage of HLM is that the problems of inadequate sample sizes that arise when conventional linear modeling is used are greatly reduced. Furthermore, aggregation bias and problems with the unit of analysis are lessened.

Data from studies of service-learning fall naturally into this model. With students serving as the unit of analysis, each student is then attached to a site. Site variables can include a range of variables such as type of service site, teacher experience, or how often students visit the site. Student characteristics might include gender, age, or prior family experience. The dependent variables can include the constructs of interest in the study and different models can be tested for different outcome variables.

HLM will work efficiently with 22 to 27 sites, allowing for variability at the site level to be evidenced as well as variability at the student level. Although problems of small sample sizes are reduced using an HLM approach, they are not eliminated and add to the complexity of the analyses. Based on both theory and an examination of the data, it may be possible to combine sites. Careful examination of the data may reveal that meaningful groupings are not the most obvious ones. For example, groups might be formed based on the type of contact students have with others at the site, such as direct contact with the same individuals each visit, direct contact with different individuals each visit, occasional contact, or no direct contact.

HLM allows for background variables such as socioeconomic status and achievement to serve as control variables and to be included for individual students and as a school average. Pre-scores can also be entered into the analyses as control variables. In many ways, HLM allows for data exploration by using different control variables and various characteristics of the site. Control variables can be selected after examining student responses and variability across schools.

A simple example of how this procedure might be applied follows. Self-efficacy might be predicted within each of 25 service sites from a pre-score and socioeconomic status. HLM then allows for examination of how the regression weights for the 25 equations function as characteristics of sites. These data provide indications of differences across sites while considering relations within sites. By varying the control variables it is possible to examine how impact varies according to site and program characteristics (e.g., intensity and nature of interpersonal contact at sites, the degree to which a collegial relation with adults is encouraged, opportunities to engage in autonomous behaviors, and characteristics of the reflection). Student pre-test data, student and program leader interviews, site questionnaires, and observation data can be as create control variables for the HLM analyses.

In summary, the types of data analyses and ways in which the information is used depend on the research questions and theoretical framework for the study. It should not occur outside of the context of the service-learning programs. As Cohen (1990) stated, "the informed judgement of the investigator is the crucial element in the interpretation of data, and that things take time" (p. 1304).

CONCLUSION

The purpose of this chapter is to consider approaches that have been used in empirical studies of service-learning and to present recommendations for new ways. The findings and approaches of earlier studies provide a useful guide for future research. Educational researchers confront many challenges as the demand increases for outcome-based evidence to support or refute the value of programs such as service-learning. The issues raised in this chapter are not unlike those confronted by researchers of other broad-based educational movements such as charter schools, progressive education, home-schooling, Head Start, and literacy. Like service-learning, each represents an approach to education designed to provide students with learning opportunities. Each is larger than a single program or series of textbooks. Instead, they are ways educators, students, parents, and the community think about learning and try to create learning environments for their students. The task of the researcher, therefore, becomes that of pulling together meaningful information from a wide range of programs and then developing some general conclusions. Because these programs are so different, this pulling together is often very difficult. This chapter briefly examined some of the challenges that researchers face and some of the decisions that may need to be made. Although it does not provide an indepth discussion of the ways to address these problems, it presents some recommendations and ideas for further exploring these issues.

REFERENCES

Alliance for Service-learning in Education Reform (ASLER). (1993). Standards of quality for school-based service-learning. *Equity & Excellence in Education, 26,* 71–73.

Allison, P. D. (2001). Missing data. Series: *Quantitative Applications in the Social Sciences, 136.* Philadelphia: Sage.

Andersen, S. (1998, September). Service-learning: A national strategy for youth development. Position paper. Washington, DC: The Communitarian Network and the George Washington University Institute for Communitarian Policy Studies (ICPS).

Anderson, V., Kinsley, C., Negroni, P., & Price, C. (1991, June). Community service-learning and school improvement in Springfield, Massachusetts. *Phi Delta Kappan, 72,* 761–764.

Arter, J. A., & McTighe, J. (2001). Scoring rubrics in the classroom: Using performance criteria for assessing and improving student performance. In T. R. Guskey & R. J. Marzano (Series Eds.), *Experts in assessment* (pp. 1–189). Thousand Oaks, CA: Sage.

Billig, S. H. (2000, May). Research on K–12 school-based service-learning. The evidence builds. *Phi Delta Kappan, 81*(9), 658–664.

Bryk, A. S., & Raudenbush, S. W. (1992). *Hierarchical linear models: Applications and data analysis methods.* Newbury Park, CA: Sage.

Campbell, D. T., & Boruch, R. F. (1975). Making the case for randomized assignment to treatments by considering the alternatives: Six ways in which quasi-experimental evaluations in compensatory education attend to underestimate effects. In C. A. Bennett & A. A. Lumsdaine (Eds.), *Evaluation and experimentation: Some critical issues in assessing social programs* (pp. 195–296). New York: Academic Press.

Campbell, D. T., & Stanley, J. C. (1963). *Experimental and quasi-experimental designs for research.* Boston: Houghton Mifflin.

Cohen, J. (1988). *Statistical power analysis for the behavioral sciences* (2nd ed.). Hillsdale, NJ: Lawrence Erlbaum Associates.

Cohen, J. (1990). Things I have learned (so far). *American Psychologist, 45,* 1304–1312.

Cohen, J., & Cohen, P. (1983). *Applied multiple regression/correlation analysis for the behavioral sciences* (2nd ed.). Hillsdale, NJ: Lawrence Erlbaum Associates.

Conrad, D., & Hedin, D. (1981). *National assessment of experiential education. 0A final report.* St. Paul, MN: Center for Youth Development and Research, University of Minnesota.

Conrad, D., & Hedin, D. (1982). The impact of experiential education on adolescent development. *Child & Youth Services, 4*(3/4), 57–76.

Cook, T. D., & Campbell, D. T. (1979). *Quasi-experimentation design and analysis issues for field settings.* Boston: Houghton Mifflin.

Cronbach, L. J., & Furby, L. (1970). How we should measure "change"—or should we? *Psychological Bulletin, 74,* 68–80.

De Fina, A. A. (1994). *Portfolio assessment: Getting started.* Jefferson City, MO: Scholastic.

Follman, J. (1998, August). *Florida Learn and Serve: 1996–97 Outcomes and correlations with 1994–95 and 1995–96.* Tallahassee, FL: Florida State University, Center for Civic Education and Service.

Grace, C., & Shores, E. F. (1998). *The Portfolio Book: A step-by-step guide for teachers.* Beltsville, MD: Gryphon House.

Hecht, D. (1997). *Annual Report to The Grant Foundation. An examination of the impact of the helper model of service-learning.* Submitted to the William T. Grant Foundation. New York.

Hecht, D. (1998). *Research of experiential programs such as service-learning: What we have learned.* Unpublished document, Center for Advanced Study in Education, CUNY Graduate Center, New York.

Hecht, D., & Fusco, D. (1996). *Student perceptions of the opportunities available form participating in service-learning.* Paper presented at the annual meeting of the American Educational Research Association, New York.

Huitema, B. E. (1980). *The analysis of covariance and alternatives.* New York: John Wiley.

Little, R. J. A., & Rubin, D. B. (1987). *Statistical analysis with missing data.* New York: Wiley.

Melchior, A. (1999). *Summary Report: National Evaluation of Learn and Serve America.* Waltham, MA: Center for Human Resources, Brandeis University.

Newmann, F. M., & Rutter, R. A. (1983). *The effects of high school community service programs on students' social development.* Final report to the National Institute of Education. Madison, WI: Wisconsin Center for Education Research.

Nunnally, J. C. (1994). *Psychometric theory* (3rd ed.). New York: McGraw-Hill.

Pedhazur, E. J., & Schmelkin, L. P. (1991). *Measurement, design, and analysis: An integrated approach* (Student ed.). Mahwah, NJ: Lawrence Erlbaum Associates.

Raudenbush, S. W. (1988). Educational applications of hierarchical linear models: A review. *Journal of Educational Statistics, 13*(2), 85–116.

Reichardt, C. S. (1979). The statistical analysis of data from nonequivalent groups designs. In T. D. Cook, & D. T. Campbell (Eds.), *Quasi-experimentation design and analysis issues for field settings* (pp. 147–205). Boston: Houghton Mifflin.

Sanders, J. R. (1994). *The program evaluation standards: How to assess evaluations of educational programs* (2nd ed.). Joint Committee on Standards for Educational Evaluation. Thousand Oaks, CA: Sage.

Scales, P. C., Blyth, D. A., Berkas, T. H., & Kielsmeier, J. C. (2000). The effects of service-learning on middle school students' social responsibility and academic success. *Journal of Early Adolescence, 20*(3), 332–358.

Schrock, K. (1995–2002). *Kathy Schrock's Guide for Educators—Assessment Rubric.* [Online]. Available:
http://www.school.discovery.com/schrockguide/assess.html

Schunk, D. H. (2000). *Learning theories: An educational perspective* (3rd ed.). Upper Saddle River, NJ: Prentice Hall.

Stevens, J. P. (2000). *Applied multivariate statistics for the social sciences* (3rd ed.). Mahwah, NJ: Lawrence Erlbaum Associates.

Switzer, G., Simmons, R., Dew, M., Regalski, J., & Wang, C. (1995). The effect of a school-based Helper Program on adolescent self-image, attitudes, and behavior. *Journal of Early Adolescence, 15*, 429–455.

Thorndike, R. M., Cunningham, G. K., Thorndike, R. L., & Hagen, E. (1991). *Measurement and evaluation in psychology and education* (5th ed.). New York: Macmillan.

Youniss, J., McLellan, J. A., & Yates, M. (1997). What we know about engendering civic identity. *American Behavioral Scientist, 40*, 620–631.

8

Practical Issues in the Conduct of Large-Scale, Multisite Research and Evaluation

Lawrence N. Bailis and Alan Melchior
Brandeis University, Heller Graduate School
Center for Youth and Communities

The design of impact evaluations needs to take into account two competing pressures: on the one hand, evaluations should be undertaken with sufficient rigor so that relatively firm conclusions can be reached; on the other hand, practical considerations of time, money, cooperation, and protection of human subjects limit the design options and methodological procedures that can be employed.

Rossi and Freeman (1993)

INTRODUCTION

Service-learning is variously described as a program, an instructional strategy, and a movement. It is, in fact, all of these things. As such, it presents immense challenges to researchers attempting to define, describe, and measure its impacts. Those who are familiar with service-learning know that no two programs are exactly alike, and no two participants have the same background and values. Therefore, no two service experiences are entirely comparable. Moreover, as an activity that is often infused within existing programs and curriculum, service-learning often takes place within a broader set of teaching and learning experiences, making it difficult to determine exactly where *service-learning* begins and other educational and developmental activities end.

Nevertheless, there is a growing recognition of the need for generalizations based upon hard data on the nature and impact of service-learning. At the program level, practitioners are increasingly aware of the need to document their programs and to assess their results, both for program improvement purposes and to make the case for service-learning with school administrators and school boards, college officials, community leaders, parents, and funders. At the national level, the passage of the National and Community Service Act of 1990

125

and the National and Community Service Trust Act in 1993 trained a spotlight on service-learning, creating a demand for new state and national service-learning evaluations and raising the stakes attached to all of the service-learning research now taking place.

Several chapters in this volume distinguish between the terms research and evaluation. However, in this chapter, both terms are used to describe systematic efforts to collect and analyze information that help those who fund or operate specific programs to decide: (a) whether their objectives are being achieved and (b) whether changes in the ways that the programs are carried out are likely to improve their effectiveness. We distinguish these terms from two other kinds of investigation that are also frequently carried out for service-learning programs: *assessment*, in which an individual teacher wants to understand how well each of his or her students are doing; and *monitoring*, in which a federal, state, college, or school administrator tracks a program to assure that their service-learning courses are being carried out according to an agreed-upon plan, that they are meeting certain standards, and so forth.

As noted in Melchior and Bailis (1996), these other types of endeavors involve many of the same issues. But these studies frequently address a limited number of program sites, thereby avoiding many of the problems that arise when one tries to compare program activities and outcomes across large numbers of sites. This chapter focuses on precisely these problems, ones that occur when one conducts research on or evaluates large-scale, multisite programs such as those funded by the Corporation for National Service (CNS), national foundations, or state agencies. These conclusions are, for the most part, based on the experience gained by the staff at Brandeis University's Center for Youth and Communities[1] in conducting more than a dozen evaluations of service-learning programs during the last eight years, as well as evaluations of a variety of other youth-related initiatives. The goal of this chapter is not to say *how to do it right*, but rather to raise some of the issues inherent in large-scale evaluations; to relate some of the experiences Brandeis University evaluators had addressing those issues; and to tease out ideas that can be helpful to those who fund, carry out, or seek to interpret the results of research and evaluations of service-learning programs that cover more than a handful of local sites.

THE CHALLENGES OF LARGE-SCALE EVALUATION

For many, the ideal research or evaluation scenario is one in which researchers are working to design the research and evaluation process in close partnership with a thoughtful funder and the people who are associated with a program. The process begins with visits to the program sites and extended discussions

---

[1] Until 2001, the Center for Youth and Communities was known as the Center for Human Resources.

about the program's history, goals, and intended outcomes. In this scenario, researchers, funders, and key program staff work together to develop or select measures for the study, determine the best data collection strategies, and introduce the larger program staff to the role of the evaluators. Logistical issues around site selection or survey administration are made easier by the limited number of sites, and the conceptual issues involved in defining the treatment or determining causality are limited in scope. Evaluating even single site programs is always fraught with complexities,[2] but the limited scale of the projects provides the opportunity to design a study in partnership with funders and program operators. This helps to keep the research conundrums in check.

Much of this begins to change at the multisite, state, and national levels. As the number and diversity of sites grows, and as the geographical distance between researchers and subjects increases, what were once relatively manageable questions of description, selection, measurement, and interpretation become much more significant challenges. When there is a high level of diversity among the programs being evaluated, as is almost always the case in service-learning, the challenges in coming up with useful generalizations increase.

Since 1992, the Center for Youth and Communities at Brandeis University's Heller School has been involved in more than a dozen evaluations of service-learning programs involving school- and college-aged youth. As noted in Table 8.1, the studies have ranged from large-scale national evaluations of programs funded by the Corporation for National and Community Service (e.g., Serve-America; Learn and Serve; Higher Education Innovative Projects; and Community, Higher Education, and School Partnership [CHESP]) to evaluations of several national programs and demonstration programs, such as Active Citizenship Today [ACT], the Earth Force Local Program, the National Community Development Program [NCDP], and the *Learning In Deed* Policy and Practice Demonstration Project [PPDP]); to statewide initiatives such as, community-based programs in Massachusetts and college level programs in Illinois; and several smaller scale demonstrations conducted for the YMCA of America and a five site effort that was funded by the America Online (AOL) Foundation.

Based on this experience, Brandeis researchers identified five broad theoretical and practical challenges in evaluating service-learning programs.

- The problem of defining and describing the programs;
- The problem of selecting sites;

---

[2] In this chapter, the authors generally use the term *site* to refer to a single community or school district, even though that site may include dozens of schools or a college that may include dozens of classes. If one treats individual classrooms as *sites*, the vast majority of service-learning studies would fit the definition of *multisite*.

- The problem of measuring outcomes and impacts;
- The difficulties of national data collection; and
- Problems of interpretation.

Each of these challenges subsumes a number of additional challenges. Moreover, each of them becomes particularly vexing as one moves from studies of a limited number of programs or sites to national or statewide, multisite, large-scale evaluations.

THE PROBLEM OF DEFINING AND DESCRIBING SERVICE-LEARNING PROGRAMS

By all accounts, service-learning (or what is claimed to be service-learning) has become a widespread phenomenon. More than 2,000 K–2 schools or school districts and hundreds of colleges are estimated to be receiving federal Corporation for National and Community Service Learn and Serve grants, and there are many additional programs operating with state funds or without outside grant support.[3]

Given the broad array of programs, one of the primary challenges in evaluating service-learning programs is that of simply describing them (and the service experience). Among service-learning programs for school-aged youth, such as those funded under the national Learn and Serve program, local initiatives include both school and community-based programs; programs serving elementary, middle, and high school-aged youth; programs that are districtwide, schoolwide, gradewide, or clusterwide, or based in single classrooms; programs that are integrated into a core academic subject, such as an English class, or that operate as elective "service-learning" courses and as after-school clubs. Service-learning programs take place in alternative schools, form the basis for at risk and dropout prevention programs, and are integrated into schools-within-schools.

This diversity raises both conceptual and practical challenges for the researcher/evaluator. At the most fundamental level, the question behind most evaluations is, "What kinds of impacts can be expected if a given program model is adopted?" But when evaluating large-scale, national initiatives such as Learn and Serve, what is the "program" the evaluators are being asked to evaluate? Is there a basic service-learning experience that represents a common, if not a core, "treatment" across the hundreds of widely varying programs, or is the task like combining apples and oranges and attempting to assess the impact of something that can only be thought of as fruit salad?

---

[3] A recent study by the U.S. Department of Education estimated that approximately one-third of the public schools in the U. S., and as many as half of the high schools, involved their students in service-learning as part of their education (see Skinner & Chapman, 1999).

Overview of Center for Youth and Communities Evaluations of Service-Learning Programs

Study	Program description	Sponsor	Dates	# Sites in program	# Sites in study sample	Includes surveys of students, teachers, and/or administrators
Serve America	Federally-funded service-learning for K–12 students	Commission on National and Community Service	1992–1994	2000+	13	✓
Learn and Serve America (K–12)	Federally-funded service-learning for K–12 students	Corporation for National and Community Service	1994–1998	2000+	17	✓
Higher Education Innovative Programs	Federally-funded service-learning for college students	Commission on National and Community Service	1992–1994	400+	12	✓
Active Citizenship Today	Building service-learning and civic education into curriculum for middle and high school students	Close-Up Foundation/ Constitutional Rights Foundation	1995–2000	3	3	✓
Earth Force Local Program	Building service-learning and environmental education into curriculum for middle school students, both in school and out of school	Earth Force	1997–present	4 (in initial program, now 7)	All sites	✓

Continued on next page

129

TABLE 8.1
Overview of Center for Youth and Communities Evaluations of Service-Learning Programs (Cont.)

Study	Program description	Sponsor	Dates	# Sites in program	# Sites in study sample	Includes surveys of students, teachers, and/or administrators
Community-Based Learn and Service	Federal- and state-funded service-learning programs operated by community-based organizations	Massachusetts Commission for National and Community Service	1996	20+	3	
Alternative Student Service Educational Trust (ASSET)	A program to integrate community service into college level co-op programs	Illinois Student Assistance Commission	1994–1995	5	5	✓
Evaluation of the *Learning In Deed* Policy and Planning Demonstration Project	An effort to promote the integration of service-learning into mainstream education at the state, school district, and school levels.	W. K Kellogg Foundation Education Commission of the States	1998–present	5 states, 36 school districts, 140+ schools	All schools and districts for surveys, 15 districts for site visits	✓
Evaluation of the National Community Development Project	Analysis of efforts to promote sustainable service-learning partnerships among colleges, K–12 school districts, and community-based organizations	National Society for Experiential Education	1997–2000	3 school districts	3 school districts	

Study	Program description	Sponsor	Dates	# Sites in program	# Sites in study sample	Includes surveys of students, teachers, and/or administrators
Institutionalization of Service-Learning Among Learn and Serve Grantees	Analysis of the extent to which Learn and Serve grantees have promoted institutionalization of service-learning at schools, higher education institutions and community-based organizations	Corporation for National and Community Service	2000–present	2000+	400+ sites for surveys	✓
Evaluation of the Community Higher Education School Partnerships Program	Analysis of a CNCS effort to promote three-way partnerships among higher education, school districts, and community groups	Corporation for National and Community Service	2001–present	20 grantees, approx. 160 subgrantees	All grantees for surveys, 6 grantees for site visits	✓
Evaluation of YMCA Service-Learning Program	Analysis of an effort to promote a model of service-learning in five YMCAs	YMCAs of America	2000–2001	5	5	✓
Evaluation of AOL Digital Divide Demonstration Program	Analysis of five efforts to use service-learning to help reduce the *digital divide* between those with and without easy access to computers and the Internet	America Online Foundation and National Service-Learning Clearinghouse	2001	5	5	✓

* NOTE: Some of these studies were conducted in association with other research organizations.

The practical solution to this dilemma is to begin categorizing programs based on clearly defined and widely accepted program characteristics. That way, evaluators can begin to define and distinguish among service-learning enterprises in ways that let them identify different structures and strategies. They can then begin to build the basis for generalizations about what *kinds* of programs work for whom.

In so doing, evaluators of large-scale service-learning programs face two major challenges. The first is the lack of any agreed upon categories for use in defining service-learning across studies. It is relatively easy to define a set of structural characteristics for service-learning programs. For example, Abt Associates and Brandeis used a simple set of structural descriptors to collect national data for the Serve-America and Higher Education Innovative Projects evaluations. But whatever their value for these studies, the Abt-Brandeis definitions have not yet become widely accepted descriptors for describing the operational characteristics of service-learning.

Therefore, one of the first tasks facing the field is to establish criteria that *can,* and *will,* be used to describe the strategies for integrating service into academic curriculum and each key element of the strategies, such as "reflection," in relatively objective, measurable terms. Without some means of differentiating program strategies in terms of their *nature,* and ultimately the *quality* of their experience, it will be difficult to draw useful general conclusions about impact across broad subsets of programs.

The second challenge is translating actual program operations into these categories once they are developed and become accepted. The Brandeis experience across many evaluations suggests that the problem of description is likely to persist even when widely accepted benchmarks have been adopted, in large part because as a process, service-learning tends to operate across, rather than within neat, easily categorized boundaries.

One example can help to illustrate this challenge. As part of the national evaluation of the Learn and Serve program, the evaluation team developed a draft series of checklists or program benchmarks to use for field visits to provide consistent descriptive information across the study's 17 local sites. The checklists included basic descriptive information about the program such as type of school, age level of participants, duration of program, and numbers of students. They also included questions aimed at describing the nature and intensity of the service experience, the quality and focus of reflection, and the degree to which the programs attempted to draw direct links between the service experience and the academic curriculum. Evaluation staff went through the checklists with the teachers or program staff at each site and then supplemented those answers with their own observations.

While the checklists helped provide some consistency in the site descriptions for the study, success in using them was mixed at best. Relatively few of the programs fit into neat categories and the programs that best met expectations for high quality service-learning (i.e., programs that linked preparation, service, reflection, and academic learning) were the most difficult to categorize. What appeared to be relatively simple questions—such as "How many hours of direct service did students provide?"—became extremely difficult to answer for programs where students were involved in substantial preparation, reflection, and academic work. If a student spent a month preparing for a public performance that lasted two hours, were there only two hours of service, or a month? In an English class that discussed literature focusing on social issues, such as those dealt with in their service placements, how much of the academic class time might be considered *service-related*? In the words of one local service-learning teacher, trying to describe his program in these kinds of terms was like *trying to catch smoke with a net*.

As is frequently the case with large-scale evaluations, the goal was not simply to describe, but also to look for connections between program characteristics (as they were described) and impacts. The way in which these questions were answered, then, had serious implications for the study. The evaluation team ultimately decided not to use the checklists in the analysis because they did not provide a valid basis for developing conclusions about the sites. But the experience was instructive and helped to highlight how difficult an issue the question of simply describing the activity can be. The CNCS-funded studies were only initial efforts in this direction, but they highlighted the degree to which the problem of description can be a major issue for service-learning and any effort to build a consistent body of research and evaluation.

Researchers/evaluators face two basic choices on this issue. The first is to accept the *fruit salad* approach to service-learning (i.e., to argue, in effect, that there is a common, core service-learning experience that is shared by all or most of the programs to be evaluated and therefore, there is no need to differentiate programs beyond some basic structural characteristics). This is how much evaluation research now takes place: the resulting research allows researchers/ evaluators to generalize about the impact of service-learning. The second option, which may be a more productive one for the field to follow in the long run, is to make an investment in developing a set of workable benchmarks or standards and in placing high priority in individual evaluations on collecting descriptive information that uses these frameworks and definitions. This way, researchers can continually refine their abilities to define, distinguish, and describe what is being measured in a way that is supportive of providing useful lessons for the future.

THE CHALLENGES IN SELECTING STUDY SITES (SAMPLE SELECTION)

One of the distinguishing characteristics of large-scale, national evaluations is the need to focus the study on a sample of programs drawn from a relatively large pool of sites. For single site programs or those operating in a limited number of sites, such as the ACT, Earth Force, YMCA, and ASSET programs that Brandeis evaluated, site selection was not an issue. The scale of the program was small enough to reasonably collect all needed data from *all* sites.

But for larger programs, particularly at the national level, it is neither feasible nor cost-effective to collect all data from every site. In those cases, some process for site selection *has* to take place. Whenever this happens, there are at least three issues that evaluators have to grapple with:

- Defining a site, or the question of the appropriate unit of analysis;
- Determining an appropriate sampling approach; and
- Learning enough about the sites to make reasonable choices before site data collection is under way.

Defining a Site

The first site selection challenge is what evaluators call the *unit of analysis* problem, more simply translated by figuring out what one means by a *site*. While this is a relatively straightforward issue for many types of programs, in this volume, Furco illustrates how the issue is relatively complicated for service-learning programs. Both K–12 service-learning and its counterparts at the college level can take place at several organizational levels. For example, among K–12 programs, service-learning may be organized as a *district-level initiative,* generally with a district coordinator working with a number of schools; as a *whole-school initiative* where all students participate in a single, coordinated initiative; as a *schoolwide initiative* in which scattered classes across all grades create their own projects; as a *single class initiative*; or as any one of a number of other variations such as subjectwide or at risk programs. At the college level, service can be organized as part of a schoolwide mission, be integrated into one or more classes, or be operated as a freestanding activity. It can be sponsored by a single college or a consortium of colleges; by a program within a college, or it can be funded directly by CNCS or indirectly through subgrants from an organization such as the National Campus Compact or State Campus Compacts that serve multiple colleges.

So how should researchers/evaluators proceed? First, define a site. Is it the school, the single classroom, or the individual student? In the Learn and Serve evaluation, Brandeis evaluators attempted to characterize the scope of the local projects for site selection by breadth of coverage (i.e., districtwide, schoolwide, gradewide, and so forth). Though the categories had been constructed based on substantial prior experience, nearly as many projects fell into the *other* category as anything else. Altogether, 240 projects examined as part of the site selection process resulted in over 30 different descriptive categories for project scope.

Ultimately, the answer to questions relating to definitions and units of analyses for multiple-site programs should grow out of an understanding of both the overall purposes of the study and the program dynamics (i.e., the shaping force and direction for the local program). Is there, for example, a consistent strategy and approach throughout a school, or is each classroom an independent operator? Unfortunately, more often than not, the latter issues can only be resolved after the evaluation is completed, not before.

Moreover, every choice has trade-offs. In general, the *real* service-learning experience often takes place at the level of the individual classroom where an adult is interacting with a student. However, focusing on a single classroom as a site makes it hard to look at institutional impacts. Conversely, while it may be valuable to look at service schoolwide, by pooling classrooms evaluators often combine very different experiences and obscure the nature of the student experience.

As always, these choices are ultimately shaped by the goals and resources of the study at hand, and evaluators need to work with policymakers and practitioners to explore the alternatives and determine the most useful and appropriate unit of analysis in terms of producing useful results.

Selecting a Sampling Approach

The second site selection issue that large-scale evaluations need to address is that of selecting site selection criteria and/or a sampling strategy that are responsive to the overall objectives of the study. One issue is pivotal in this regard. Is the goal of the study to document the impact of an average service-learning program, or to examine the effects of exemplary program models? In many cases, large-scale evaluations begin with the assumption that a random sample is the best way to proceed. However, it is not always that simple.

If generalizability to all programs is the overriding objective, simple random selection is clearly the best choice. But there are times when generalizability to all programs is *not* the primary criterion. For example, in the Learn and Serve evaluation, Brandeis evaluators sought to develop indications of the kinds of outcomes that could be expected from well-designed, well-implemented service-learning programs. These outcomes would, presumably, be greater than those that could be expected from a representative sample of programs, since many programs in the random sample would likely not be well-designed and/or well-implemented. A sampling scheme was adopted in which sites were selected based on a specific set of criteria, with those criteria based on a set of assumptions about the relationship between program characteristics and participant impacts. This kind of approach requires a careful effort to ensure that readers understand how the sites were selected and that they should *not* try to generalize the results to all sites in the program, or to the program as a whole.

The point here is *not* that one way of drawing a sample is better than any others *per se*. Rather, the approach to sampling needs to be dependent upon the overall purpose of the study. For example, it is important to be clear whether the study is meant to be an evaluation of *Learn and Serve* as it now exists, an effort to spell out the potential for a well-implemented Learn and

Serve program, or simply basic research about the potential impacts of service-learning under specific conditions.

Identifying Sites

The third site selection challenge is that of knowing enough about the sites to make reasonable choices. Simply put, Brandeis evaluators found that existing data are rarely sufficient for making the kinds of choices that are necessary. They are frequently incomplete and/or not provided in a consistent fashion from site to site. Once again, the diversity of the service-learning activities, distance, and the problem of description set the terms. Increasingly, as researchers try to fine tune their understandings of service-learning, they need to be able to target evaluations to specific types of programs or to stratify sampling to ensure representation of a variety of different program approaches. But how does one know enough about the candidate sites to do this in an intelligent fashion?

Again, the Learn and Serve experience was instructive. Early on in that evaluation it was decided to focus the study on more intensive, fully-implemented service-learning programs: in this case, programs that were more than a year old and had reported higher than average service hours per participant, had documented regular written and oral reflection, and were linked to a structured curriculum. To identify sites, the evaluators constructed a multi-step selection process in which a random sample of Learn and Serve subgrantees, generally school districts or individual schools that had received a Learn and Serve grant, were identified. Evaluators then conducted telephone interviews with the subgrantees, and in many cases their sub-subgrantees, generally individual schools or classrooms that actually conducted service-learning, in order to confirm or collect program information. Each interview lasted approximately 20 minutes. Ultimately, evaluators collected information on a sample of 240 local programs and used those data to set the benchmarks for selection; for example, calculating the median hours of service and identifying programs that met the selection criteria.

Next, those programs were contacted for a one-hour interview to confirm that the program met criteria and to check their interest in participating in the evaluation. Finally, in most cases, evaluators made a one day site visit to the final list of sites, again to confirm information and finalize their involvement in the study.

The Higher Education Innovative Projects evaluation involved a similar, though less extensive process. Evaluators began with review of documentation about each site that had been provided to CNCS. They then conducted telephone interviews to obtain more information about the sites, but did not make any final decisions until the team was able to spend at least one day at each candidate college or university.

In both cases, the process 'worked.' Evaluators were able to identify sites with some degree of confidence that they met the criteria established for the studies. However, through these and other nationwide studies, Brandeis evaluators learned that it is often extremely difficult to get accurate information about a program even with a carefully constructed, resource intensive interview and screening process. Not too surprisingly given service-learning's problem of description, it was often not until the second or third telephone conversation, or in some cases the site visit, that field staff began to feel that they were clear on the major elements of each local program. More importantly, in at least several cases, observations of local programs differed substantially from the programs' own descriptions of program operations (particularly their assessments of their use of reflection). The differences in description highlighted the degree to which perceptions vary and the fact that questions left substantial room for interpretation.

There are several practical lessons learned through these experiences. The first is the need for large-scale evaluations with sufficient resources to make a substantial up-front investment in learning about and describing the programs to be evaluated. Sponsors of multisite programs should make an investment in a basic program reporting system as a prerequisite to, or first step in, a large-scale research or evaluation effort. Even where a reporting system exists, one cannot rely on written materials prepared by program personnel sites in deciding which sites to include in a study. More often than not, before site selection decisions can be made with any degree of confidence, it is necessary to complete telephone mini-surveys of representatives from each site to select a group of site finalists and to visit sites to confirm the data provided in the mini-surveys and to learn enough additional contextual information.

It is worth noting that the site selection process, particularly a well-conducted initial site visit, can also help to bolster the site *recruitment* process. Telephone interviews and site visits both provide opportunities to build a relationship with key people at the potential sites and to ensure that they understand the benefits and costs of participating in the study. Evaluators found that schools and colleges, contacted as part of the larger site selection process, often asked to be included in the study and that the relationship built during the early calls helped smooth the way later on.

The second related lesson was to build the interview and selection process on as clearly defined and stated criteria as possible. Both in terms of consistency of selection, and the eventual ability to generalize results, evaluators need to be as clear as possible about selection criteria and the nature of the evidence being used in making those decisions.

THE PROBLEM OF MEASURING IMPACTS

Do service-learning programs produce measurable results? Are the participating students better off than similar colleagues who were not part of the service-learning enterprise? Are these students able to produce clear benefits for the communities that they intend to help? There are at least three distinct challenges that have to be faced before these kinds of questions can be answered. First, it is important to begin with clear understandings about the kinds of outcomes that are expected. Second, the necessary data need to be collected in a uniform manner, and third, the causality issue must be resolved.

Identifying and Utilizing Appropriate Measures

During the course of more than a dozen studies, Brandeis evaluators discovered that proponents and practitioners rarely agree on the types of results to expect. The decisions for multisite research and evaluations need to be made by balancing program goals, the limited teacher and student time available for student assessments, and the ready availability of appropriate measures that one can realistically expect to be utilized in a consistent manner across all of the sites. As in so many other areas of research design, the fundamental lesson here is for multisite researchers and evaluators to work with program practitioners, as well as the existing research base, to clarify the kinds of outcomes that are expected and develop operational measures of those that represent the highest priorities.

In many cases this work can draw on and effectively use existing resources thus avoiding the challenge of re-inventing the wheel. A considerable body of research and evaluation work has already produced a number of measures that have been used over the years in assessing service-learning outcomes, including measures of:

- Citizenship and civic development, including civic attitudes, actual volunteer activity, and planned activity in the future;

- Academic achievement, including measures of impact upon individual students as well as schoolwide measures such as attendance rates, engagement, and dropout rates; and

- Personal development, including measures of self-esteem, locus of control, and measures of the extent to which students are engaged in various types of "risk behavior."

With relatively small-scale studies, evaluators can review shopping lists of these kinds of measures with key policymakers and practitioners at the sites in a participatory research fashion and then develop a consensus about which are believed to be the most important outcomes. Procedures can then be developed to collect information about each of them. Unfortunately, the need for consensus is just as great for large-scale, multisite programs, but it is far harder to obtain the degree of consensus before the study gets under way. In the case of publicly-funded programs, evaluators can begin with the formal goals of the enabling legislation. But even in those cases, the actual goals and priorities of those that operate service-learning programs may be very different from those outlined in the legislation. Thus, as was the case with site selection, it can be highly useful to spend time with representatives of programs being evaluated while such decisions are being made.

As the interest in, and the stakes attached to, service-learning research and evaluation are growing, it is becoming increasingly clear that the available measures and methodologies are in need of updating and improvement. Much of the recent research into service-learning, including the studies that are that discussed here, has relied heavily on paper and pencil instruments that were developed a decade or more ago. In many cases, the survey scales commonly used were developed for purposes other than assessing service-learning and only indirectly addressed high priority service-learning outcomes. Most of the scales have never been normed on minority or at risk populations and, in most cases, have not been reviewed or revised in some time.

Moreover, as the emphasis on cognitive and applied skills, such as critical thinking and problem solving skills, has grown, it is also increasingly clear that traditional, multiple-choice paper and pencil tests simply cannot capture many of the kinds of skill, knowledge, and behavioral changes most commonly associated with service-learning. Those changes include: understanding of the community, an ability to acquire and apply information in new ways, and the capacity to work effectively with diverse others. As in the broader field of education, there is a growing consensus among practitioners and researchers that these kinds of gains need to be assessed through more "authentic," performance-based assessment strategies.

Before the development of those instruments can take place, however, researchers and policymakers need to begin to develop collaborative endeavors to more carefully define the many outcomes that are attributed to service-learning. What do researchers really mean, for example, when they talk about "civic responsibility"? Is it knowledge of community issues? A set of beliefs about civic participation? Intending to vote regularly or active participation in a range of civic activities? Or all of the above? What benchmarks or indicators would researchers look for on each of these as the basis for assessment? Similarly, what do researchers really mean when they talk about critical thinking or problem solving skills? Thus, at this point in time, one of the major barriers to effective assessment of service-learning outcomes is the lack of a consensus on which outcomes are most likely to result from service-learning programs, on clear or consistent definitions of what these outcomes really mean, and/or which outcomes one can reasonably expect to measure effectively. Developing outcome typologies and widely accepted measures within these typologies are among the highest priorities for the field of service-learning.

In the evaluation of ACT, an initial effort was made to address this issue, though not in terms of reaching a *national* consensus on measures. ACT was a civics education/service-learning initiative operating in approximately 45 middle and high schools in three school districts: Jefferson

County, CO; Jackson, MS; and Omaha, NE. The program was built around a five-part framework in which students learn about their community, identify issues, explore policy, and plan and carry out a community project. The goal of the program was to teach a wide range of skills that students needed to act as effective citizens in their communities.[4]

The challenge for this evaluator, as in many service-learning programs, was how to assess the achievement of core ACT skills such as ability to analyze community problems and evaluate policy options, an enterprise which clearly required something other than a multiple-choice, short-answer assessment instrument. Evaluators convened a group of teachers and site coordinators from the three districts for a two-day working session aimed at outlining an alternative assessment strategy. The workgroup identified roughly 30 possible strategies, ranging from having a sample of students conduct a second project during the summer to using video observation to document student skills. After adopting a number of criteria to help shape the decision making process, including the need to complete any pre-/post-assessments during a single class period, the group chose to create a simulation exercise in which small groups of students were given a description of a community problem and asked to respond to a series of planning and analysis questions.

During the course of the two-day meeting, the workgroup outlined the scenario to be used, developed a list of questions, and brainstormed a rough scoring rubric for the assessment. The evaluation team then refined the design, which was piloted in several sites and further revised that year. The final outcome was an *ACT Community Problem Solving Exercise* that was pilot-tested in selected ACT schools and incorporated into the study.

As before, lessons were learned from this process. The first was the difficulty of constructing an alternative assessment that can be used reliably at scale. Even after substantial work with the pilot tests to refine a scoring rubric, scoring the assessments consistently remained a significant challenge. The use of alternative assessments was also time consuming, both in administering the assessments and in scoring them.[5] Finally, the most effective assessments appeared to be those that were tailored to the specific skills being taught in the program, which makes the idea of a single set of widely accepted tools for multiple sites much harder to achieve.

The second, perhaps more positive lesson, was the extraordinary value of involving the ACT teachers and site coordinators in the development process. Their insights into the expected skills of the students, the issues that the assessment needed to address, the time constraints teachers faced, and the specific language needed to motivate their students to respond made the

---

[4] Further information about ACT can be obtained from its two national sponsors, the Constitutional Rights Foundation and the Close-Up Foundation.
[5] Despite researchers' efforts, the final ACT exercise ended up taking between one and two class periods.

design process easier and resulted in a much more useful tool than would have been otherwise possible. This suggests that efforts to design newer, more targeted assessments for service-learning are much more likely to be fruitful if they are built on a foundation of practitioner involvement.

THE CHALLENGE OF ASSIGNING CAUSALITY

Unlike the teacher in the classroom, the multisite program evaluator needs to distinguish between *outcomes* (i.e., the things that happen after a service-learning course is completed) and *impacts* (i.e., the things that have happened *because of* the course). In other words, efforts have to be made to identify those things that would have happened even if the course had not taken place and then subtract them out from the observed outcomes. Even if evaluators can demonstrate that young participants in service-learning programs, or the communities they seek to help, are better off after they are in these programs, the evaluator cannot be sure that the programs have caused the observed outcomes without developing some means of estimating what the observed outcomes would have been had the programs not taken place.

Many of the issues raised in this section concerning measurement and causality apply in broad terms equally well to efforts to assess institutional and community impacts of service-learning, an area of research that has received considerably less attention than that of participant impacts. Measuring the economic impact of service is extremely difficult when projects vary so widely in the service provided. While one can go project by project to assess some impacts, that process is difficult to sustain in a large-scale study. Similarly, many community impacts are not easily measured. For example, changed relationships and attitudes may ultimately result in regeneration of a neighborhood, but how does one measure those changes and how are they related to their proposed cause?

To be sure that a service-learning program has *caused* a given set of observed outcomes, it is necessary to separate out the effects of normal growth and development (sometimes called maturation effects), other activities in the schools or colleges, and other influences from outside the educational institutions. Within the schools, it is necessary to distinguish between changes in curriculum and the impact of leadership. Within curriculum, it is necessary to distinguish between the service-learning offerings and the other courses and extra-curricular activities with which young people may be involved.

Long before Campbell and Stanley (1963), the evaluation orthodoxy tended to argue that experimental designs, using random assignment, was the preferred way to prove causality because the outcomes experienced by the students who were randomly assigned to the control group could be assumed to be very close to those that the program participants would have experienced had they not been in the program. The researcher can estimate the impact of the program by subtracting the outcomes experienced by the control group from those of the program participants in the experimental group, using the difference as the estimate of program impact.

However, experience with numerous multisite studies has shown that this approach is neither desirable nor feasible in most large-scale service-learning programs. The in-school nature of most service-learning offerings at the elementary, secondary, and post-secondary levels generally precludes random assignment of students into a class. Even if this were possible, the key role of the teacher/professor and the community experiences would still make it difficult to argue that the experimental and control groups were suitably similar unless the same teacher/professor were overseeing both classes, and the community experiences were obviously very similar.

On the other hand, the evaluation literature often stresses the shortcomings of the so-called quasi-experimental designs that rely on comparison groups, particularly the inability to adequately adjust or control for differences in motivation and outside circumstances affecting the two groups. The concern here is that the measured impacts ultimately reflect some fundamental difference between the participants and comparison group members rather than the program itself. Ideally, the researcher/evaluator needs to work with the local program staff to design a comparison group strategy that eliminates as many of the uncontrollable variables as possible.

- If comparison classes are being used, is it possible to use another class with the same teacher who teaches the service-learning course (to control for differences in teaching style)?

- Are the comparison students as comparable as possible in terms of academic performance, as well as traditional demographic measures (age, gender, race, socioeconomic status)? For example, one would not want to use a "general teacher" course as a comparison to an honors course.

- Are the experimental and comparison courses as similar in their role in the curriculum as is possible (e.g., both voluntary electives or both required courses) so that issues of differential instruction do not complicate the analysis.

- Are the comparison students really non-participants, or are there schoolwide program events that will pollute the comparison group? If so, it may be necessary to look for a comparison school, in which case it is critical to look at school philosophy and characteristics in making your choice and to ensure that the schools have similar grading and attendance policies.

However, the complexity of making decisions based on criteria like these increases exponentially as the number of sites goes up and it is no longer possible to engage in person-to-person discussions with each of them. Decision rules that make sense in one setting are often contradicted in others.

It is extremely valuable to visit candidate program sites and potential comparison classes and/or schools as part of the design phase of a study. One benefit of those visits is that the researcher can explore some of the possible differences between the participant and comparison group students and use that information in interpreting the final results. It is equally important to visit as a means of investing the comparison group teacher in the study and ensuring that he or she understands the steps that need to be taken to ensure fair administration of the study design. The biggest danger in a comparison group approach may be the differences in motivation between the service and the comparison teacher, rather than the differences between the students themselves. Things work best when the researcher/evaluators and those closest to the program can work together review the rationales behind using different kinds of comparison groups and then work with the school-based personnel to come up with the groups that (a) are feasible and (b) have the greatest likelihood of coming up with useful, convincing results.

Causality and Infusion

Random assignment and comparison groups are designed to address one aspect of determining causality, that is, what would have happened in the absence of the program? However, there is a second, even more intractable issue that service-learning researchers are increasingly likely to need to address: the problem of infusion. Most traditional evaluation strategies, both local and large-scale, are built on the idea of a stand-alone *program* in which the *treatment* can be identified and separated out through the use of control groups. However, service-learning is increasingly being used as an integral part of broader, more comprehensive strategies. Two examples here are the Teen Outreach Program, that has used community service as part of a comprehensive pregnancy prevention initiative for teenage girls, and the Quantum Opportunities Program, that has used service as part of a comprehensive dropout prevention program. In these kinds of instances, the impacts of service-learning may be inextricably bound up in the impacts of the broader program in which it was embedded; hence, the question of the impact of service-learning *per se* may ultimately turn out to be impossible to answer. Using interviews and observation at specific sites, evaluators may be able to make judgments about the relative value and impact of different program components, but they may also need to acknowledge that the ability to use statistical techniques to isolate the service-learning as a determining factor in the program's observed outcomes will likely decrease.

THE CHALLENGE OF COLLECTING VALID DATA
IN A TIMELY FASHION

In addition to meeting the conceptual and practical challenges discussed thus far, those who hope to develop useful findings in large-scale evaluations must find ways to overcome the seemingly inescapable logistical nightmares of data collection on program descriptions and outcomes across widely separated geographic sites. As much as 90% of the day-to-day work involved in any large-scale, multisite research or evaluation project revolves around the challenges of getting data from scattered local sites in a timely and consistent manner.

The data collection challenge is easy to articulate, but hard to meet. While no simple responses to the data collection challenges exist, there are several promising approaches that are worthy of consideration.

Find a Creative Partner

Unlike single-site studies, the evaluation of multisite programs generally means that the core evaluation team members cannot do the job of data collection for themselves. In those cases, Brandeis evaluators have generally tried to identify and recruit site-based program managers to directly oversee data collection. They may be college or school employees whose multiple responsibilities include the program being evaluated, as was done in the Illinois ASSET study; college or school employees who are supported by funding from the program being evaluated, as was done for the ACT study; or site-based employees of the program itself, as has been done for the Earth Force study. In all cases, the key is to find someone who cares, an individual with a clear commitment to getting the study done well and on time, and the ability to work directly with the teachers/professors who have the responsibility to actually collect student data. This approach introduces a possible source of bias that must be dealt with in the study design phase, but such problems can be dealt with and the value of utilizing site-based data collectors far outweighs the risks.

Offer Targeted Incentives

Particularly in public schools where flexible funds are hard to come by, it helps to be able to offer some modest incentives. In several of the national evaluations, Brandeis evaluators gave each participating school grants of up to $1,000 as an acknowledgement of the effort involved in supporting the evaluation. While the payment may not have covered the true costs of data collection, it was a means of recognizing the effort that was involved, and often served the practical goal of securing the interest of the building administrators. In some cases the grants went directly to the program staff to compensate for overtime, and in others it was used to pay for school or program events. The key, however, was in being able to provide something that schools and local programs often have a hard time acquiring: flexible funding.

For some tasks, such as collecting school record data, the best approach is to ask the program staff or administrators to identify someone who will collect the information and be paid directly. In many cases, the school secretary, counselor, a substitute teacher, or in one case, the school security guard, were willing to spend a day or two pulling together needed records for a relatively modest sum. Different circumstances may make it advisable to provide the incentives to a school or to an individual within the school.

Provide Feedback

The other effective currency in many schools is information. In return for participation in the study, many local program staff want the information fed back to them for use in grant proposals, presentations to school boards or college committees, and for school accreditation decisions. Feeding information back to the sites will buy substantial cooperation and commitment to the study.

Keep It Simple

The larger the number of sites, the less control the evaluator has on data collection at each site. Given this situation, the "keep it simple" approach cannot be over-emphasized. This involves limiting the number of people who need to supply the data, limiting the different approaches to data collection, and limiting the number of data items that are requested. The obvious trade-off is that of having to limit your methodology in order to get *any* results. But in most cases, the discipline of focusing data collection on priority items pays off in a better rate of return, and hence more convincing results.

THE PROBLEM OF INTERPRETATION

If all has gone well, the large-scale research project or evaluation provides reams of data that document program operations and estimate impact at each of the sites as well as across sites. But the bottom line questions that still remain are "So what?" and "What are the practical implications of the findings?"

There is little guidance on this issue in the literature. Does the presence of *any* statistically significant change in students in the desired direction automatically make a program worthwhile, or are there minimum amounts of change that are necessary? The evaluators' Serve-America evaluation, for example, found a 5% increase in some measures of civic responsibility. It was *statistically* significant, but it was not clear what its practical impact was. One can make the case that it confirms service-learning's role as reinforcing and supporting existing attitudes or one can say that a 5% change in an amorphous-sounding indicator has no practical significance.

What kinds of steps can be taken in this regard? First, it would be useful to work with policymakers and practitioners during the design phases of a study to clarify what *their* expectations are, and then use these expectations as a standard against which actual results are assessed. Second, and more broadly, researchers and evaluators need to begin putting service-learning programs in the broader educational and youth program context and thus begin to compare the results of service-learning programs to other kinds of educational and related youth development initiatives for the same kinds of young people. How, for example, do the results of service-learning programs compare to those of work-based or project-based learning as a means of improving academic skills? How do they compare to other forms of civic education as a means of teaching citizenship skills?

None of this will be easy, and the efforts to compare the results of programs will be challenged by the same factors that have been addressed in this chapter. But, much can be accomplished when evaluators, policymakers, and practitioners get together to discuss the issues and begin to come up with ways to put results into this kind of context, and again, this works best when there are representatives of at least some of the sites present at the table.

SUMMARY AND CONCLUSIONS: WHERE DO WE GO FROM HERE?

Each of the challenges outlined here represents important barriers to effective research and evaluation on service-learning. Each is particularly vexing when faced by the challenges of large-scale research and evaluation. While none is impossible to address, few are open to simple, straightforward, easy, short-term solutions. So, what do researchers/evaluators do?

First, and perhaps foremost, the research and evaluation field can do a better job of sharing experiences and using them to adjust practice. The problem of description, for example, has a number of practical implications for national data collection, site selection, and the other issues addressed in this chapter. In the short-run, it is clear that paper forms are not going to provide enough high quality descriptive information and that site selection based on reporting is similarly inadequate. For national reporting purposes, researchers need to build more finely-tuned data gathering, probably based on intensive interviews with smaller samples of programs. Those in the evaluation field need to talk to and listen to each other more.

Second, service-learning researchers and evaluators need to talk sooner, more often, and more honestly with those who fund and operate service-learning programs. As Curnan and LaCava (1997) noted:

> Just as people participate in project activities, people must participate
> in project evaluation. The best evaluations value multiple perspectives
> and involve a representation of people who care about the project.
> Effective evaluations also prepare organizations to use evaluation as an
> ongoing function of management and leadership. (p. 2)

It is easier to conceptualize and implement participatory approaches with single site evaluations and research projects. But those who seek to conduct multisite research and evaluation must also find ways to make it happen.

Third, it is time to invest in the development, pilot-testing, and refinement of up-to-date and appropriate instruments that could be used across different studies in order to promote greater ability to develop generalizations.

Answering yes to questions like these will require researchers to work together in a more collaborative fashion than has been traditional in the service-learning field.

Fourth, researchers and evaluators need to work with policymakers to educate them about both the benefits *and* the limitations of research and evaluation of large multisite programs. In particular, policymakers and program operators need to understand problems of measurement and causality and the unavoidable uncertainties that they introduce.

Fifth, given what seem like inevitable handicaps faced by those who carry out large-scale research and evaluations of service-learning programs, those seeking to understand the impact of and improve service-learning programs should adopt broad research and evaluation strategies that incorporate multiple approaches. Multisite studies can be invaluable, but they should not be the only approach. The more diversified national research and evaluation strategy should combine large-scale studies with more targeted and controllable research into smaller groups of programs, including richly detailed case studies of individual programs—or even the experiences of individual participants.

Researchers need to recognize that this is a long journey. Service-learning researchers have learned a lot, but still have a lot to learn.

REFERENCES

Campbell, D. T., & Stanley, J. C. (1963). *Experimental and quasi-experimental designs for research.* Boston: Houghton Mifflin.

Curnan, S., & LaCava, L. (1997). *Evaluation handbook for W. K. Kellogg Foundation Grantees.* Waltham, MA: Brandeis University, Center for Human Resources.

Melchior, A., & Bailis, L. (1996). Evaluating service-learning: Practical tips for teachers. *Constitutional Rights Foundation Network* 5(4), 1–4.

Rossi P., & Freeman, H. (1993). *Evaluation: A systematic approach.* Newbury Park, CA: Sage.

Skinner, R., & Chapman, C. (1999). *Service-learning and community service in K–12 public schools.* Washington, DC: U.S. Department of Education, NCES Statistical Brief, 1999-043.

9

Self-Assessment for Service-Learning

Robert Shumer
University of Minnesota

INTRODUCTION

Service-learning is an educational philosophy and pedagogy that connects community service with intentional learning (Shumer, 1993; Stanton, 1990). Often, in school-based and community-based settings, it is tied to academic or formal learning programs. Students meet real community needs, learn how formal learning connects with real world experiences, frequently reflect on the nature of the service and the learning, and document learning and change through evaluative processes. Service-learning has grown tremendously in the last decade, involving more than six million students at the secondary level (Shumer & Cook, 1999; Skinner & Chapman, 1999).

As a field, service-learning has developed a set of guiding principles of good practice (ASLER, 1995; Honnet & Poulson, 1989; National Service-Learning Cooperative, 1998). These guides to practice were developed by experts and practitioners, producing standards through meetings and discussion. Up to this time, no one had attempted to develop a system for having practitioners measure quality of practice by actually field testing an instrument over several years to determine the form and content of the document or process. This chapter examines what happened over a three-year period when researchers and practitioners joined forces to field test a self-assessment instrument (and process) to learn how to improve the practice of service-learning.

BACKGROUND AND THEORY

Service-learning, in its best form, involves action and reflection (Rhoads & Howard, 1998). Its very nature requires that every service activity be connected to a reflective component in which the actions of service are assessed for their learning and impact dimensions. The development and implementation of service-learning programs also are a process of action and reflection. Each element of program development requires assessment of its effectiveness and quality. Such assessment and evaluation can be done through external sources, through internal self-assessment, or a combination of the two. In order to make the evaluation process more sustainable and have more immediate impact, self-assessment seems to provide the best model for critical examination of any program.

Self-assessment is a desired process because engaging practitioners in the evaluation process potentially leads to constant and appropriate change. Such efforts allow for a transfer of power from outside sources to internal, intimately connected personnel who can take the information and immediately put the recommendations to use. Self-assessment can lead to effective personal learning, the kind necessary for more successful direct application. It also allows program operators to engage in critical analysis, a process necessary for improved professional practice (Schon, 1987).

One of the primary goals of self-assessment is empowerment of individuals to study their own programs to make changes for improvement. The work of Fetterman, Kaftarian, and Wandersmann (1996) helps frame some of the theoretical underpinnings for the self-assessment presented here.

One of the primary goals of self-assessment is self analysis, that is, helping program implementers develop the analytical skills to determine what works in their program and what actions need to be taken to improve their design and implementation. The empowerment evaluation process involves four steps: taking stock, setting goals, developing strategies for improvement, and providing evidence of credible progress (Fetterman et al., 1996, p. 18). Developing an effective self-assessment system requires instrumentation and a process that first allows people to take stock of their program and determine what is working and what needs improvement. Second, they need to use this baseline information to set goals for change that lead to improvement. Third, they need to translate their goals into programmatic actions that produce the desired goals. Fourth, they must assess the new actions to determine whether or not their program is indeed improved.

Another factor that influences self-assessment is the quality of an assessment instrument or process itself in measuring program quality and strength. The primary purpose of this research project was to develop an effective instrument to help measure program quality. Part of the discussion that follows focuses on the issues encountered in developing a good, effective instrument. The complexity of service-learning, the variety of purposes and program designs, and the differing program goals all made the instrument development process quite complicated.

METHOD AND PROCESS

It took three years to design, develop, and implement a self-assessment program to help practitioners and researchers produce a useful system to measure the quality of service-learning initiatives. The project involved working with teachers and administrators in five states (California, Georgia, Minnesota, South Carolina, and Wisconsin) for a period of two years. The initiative was expanded to include three additional states in the last year: Colorado, Florida, and Iowa. In the first two years, five to eight teachers and/or administrators completed the self-assessment instrument. Several weeks later they discussed the instrument questions and process with a researcher from either the University of California, Berkeley, Clemson University, or the University of Minnesota (the closest university to their state). The research interview lasted between one and two hours and was based on a common protocol that included questions about each survey item and additional questions about the actual process of carrying out a self-assessment.

University research staff, from UC Berkeley, Clemson University, and the University of Minnesota, met once each year to review research data and to evaluate the recommendations for change. Discussion of data and feedback from each state produced the guidelines for modification of the instrument and directions for the process. These meetings were sometimes attended by graduate students who were involved in the data collection process; their input was also reviewed. Discussion and actions at these meetings produced the actual modifications in the instrument and self-assessment process each year.

The three-year project was also monitored by an advisory committee consisting of representatives from Northwest Regional Educational Laboratory, the Center for 4H Youth Development, and Brandeis University. National experts in experiential learning, research design and practice, and service-learning from these sites reviewed annual progress reports about the project. They provided feedback to the research staff and critiqued the instrument and process each year.

The initial instrument was based on theories of experiential learning and existing principles of good practice. The instrument had 30 questions, all requiring Likert scale responses. Initially, there was no formal breakdown of categories, although the questions were grouped around topics related to administration and instruction. The instrument was sent to a group of teachers and administrators from each state that was recommended by the state Learn and Serve coordinator, then followed with an in-person interview by one of the research staff.

After participants completed the instrument and interviews were completed, data were analyzed. Responses were recorded on a master list. They were then grouped by using a common words or phrase analysis. The goal was to describe what was meant by each numerical response; what *1* meant, a *2*, and so forth. The intent was to create a standardized instrument that could identify distinct elements in a service-learning program.

Analysis revealed a major problem. The phrases used were not consistent with the numbers. For example, when asked about having strong administrative support, one person indicated that their superintendent and school board were great supporters of the program. They rated their district a 5 (highest score) on that question. Another respondent also rated their district a 5 for administrative support, but they focused on their school principal and department chairman being the strong supporters, not the school board or superintendent. Thus, the effort to develop a consistent description of administrative support that would be meaningful on a Likert scale proved elusive. People meant different things, even though their numerical ratings were the same.

Based on feedback and data analysis, the instrument was modified for the second year. Changes included making it shorter, adding questions for administrators, and providing other options besides Likert scale responses.

The next version was completed by the same participants who completed the instrument in Year 1. Follow up interviews ensued. Data were analyzed for topical or phrase patterns for each question, as well as trends for the self-assessment process itself. Modifications were again made based on recommendations. The most significant change was in response to consistent concerns about the instrument length and time of completion. Almost all participants found the instrument too long and too time consuming to complete at one time (even though they were instructed not to complete it in one sitting). Participants indicated that they liked the questions and found them to be stimulating in promoting critical examinations of their programs.

Based on recommendations from the Advisory Committee and feedback from the interviews, the actual survey for Year 3 was divided into two separate sections: a quick assessment and an indepth form. Each version had 23 questions. The first section, Part I, requested only three responses: Barriers, Needs Improvement, and Strengths. The second survey, Part II, contained the same 23 questions as before, only this form had subquestions that further focused on issues and elements considered necessary for good service-learning. Time for completion of Part I was 10 to 15 minutes. Part II took from 20 to 30 minutes.

In the third year, focus groups to gauge personal reactions were conducted in each state. Participants discussed the instrument and the process for self-assessment in detail. Recommendations were made for final modifications.

In addition, site visits were made to one program in each of the eight states. The visit consisted of spending one to two days observing and interviewing teachers, administrators, students, and community members. Its purpose was to gather information to allow the researchers to complete the instrument (Part I). In addition to understanding how the process actually occurred in the field, one goal of this activity was to determine how well the instrument fared when insider knowledge was compared with someone from the outside. Plans were made to correlate practitioner responses with outside evaluators to determine some level of reliability.

DATA ANALYSIS AND DISCUSSION

There were several important things learned during the course of the three-year study. Perhaps the most important understanding was that developing a self-assessment instrument is only part of producing a self-assessment system. Participants almost unanimously said that the instrument had value because it stimulated thought about the issues involved in developing a service-learning initiative. They also said that the instrument could never have questions that satisfied everyone and were accepted by all. Improvement came when the instrument was combined with thoughtful discussion among peers and experts—where each issue on the survey could be discussed, refined, and explained. It was only through this conversation that the instrument took on a significant role in helping practitioners to understand the complexity and context of implementing good service-learning.

It was also important to create two separate forms of the document, a short triage form that only required 10 minutes to complete, and a longer, more detailed version with the same questions. Those variations allowed practitioners to use the assessment system for varied purposes. Almost everyone responded positively to the two-part system because they were able to do a quick assessment of their program initially, and then do a more thoughtful investigation later on. Most states wanted to implement the use of the instrument as it was designed, with both parts completed in close time proximity at the beginning of the year and then completed again at the end of the year as a post-evaluation and planning document for the next year.

Some states, however, intended to use the instrument in different ways. In a few of the meetings, participants wanted to use Part I as an early program assessment, usually in October, as a pre-test. Part II would only be used later, around February or March, to serve as an indepth check on areas of improvement. Other states decided to use Part I as a pre-test, but did not want to use Part II in its entirety as a post or monitoring check. To simplify the process, these states would only send the sections of Part II that addressed the issues identified in Part I. If, for example, the participants identified Questions 8 and 14 in Part I, as needing improvement, the state director would only send them Questions 8 and 14 from Part II for completion. These state-level respondents believed that this approach would make the process easier for busy practitioners, and therefore, more likely that they would actually use the instrument.

These variations in using the instrument led to further recommendations for modification. Several states wanted to alter the instrument by tailoring it to different audiences. Meetings revealed that the instrument would be more effective if they could actually rearrange the questions to suit the audience. For instance, some people thought that by placing the *Pedagogy and Practice* section first, it would appeal more to teachers, and thus more of them would complete the document. Others thought that by placing the *Policy and Parameters* section first, more administrators would be satisfied with the information they received. The point of these recommendations was that people tire when they complete surveys. It was important to put the most critical issues first, so participants responded with their fullest attention. It is not that the other sections are not as important. They simply are not as connected to the scope of work identified by the area of focus: practice for teachers, policy for administrators.

This discussion pointed to one of the major findings about creating self-assessments. In order for the process to be useful for practitioners, it had to be simple, take little time, and be fairly easy to complete. Perhaps the biggest success of the entire effort was the production of Part I of the instrument. Placing all the questions on one page so that the instrument took only 10 minutes to complete made the self-assessment more useful for practitioners. Although other self-assessment documents and rubrics exist in the field of service-learning, none had a 10 minute component that allowed practitioners to get a quick overview of their program strengths and weaknesses. For this reason alone the instrument development process could be called a success because it produced a document that was more useful for busy practitioners.

The development of the instrument and the process of dialogue about the instrument showed us that the self-assessment system was not linear—that the questions posed by the document caused practitioners to revisit their goals, their practice, and their assessment of progress. The instrument provided a unique contribution to the act of self-assessment. It provided a consistent set of questions and issues by which to measure service-learning operations. The questions were based on common notions of theory and practice and participants felt they were extremely helpful and important. The questions and the discussion caused participants to measure their work more regularly and consistently by examining the five dimensions of service-learning programs. The instrument provided structure and guidance necessary for professional growth and development.

COMPARISON OF SCORES: PROGRAM STAFF WITH OUTSIDE EVALUATORS

Comparison of participant scores with those of outside evaluators was conducted only on Part I of the instrument. Of the four programs that actually completed the surveys, the average number of matches was 16. The correlation between the scores was 0.70 ($r = .70$). Although this correlation is not as high as one might hope, it does indicate that when people have a chance to observe and discuss program elements, there is a better than average chance that they will be talking about the same dimensions from similar perspectives. Future efforts should involve a large-scale comparison with a sufficiently large population of practitioners and outside evaluators to determine a more reliable correlation.

SELF-ASSESSMENT AND EMPOWERMENT EVALUATION CRITERIA

The instrument and system fulfilled the requirements for good empowerment practice. Both Parts I and II, in their final forms, served to help program operators take stock of their programs (Criterion 1). It assisted them in determining what areas of their program needed change. Taking this information and completing the planning sections of Part I met Criterion 2; it helped them set goals for change. Implementing the change, Criterion 3 in the empowerment process, was fulfilled through questions at the end of Part II, where specific plans for actually making the change were developed to address the areas of concern identified. Several participants in the study mentioned that the planning document at the end of Part II was particularly helpful in describing what actually had to be done in order to improve the program. The final phase, monitoring and assessing change, was fulfilled by using the instrument as a post-test, measuring the change that had to be implemented. Thus, the instrument and process identified in this study met the criteria for empowerment evaluation and added the dimension of uniformity of assessment to the process.

The experience of improving the instrument over the three years reinforced the notions of reflective practice described by Schon (1987) in *Educating the Reflective Practitioner*. He suggested that "The problems of real-world practice do not present themselves to practitioners as well-formed structures. Indeed, they tend not to present themselves as problems at all but as messy, indeterminate situations" (p. 4).

Although this instrument tended to provide some sense of order and theory to program analysis, the fact that no perfect questions could be constructed showed that situations were indeterminate; they needed to be placed in context and examined for their uniqueness and their instructive potential. Respondents continuously said that answering the questions was difficult because they never quite knew the frame of reference for the response. Should they answer the questions based on one student, on an average student (who really does not exist), on the basis of one person's opinion, or on group consensus? Users of the instrument were always coming back to explanations of context for understanding. This was required because of the simple messiness of real-world work.

The uncertainty of real-world work also reinforced the need to have some form of dialogue attached to the self-assessment. No instrument by itself could capture the complexity of service-learning initiatives. It was only when the instrument became attached to a discussion group with others who were familiar with service-learning that participants could maximize the impact of the self-assessment on their program. In the many state level discussions, as well as the local discussion groups that emerged throughout the study, participants reiterated the fact that through discussion they were able to explain exactly what they meant by their responses to the instrument questions. They were also able to get feedback from others as to the relationship between context and action: what the context was for their programs and what possible solutions could be developed to deal with the problems identified.

Developing a self-assessment instrument and process is an important exercise in professional practice because it requires systematic analysis of the context and activities that make up a program. The instrument helps to structure the self-reflective work and provides benchmarks to measure strengths, weaknesses, growth, and decline. It becomes a referent, a quasi-standardized document that forces practitioners to ask specific questions of merit and substance. One does not need this particular instrument to perform self-assessment, but if improvement of professional practice in a rigorous, systematic way is a goal, it seems to help.

Appendix

The Appendix on the following pages contains the final version of the Shumer's Self-Assessment for Service-Learning instrument.

It can also be found by contacting the National Service-Learning Clearinghouse and looking under the topic: Frequently Asked Questions—Self-Assessment. The web address is: http://.www.servicelearning.org or you can contact Dr. Shumer directly at drrdsminn@aol.com

The Shumer Self-Assessment for Service-Learning (SSASL) is designed as a self-reflective system for professionals in the service-learning and experiential learning fields. What follows is a series of instruments and analysis worksheets arranged to help individuals evaluate their current service-learning initiatives to improve and strengthen them.

SHUMER'S SELF-ASSESSMENT FOR SERVICE-LEARNING

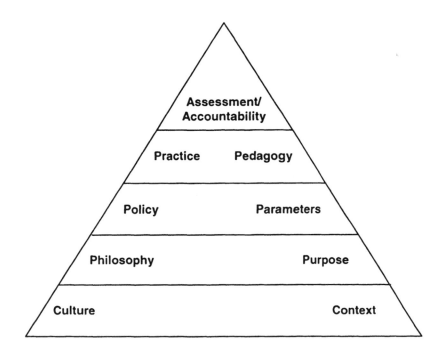

QUINTESSENTIAL ELEMENTS OF SERVICE-LEARNING

Primary Author
Rob Shumer

Contributing Authors
Pat Duttweiler, Andrew Furco, Madeline Hengel, and Gwen Willems

PART I: Quick Assessment

Before turning to Part I, examine

Your Service-Learning Context

To better assess your initiative, please explain the context in which you do service-learning.

We define service-learning as:

_____

_____

The purpose of our service-learning initiative/program is:

_____

_____

Our primary goal(s) for service-learning is (are):

_____

_____

Typical activities performed by students doing service-learning include:

_____

_____

We typically assess student learning and impact of service by:

_____

_____

This self-assessment is focused on our __ district __ school __ other:

_____

What aspect of our service-learning initiative do we especially want to evaluate?_____

_____

DIRECTIONS FOR PART I

For each of the 23 statements, choose and check off one response that indicates the current status of your service-learning initiative. Each statement represents a positive, desirable goal for effective service-learning. Consider having students and your colleagues (teachers, administrators, parents, and other community members) fill out Part I and discuss reflections as a group.

- Select **"Weak"** if the area or element is not in place or there are conditions that work against it. This is where you encounter "**Barriers.**"
- Select **"Needs Work"** if the area or element is in place, but needs improvement for effective practice.
- Select **"Strong"** if you think the area or element is in place and operating at a highly effective level. This is where **"Assets"** contribute to your initiative.

UPON COMPLETION

Note which of the 23 statements you checked as "Weak" or "Needs Work." For a more indepth analysis of the areas you consider most important to change or most in need of improvement, complete only the corresponding questions on Part II. The second part provides more indepth questions for each part of items in Part I.

FIGURE 9.1
Shumer's Self-Assessment for Service-Learning Part I

I. Culture and Context *The social and personal climate, as well as the larger setting, in which service-learning is planned and implemented*	**Weak (Barrier)**	**Needs Work**	**Strong (Asset)**
1. Cooperative connections between school and community are valued.			
2. The role of service in improving individual and community quality of life is valued.			
3. Involving students in the development of the learning program is valued.			
4. Learning through real world experience is considered integral to the school and community.			

II. Philosophy and Purpose *The ideas, reasons, intentions, and rationale that guide your service-learning practice*	**Weak (Barrier)**	**Needs Work**	**Strong (Asset)**
5. The purpose(s) of our S-L program is (are) clear to everyone involved.			
6. We consider S-L important in improving teaching and learning.			
7. Our school and/or district's philosophy includes service as a vehicle for learning.			
8. The purpose of our initiative is clearly linked to meaningful activities and learning objectives.			

III. Policy and Parameters *Formal, organizational elements that define service-learning through administrative policies and support, state and district mandates, board of education policies, school structures, and the like.*	**Weak (Barrier)**	**Needs Work**	**Strong (Asset)**
9. Our schedules are flexible enough to allow us to meet S-L participant needs.			
10. We have specific curricular goals and guidelines that support S-L initiatives.			
11. There is sustained administrative commitment for developing and implementing S-L initiatives.			
12. The district's and/or school's policies support effective S-L.			

	Weak (Barrier)	Needs Work	Strong (Asset)
13. There is ongoing pertinent staff development for all members of our S-L initiative.			
IV. Practice and Pedagogy *What teachers, students, community partners, and administrators do to implement service-learning*			
14. Students play an active role in selecting, developing, implementing, and assessing S-L initiatives.			
15. Structured student reflection encourages critical thinking and is central to fulfillment of curricular objectives.			
16. Our program includes training, supervision, and monitoring of S-L and all people involved.			
17. S-L students are engaged in responsible and challenging actions for the common good that meet genuine needs in the school or community and have significant consequences.			
18. Student learning through service is directly tied to regular class objectives and activities.			
19. S-L occurs during regular school hours.			

	Weak (Barrier)	Needs Work	Strong (Asset)
V. Assessment and Accountability *Evidence that the service-learning initiative is meeting its goals and the process and results are being reported*			
20. Our assessment plan is clear, purposeful, and linked to state standards and district learning objectives.			
21. Our assessment process is appropriately frequent and thorough.			
22. Our assessment looks at the different sectors (students, teachers, parents, community, school, etc.) involved in S-L.			
23. Our assessment secures enough pertinent data to measure effectiveness and guide improvement.			

161

SUMMARY OF PART I

Planning for Part II

To establish priorities for a more in-depth analysis of your initiative, please write on this page the three statements or sections you identified in Part I as highest priorities for improvement. These are statements to which you answered either *Weak* or *Needs Work*. Also include the top three strengths, with *1* being the highest priority.

Priorities for improvement

1. _____

_____

_____

2. _____

_____

_____

3. _____

_____

_____

Strengths

1. _____

_____

_____

2. _____

_____

_____

3. _____

_____

_____

PART II: INDEPTH ANALYSIS

DIRECTIONS FOR PART II

Use your Part I responses to complete only the comments and questions in Part II that correspond to the numbered statements in Part I that you considered *Weak* or *Needs Work*. (For example, if you checked *Weak* for Statement 4, *The purpose of our S-L program is clear*, make comments and answer the two statements under Number 4 in this part of the assessment.)

Part II of this instrument is designed to help you examine in more detail portions of your program that you want to improve. The same 23 statements that you answered in Part I are repeated here. The major difference is that each statement has a series of sub-statements that will help you think more critically about what components of the issue need to be addressed. When the statements have relevance to more than one section, they are repeated in the appropriate sections.

A primary purpose for this survey is to help you examine issues about your program that need improvement. If any question is unclear, answer it as best you can, knowing that the instrument will serve as a point for discussion as you become further engaged in the self-assessment process. It is not necessary to complete this survey; address those questions that will help you further analyze areas for improvement.

Section I. Culture and Context
The social and personal climate, as well as the larger setting in which service-learning is planned and implemented

Please use the following to assess your overall "impression" of service-learning **in your setting**. If you work in service-learning in multiple settings, please choose one on which to concentrate. Write your answers in the space provided and/or use additional paper, if necessary. *Mark the response that most closely describes the culture and context that exist in your school or district.* District culture is the overall climate created by all of the stakeholders together—students, teachers, administrators, and community members.	
1. **Cooperative Connections Between School and Community Are Valued.**	
A. Students value cooperative educative connections between school and community	

Choose One:
  O Weak Value
  O Medium Value
  O Strong Value
	Comments:

Continued on next page

B. Teachers value cooperative educative connections between school and community.	

Choose One:
  O Weak Value
  O Medium Value
  O Strong Value
	Comments:

C. Administrators value cooperative educative connections between school and community.	

Choose One:
  O Weak Value
  O Medium Value
  O Strong Value
	Comments:

D. Community members value cooperative educative connections between school and community.	

Choose One:
  O Weak Value
  O Medium Value
  O Strong Value
	Comments:

E. We value cooperation among all stakeholders: students, teachers, administrators, parents, and other community members.	

Choose One:
  O Weak Value
  O Medium Value
  O Strong Value
	Comments:

2. The Role of Service in Improving Individual and Community Quality of Life Is Valued.	
A. District and school values are consistent.	

Choose One:
  O Weak Value
  O Medium Value
  O Strong Value
	Comments:

Section V. Assessment and Accountability
Evidence that the service-learning initiative is meeting its goals and the process and results are being reported.

Mark the response that most closely describes the assessment and accountability that exist in your school or district. Write your answers in the space provided and/or use additional paper, if necessary.
20.   Our Assessment Plan Is Clear, Purposeful, and Linked to State Standards and District Learning Objectives.
A.   Our assessment/accountability plan can be characterized as follows:

i)   Purpose of assessment
No clear purpose ① ② ③ ④ ⑤ *Purpose is clear to all parties*   Comments:

ii)   Development of plan
Few involved ① ② ③ ④ ⑤ *Wide involvement of teachers, administrators, students, and community*   Comments:

iii) Clarity of plan
No clear or specific plan ① ② ③ ④ ⑤ *Clear and measurable goals and objectives*   Comments:

B.   Our assessment plan is linked to state and/or other standards.
Never ① ② ③ ④ ⑤ *Always*   O State standards   O Other standards_____   Comments:

C.   Our assessment plan is linked to district learning objectives.
Never ① ② ③ ④ ⑤ *Always*   Comments:

21. Our Assessment Process Is Appropriately Frequent and Thorough.
A.   Our assessment process includes the following:
i)   Frequency
No evaluation ① ② ③ ④ ⑤ *Continuous evaluation*   Comments:

Continued on next page

ii)   Participants
No one involved in evaluation ① ② ③ ④ ⑤ *Key participants are involved in evaluation* Comments:

iii)   Types of Data
Single data source (limited methods) ① ② ③ ④ ⑤ *Multiple data sources and methods* Comments:

iv)   Accountability
No accountability ① ② ③ ④ ⑤ *Data tied to local/state accountability measures such as standards or curriculum guidelines* Comments:

22. Our Assessment Looks at the Different Sectors (Students, Teachers, Parents, Community, School, etc.) Involved in S-L
A.   The assessment of the effectiveness of our activities indicates the following:
i)   Impact on students
Not considered in evaluation ① ② ③ ④ ⑤ *An important evaluation component* Comments:
ii)   Impact on community
Not considered in evaluation ① ② ③ ④ ⑤ *An important evaluation component* Comments:
iii)   Impact on teachers

Not considered in evaluation ①	②	③	④	⑤ *An important evaluation component*	

Comments:

iv) Impact on school

Not considered in evaluation ①	②	③	④	⑤ *An important evaluation component*	

Comments:

v) Impact on district

Not considered in evaluation ①	②	③	④	⑤ *An important evaluation component*	

Comments:

vi) Other areas of impact

Please list other areas of impact:

23. Our Assessment Secures Enough Pertinent Data to Measure Effectiveness and Guide Improvement.

A. We use assessment to plan future activities.

Never ① ② ③ ④ ⑤ *Always*

Comments:

B. We use assessment to monitor the implementation of the program (continuous program improvement).

Never ① ② ③ ④ ⑤ *Always*

Comments:

Continued on next page

C.	We use student learning outcome data for program improvement.
	Never ① ② ③ ④ ⑤ *Always*
Comments:	

D.	We use community assessment data for program improvement.
	Never ① ② ③ ④ ⑤ *Always*
Comments:	

E.	We use assessment data to demonstrate cost-effectiveness of the service-learning initiative.
	Never ① ② ③ ④ ⑤ *Always*
Comments:	

Other Issues of Assessment and Accountability You Consider Important:

WHAT'S NEXT? CREATING AN ACTION PLAN

Remember that the purpose of this self-assessment process is to provide you with useful information that can guide improvements of your service-learning initiative. To move from information to action, use this sheet to help develop an explicit plan and decide how to assess progress toward improvement of your initiative.

Strengths of our service-learning initiative

1. _____
2. _____
3. _____

Areas for improvement

1. _____
2. _____
3. _____

Action steps to improve our service-learning initiative

Action priority 1

What? _____
By whom? _____
By when? _____
How to assess changes? _____

Action priority 2

What? _____
By whom? _____
By when? _____
How to assess changes? _____

Internal resources (e.g., other teachers, parents):_____

_____

External resources (e.g., university, state department of education):____

_____

Now that you have identified strengths and weaknesses of your initiative, it will help to share this with other service-learning practitioners, especially those who will help you improve your practice. Follow up with colleagues in your school, district, and larger service-learning community to both discuss the results of this assessment and choose ways to make the improvements you have identified as most needed for your service-learning initiative.

MONITORING THE ACTION PLAN

Use copies of this sheet to periodically review progress and revise plans for improving your service-learning initiative.

DATE _____

Current strengths of our service-learning initiative

1. _____
2. _____
3. _____

Areas currently needing improvement

1. _____
2. _____
3. _____

Action priority 1: _____
Progress: _____
_____
_____

Obstacles: _____
_____
_____

What to do next: _____
_____

Action priority 2: _____
Progress: _____
_____
_____

Obstacles: _____
_____
_____

What to do next: _____
_____

Overall assessment (did things improve?):
_____
_____

REFERENCES

Alliance for Service-Learning in Educational Reform. (1995). *Standards of quality for school-based and community-based service-learning.* Chester, VT: SerVermont.

Fetterman, D., Kaftarian, S., & Wandersman, A. (Eds). (1996). *Empowerment evaluation: Knowledge and tools for self-assessment and accountability.* Thousand Oaks, CA: Sage.

Honnet, E. P., & Poulson, S. J. (1989). *Principles of good practice for combining service and learning.* (Wingspread Special Report). Racine, WI: The Johnson Foundation.

National Service-Learning Cooperative. (1998). *Essential elements of service-learning.* St. Paul, MN: National Youth Leadership Council.

Rhoads, R., & Howard, J. (Eds.). (1998). *Academic service-learning: A pedagogy of action and reflection* (pp. 39–46). San Francisco: Jossey-Bass.

Schon, D. (1987). *Educating the reflective practitioner: Toward a new design for teaching and learning in the professions.* San Francisco: Jossey-Bass.

Shumer, R. (1993). *Service-learning: A Delphi study.* St. Paul, MN: The Generator Center, University of Minnesota College of Education, Department of Work, Community, and Family Education.

Shumer, R., & Cook, C. (1999). *Service-learning: A status report.* St. Paul, MN: University of Minnesota, Learn and Serve America National Service-Learning Clearinghouse, Department of Work, Community, Family.

Skinner, R., & Chapman, C. (1999). *Service-learning and community service in K–12 public schools.* Washington, DC: U.S. Department of Education, National Center for Education Statistics.

Stanton, T. (1990). Service-learning: Groping for a definition. In J. Kendall (Ed.), *Combining service and learning* (pp. 65–67). Raleigh, NC: National Society for Internships and Experiential Education.

10

Teacher Research in Service-Learning

Susan Root
Alma College

Efforts to identify the outcomes of service-learning and variables that mediate its impact in P–12 settings are increasingly the focus of research (Eyler & Giles, 1999; Melchior, 1998; Weiler et al., 1998). Studies have shown effects for service-learning on a range of outcomes including grades, motivation to learn, social and personal responsibility, self-esteem and attitudes toward diversity (Billig, 2000; Melchior, 1998; Weiler et al., 1998). To date, however, service-learning investigations in P–12 classrooms have primarily been the domain of those external to the classroom (i.e., college and university researchers or evaluation specialists interested in its effects). Studies by the teachers who actually design and implement service learning projects have been notably absent.

The exclusive emphasis in the field of service-learning on researcher-generated studies stands in contrast to developments in the larger field of research on teaching (Richardson, 1994). For almost 20 years, educational researchers have acknowledged the difficulty of establishing generalizable laws about teaching and learning given the multivariate world of the classroom and the contextualized nature of these processes. In response, many have adopted qualitative forms of inquiry such as ethnography in order to obtain a more textured understanding of the ways in which particular curricula or techniques are experienced by participants. Teacher research is consistent with this recognition of the indeterminacy, complexity, and tenuousness of educational findings. Proponents of this point of view argue that teachers, as insiders to a classroom community, are in the best position to articulate the frameworks within which members apprehend classroom life (Cochran-Smith & Lytle, 1990; Henson, 1996; McKernan, 1991). Interest in teacher research has also been stimulated by concerns about the marginalization of teacher knowledge and the desire to add teachers' power and voice to the field of educational research.

The purpose of this chapter is to suggest an increased role for teacher research on service-learning. Teacher research can provide insight into the situational variables that mediate service-learning, as well as into the lived experiences of participants. Encouraging teachers to contribute to the dialogue on service-learning is consistent with the democratic and emancipatory purposes of this approach. Conducting teacher research can enhance teachers' autonomy

173

in analyzing and solving the problems of designing, implementing, and improving service-learning in their classrooms. Finally, investigations by practitioners may be more accessible to teachers, increasing the likelihood that they will apply the results of service-learning research to their own practice.

DEFINITION

Although teacher research is a family of approaches rather than a single method, definitions share some agreement about its nature, goals, and agents. According to Hopkins (1993), teacher research is "research in which teachers look critically at their own classrooms primarily for the purpose of improving their teaching and the quality of education in their schools" (p. 9). Carr and Kemmis (1983) defined teacher research as

> a form of self-reflective enquiry undertaken by participants in social situations in order to improve the rationality and justice of practices, their understanding of these practices, and the situations in which these practices are carried out. (p. 162)

Noffke (1995) noted that teacher research is "at once . . . a set of things one can do, a set of political commitments that acknowledges that . . . lives are filled with injustice . . . and a moral and ethical stance that recognizes the improvement of human life as a goal (p. 4).

The literature on teacher research reflects disagreement over issues such as the appropriate focus of inquiry or level of collaboration between teachers and university researchers. However, there seems to be agreement that formal investigations of teaching and teacher research differ in several key epistemological principles including their assumptions about the sources, purposes, and use of knowledge about teaching. Formal investigations, even those concerned with problems of learning and instruction, tend to address theoretical or methodological questions, many of which derive from disciplines other than education, such as anthropology and psychology. In contrast, the questions for teacher research studies originate from teachers' own experiences. Thus, the questions for teacher research projects are highly reflexive, and typically concern immediate classroom problems (Cochran-Smith & Lytle, 1990; Henson, 1996; Lytle & Cochran-Smith, 1994; McKernan, 1991).

Results of formal research typically take the form of propositional knowledge about teaching and learning, whereas those of teacher research assume the shape of practical knowledge, such as procedural knowledge or narrative (Connelly & Clandinin, 1995; Elbaz, 1983). By meeting scientifically established standards for proof, the results of formal research are characteristically intended to generalize beyond the research setting, while the results of teacher research are intended mainly to exert influence on one or several teachers' practice.

HISTORY OF TEACHER RESEARCH

Most authors (e.g., McKernan, 1991; Noffke, 1997) trace the origins of teacher research to action research, a method pioneered by Collier (1945) and Lewin (1946). Collier, a Commissioner of Indian Affairs, assisted Native-American communities to conduct research on local problems. Lewin (1946), a social psychologist, defined action research as "research on the conditions and effects of various forms of social action and research leading to social action" (pp. 202–203). He proposed a cycle of "action-research-action" that would yield both the advancement of knowledge and also social change.

The leading early figure in the application of action research to education was Corey (1953). Corey and teachers associated with Teachers' College Columbia conducted numerous research projects on curriculum and instruction.

In the late 1950s and 1960s, as support for a formal science of education housed in universities and research and development laboratories increased, acceptance of teacher research waned. Proponents of teacher research, such as Taba (Taba & Noel, 1957), continued to promote the activity, not as an instrument for education reform but as a tool for teacher change (Noffke, 1997).

In the 1970s, Lawrence Stenhouse (1970, 1975), at the Centre for Applied Research in Education, advocated teacher research in order to include teachers in the processes of curriculum development and evaluation. Reacting against the outside-in nature of contemporary curricular reform, Stenhouse argued that curriculum was a set of hypotheses to be tested and revised by the teacher. Teacher research was also viewed as a means to professional emancipation, allowing teachers, rather than external evaluators, to control their professional development.

Teacher research achieved additional momentum in the 1980s. Cochran-Smith and Lytle (1999) pointed out that the several movements that contributed to its renewal collectively rejected a view of the teacher as technician rather than creator and mediator of knowledge. In many cases, too, proponents of teacher research shared a commitment to altering the fundamental social and political organization of schools.

In the field of language arts in the 1980s (e.g., Atwell, 1987; Berthoff, 1987; Goswami & Stillman, 1987), an emphasis on process models of learning led to a view of reading and writing as active, personal, and meaning centered. Literacy performances were understood as holistic efforts, inseparable from the student's membership in a language community and from family and social influences. In order to grasp the complexity of students' literacy acts, the teacher him or herself needed to become a "RE-searcher."

The 1980s also marked the integration of teacher research with critical social theory (Carr & Kemmis, 1986). Critical social theorists encouraged teachers to analyze the ways in which educational practice could perpetuate the race and gender-based inequities of the broader society and to collaboratively seek the transformation of schools.

In the 1990s, teacher research gained broad acceptance in schools and in teacher education programs as a component of professional development and programmatic reform initiatives (Cochran-Smith & Lytle, 1999). However, during this period, teacher research was also subject to increased scrutiny on both epistemological and methodological grounds (Cochran-Smith & Lytle, 1999; Fenstermacher, 1994; Huberman, 1996). Proponents (e.g., Cochran-Smith & Lytle, 1990) argued that teacher research permitted the elaboration of a unique form of knowledge about teaching: practical knowledge or understandings gleaned from experience and grounded in the contingencies of specific teaching situations rather than formal knowledge. However, Fenstermacher (1994) noted that, "There are serious epistemological problems in identifying as knowledge that which teachers believe, imagine, intuit, sense, and reflect upon" (p. 47). As with the formal science of teaching and learning, the claims of teacher researchers needed to be supported by epistemic warrants that, ideally, render them objectively reasonable (Fenstermacher, 1994).

Teacher research was criticized on methodological grounds. For example, Huberman (1996) argued that the closeness to the classroom enjoyed by the teacher researcher can provide unique opportunities to generate interpretations, observe events as they unfold, and revise one's understandings. However, he also cited the difficulties of conducting research as an intimate participant. As Huberman stated, "caught up in our limited milieus . . . filled with complexities, we can seldom make out, much less reflect on the rational and nonrational forces acting on those milieus" (p. 137). According to Huberman, to guard against distortion and bias there must be "a body of research, some robust methods, and a set of plausible constructs" (p. 132).

CONCEPTUAL FRAMEWORKS IN TEACHER RESEARCH

McCutcheon and Jung (1990) argued that teacher research studies can be based in different epistemological frameworks, each of which makes particular assumptions about the nature of reality, the relationship between the researchers and the objects of knowledge, and the goals of research. One potential source of teacher research projects is the informal epistemology of the classroom teacher (i.e., theories, scripts, etc., about students or classroom events constructed out of practical experience). Alternatively, teacher research can be grounded in formal epistemologies.

One such epistemology, positivism, assumes that there is an objective reality that exists separate from the observer and that the nature of this reality can be determined through rigorously controlled observation. Positivist researchers also assume that phenomena are governed by general laws and that the goal of science is to discover these relationships. Teacher researchers investigating service-learning from a positivist perspective might ask questions such as, "What is the impact of service-learning on students' mastery of standards and benchmarks?" "What correlations exist between the number of hours students have spent volunteering prior to this project and their attitudes toward service-learning?"

A second model of knowing is the interpretivist perspective. Interpretivism does not presuppose an external knowable reality. Instead, knowing is personal and involves the interaction of features of situations and the cognitive structures of their participants. The purpose of research in the interpretivist framework is to determine the nature of the meanings assigned by insiders to a social situation. A teacher conducting an interpretivist study of service-learning might ask questions, such as, "How do students understand the meaning of service-learning?" "How do students construct the causes of social problems or the individuals they are seeking to serve?"

A third perspective is the critical theory perspective. Critical theorists such as Carr and Kemmis (1986) reject the positivist model of teacher research and discount interpretivism as well because of its failure to empower participants to alter their situations. Critical theorists assume that social behavior, including teaching and research, reflects social, political, and economic categories. From the critical perspective, the goal of teacher research is to liberate teachers and students from oppression based on race, gender, or other aspects of personhood through praxis—a cycle of action and reflection. Praxis is viewed as the means by which practitioners can uncover their own and others' biases and create more just practices. Teachers conducting investigations of service-learning within a critical theory framework would view themselves as agents of social change. They would be concerned about the effects of service-learning on students' critical social consciousness and on problems such as inequity and discrimination. These teachers would also want to ensure that the service-learning project itself not perpetuate differences in power and status between participants and those they sought to serve.

RATIONALES FOR TEACHER RESEARCH IN SERVICE-LEARNING

Regardless of its epistemological foundations, there are several rationales for promoting teacher research on service-learning. Conducting research on service-learning has the potential to be an effective tool for preparing teachers to use this approach. Current perspectives on teacher thinking suggest that practitioners actively construct knowledge about students and teaching situations. Teacher knowledge appears to be in the form not of declarative prescriptions, but of personal theories, scripts, and metaphors. Further, recent research suggests that teaching itself is not the routine application of empirically derived generalities, but a complex cognitive activity involving planning, interpretation, and decision making. Finally teacher change appears to be self-directed, a natural response to the need to create more workable practice, rather than the result of externally mandated training. The implication of these findings is that if teachers are to incorporate service-learning into their practice, they must be actively involved in the conceptualization, design, and assessment of service-learning activities. This view is supported by the results of the curriculum development efforts of the 1960s and 1970s, which indicated that teachers seldom directly replicate innovations in their classrooms, but interpret, modify, or abandon them according to their perceived fit with their beliefs about practice. Opportunities to conduct their own classroom research may facilitate teachers' adoption of service-learning. In addition, teacher research may help teachers become more effective in their use of service-learning (Forward, 1989; Henson, 1996). For example, Bennett (1993) found that "teacher researchers viewed themselves as . . . better informed . . . as experts in their fields who were better problem solvers and more effective teachers" (in Henson, 1996, p. 55).

Conducting research on service-learning may also empower teachers to act as agents of educational and social change (Glesne, 1991; McKernan, 1991; Strickland, 1988). Several authors (e.g., Anderson & Guest, 1995; Root, Moon, & Kromer, 1995; Wade, 1995) have argued that service-learning is consistent with more holistic, authentic, socially constructed, and responsive educational practice. To articulate the linkages between service-learning and district or school improvement, however, teachers need to have a thorough understanding of this approach. Conducting teacher research studies can be one route to understanding. In addition, teacher research can help teachers acquire the "communicative competence" to structure district discussions of service-learning to include their concerns (Rogers, Noblit, & Ferrell, 1990). Conducting teacher research on service-learning can also enhance teachers' awareness of the degree to which schooling is coextensive with historical and political problems (Beyer, 1991). Such awareness may strengthen teachers' willingness to act as public advocates for learning and for children and families and to reflect on the ways in which they create the conditions for social justice or injustice in their own practice (Noffke, 1995).

Finally, findings from teacher research can be an important addition to the knowledge base on service-learning. Dewey (1929) argued that teachers should be producers as well as consumers of educational research, stating, "A constant flow of less formal reports on special school affairs and results is needed" (p. 46). Existing research in service-learning has identified several variables that mediate the impacts of service-learning, such as opportunities for structured reflection (Conrad & Hedin, 1982; Krug, 1991; Waterman, 1993); integration of service and academic goals (Dewsbury-White, 1993); and characteristics of individual students' experiences (Conrad & Hedin, 1982; Crosman, 1989; Krug, 1991; Melchior, 1998). By tapping into teachers' extensive practical knowledge of students and the conditions under which particular teaching approaches work, teacher research studies can contribute information about how, why, and for whom service-learning is effective. Teacher research studies can also provide a body of case studies about service-learning.

Cochran-Smith and Lytle (1993) argued that teacher research can contribute to two general knowledge bases: local and public. In addition, they have identified several types of knowledge that can be generated by this research. Locally, teacher research can contribute to the teacher's professional development. For example, it can inform teachers about how a particular curriculum is constructed in their classrooms, or how students learn. In addition, teacher research can contribute knowledge to the local community of teachers (i.e., it can inform teachers about the ways in which a particular method is being implemented across classrooms or contribute to decisions about district reform). Publicly, teacher research can contribute case studies to the educational research community and questions for further research.

Teacher research on service-learning has the potential to contribute similar information to local and public knowledge in education. However, because service-learning involves the integration of local or public social problem solving with academic learning, it has the potential to contribute insights and questions and to influence decision making in local and public knowledge communities beyond those concerned with educational practice. Table 10.1 on the next page illustrates the knowledge domains to which teacher research on service-learning can contribute and examples of the knowledge such research could provide:

TEACHER RESEARCH IN SERVICE-LEARNING: AN EXAMPLE

The following example illustrates a teacher research project in service-learning. Between 1993 and 1994, researchers from Central Michigan University, Michigan State University, and Alma College directed a project in which four K–12 teachers conducted teacher research studies of service-learning. In the first session of the project, the teachers articulated concerns about their students or their teaching that they felt might be addressed by service-learning. Using the technique of graphic representation (Sagor, 1992), they created maps identifying these dependent variables, as well as antecedent variables and possible mediating variables. From these representations, the teachers were able to formulate researchable questions for teacher research projects. For example, Jeri, a third-grade teacher, was interested in the effects of a project that paired elementary students who needed special attention with at risk middle school "buddies" on participants' attitudes toward school and attendance. Linda, a middle school teacher, wanted to engage all the students in her team in a community restoration project at a local opera house. She was concerned about the impacts of the project on students' self-esteem and attitudes toward their class and their community. Warren, a high school social studies teacher, wanted his students to become more active, self-directed learners. He developed a research project in which students investigated the consequences of a proposal to locate a low-level radioactive waste facility in their community. Warren was curious about the consequences of the research project for students' engagement (e.g., participation, being prepared for class) and meaningful learning.

TABLE 10.1
Types of Knowledge and Teacher Research on Service-Learning

	Local Knowledge		*Public Knowledge*	
To the teacher's professional development	For the local community of teachers	For the local social-political community	For the larger community of educators	For the larger social-political community
• How service-learning is enacted in specific class-rooms or contexts • How student learning and development (e.g., ability to apply learning, acceptance of diversity) are influenced by service-learning • Curriculum development • Relationship of the class-room to the larger community	• How teachers and students enact service-learning as an approach across local classrooms • Justifications and effects on the local community of incorporating service-learning	• Local problems and the effects of possible solutions • How local students are developing as citizens • Relationship of the class-room to the larger community • Alternative conceptions of know-ledge, teachers' and students' roles	• Case studies of students, classrooms, and schools engaged in service-learning • Additional research questions	• Case studies of social problems and how they are experienced and addressed in local communities • Case studies of civic development in students

The second session of the teacher research training focused on methodology. The differences between formal and teacher research in goals, audience, and methods were discussed. Teachers were introduced to the steps in the action research process. The session addressed research ethics, constraints on teacher research, and techniques for enhancing the validity of teacher research findings such as triangulation. The majority of this session was devoted to data gathering techniques. Each teacher developed a data collection matrix for his or her project that listed the research questions for their project and three data gathering techniques appropriate to each question. For homework, teachers were given additional readings on data collection methods and asked to prepare a detailed design for their project for the next session.

In the third session, teachers shared the methods they had chosen. They had selected a range of methods such as teacher and student journals, observation, standardized and teacher-developed questionnaires, interviews, and student work. For example, Jeri created two questionnaires to assess the attitudes of the middle school and elementary children toward school. In addition, she had students complete evaluations of each buddy session. Linda decided to ask the school counselor to administer a standardized self-esteem index to students. Their parents were also asked to complete the same survey to reflect their perceptions of their children. Linda also used a teacher log, interviews, and photographs. Warren decided to use to use two of his traditional classes as a comparison group. The primary data source for his study was self-report sheets on which students recorded the types and settings of learning tasks they engaged in each day. Warren also used a teacher journal, interviews, student work, and video recordings.

Over the next several months, teachers implemented their projects and collected data. The next phase of the project that involved data analysis and report writing was the most difficult. Teachers received a manual on data analysis in teacher research created by the project directors. In the next group session, the teachers discussed and practiced techniques for analyzing their narrative data, such as coding, thematic analysis, and creating maps. Warren, for example, developed a system for coding the level of intrinsic motivation for learning apparent in students' questionnaires. After the session, the teachers continued analyzing data and writing and occasionally meeting individually with researchers to clarify questions.

The teachers presented the results of their projects at a national service-learning conference. The results of Jeri's project showed no change in self-esteem for the students; however, both middle school and elementary students showed improved attitudes toward school. Linda found that the community restoration project required a much greater investment of time than expected and was not able to give the self-esteem post-test before the end of the year. However, interviews with a subsample of her students indicated that the project had caused them to have more positive feelings toward their classmates and their town. Warren found that the self-reports of students involved in the service-learning research project more frequently indicated intrinsic interest in learning than did the self-reports of learners in his traditional classes. For example, participants were more likely to describe learning tasks in terms of task-internal features, such as the types of cognitive activity involved, rather than external features, such as grades. They were also more likely to report working on and thinking about the project outside of class.

In each of these cases, the teachers were able to use teacher research to arrive at conclusions about the effectiveness of service-learning in the context of their specific classrooms and to modify their classroom planning and practice based on these conclusions.

In summary, as these cases suggest, teacher research offers several potential benefits:

1. Although formal research can provide normative information about the effects of service-learning and mediating variables, a body of teacher research cases is needed if we are to gain a more precise understanding of the influence of contextual variations and the specific processes involved in designing and implementing service-learning activities effectively.

2. Curricular innovations and research-based principles are not implemented directly by teachers, but interpreted, or modified based on their consistency. Knowledge about teachers' models of practice suggests that a different perspective on teacher training in service-learning is needed. Specifically there is a need for training programs that actively engage teachers in the conceptualization, design, and evaluation of service-learning experiences. Teacher research projects can be a key component of such training programs.

3. One goal of service-learning as a curricular method is to enhance students' capacities for productive citizenship. Although most teachers accept some responsibility for promoting the personal and moral development of their students, a concept of teaching as a "bounded," technical activity has dominated the profession. Conducting inquiry on the effects of service-learning may heighten teachers' awareness of their responsibilities in civic education and public advocacy. Involvement in teacher research may also make teachers more cognizant of injustices in their own teaching.

The potential effects of teacher research on service-learning are recursive and multidimensional. Engaging in spirals of action, research on practice, and new action can provide teachers with a continuously improving knowledge and pedagogy in service-learning. Teacher research can simultaneously bridge the gap between service-learning theory and practice by adding to the knowledge base in service-learning the voices and concerns of teachers themselves.

REFERENCES

Anderson, J., & Guest, K. (1995). Linking campus and community: Service leadership in teacher education at Seattle University. In B. Gomez (Ed.), *Integrating service learning into teacher education: Why and how?* (pp. 11–30). Washington, DC: Council of Chief State School Officers.

Atwell, N. (1987). *In the middle: Writing, reading and learning with adolescents.* Portsmouth, NH: Boynton/Cook.

Bennett, C. (1993). Teacher-researchers: All dressed up and no place to go. *Educational Leadership, 51*(2), 69–70.

Berthoff, A. (1987). The teacher as researcher. In D. Goswami & P. Stillman (Eds.), *Reclaiming the classroom: Teacher research as an agency for change* (pp. 28–38). Upper Montclair, NJ: Boynton/Cook.

Beyer, L. (1991). Schooling, moral commitment, and the preparation of teachers. *Journal of Teacher Education, 42,* 205–215.

Billig, S. H. (2000, May). Research on K–12 school-based service-learning: The evidence builds. *Phi Delta Kappan, 81*(9), 658–664.

Carr, W., & Kemmis, S. (1983). *Becoming practically critical: Education, knowledge, and action research.* London: The Falmer Press.

Cochran-Smith, M., & Lytle, S. (1990). Research on teaching and teacher research: The issues that divide. *Educational Researcher, 19*(2), 2–11.

Cochran-Smith, M., & Lytle, S. (1993). *Inside/Outside: Teacher research and knowledge.* New York: Teachers College Press.

Cochran-Smith, M., & Lytle, S. (1999). The teacher research movement: A decade later. *Educational Researcher, 28*(7), 15–25.

Collier, J. (1945). United States Indian relations as a laboratory on ethnic relations. *Social Research, 12,* 265–303.

Connelly, F., & Clandinin, D. (Eds.). (1995). *Teachers' professional knowledge landscapes.* New York: Teachers College Press.

Conrad, D., & Hedin, D. (1982). Youth participation and experiential education. *Child and Youth Services, 4*(3/4).

Corey, S. (1953). *Action research to improve school practices.* New York: Teachers College Press.

Crosman, M. (1989). *The effects of required community service on the development of self-esteem, personal and social responsibility of high school students in a Friends school.* Unpublished doctoral dissertation, Lancaster Theological Seminary.

Dewey, J. (1929). *The sources of a science of education.* New York: Horace Liveright.

Dewsbury-White, K. (1993). *The relationship of service-learning project models to the subject matter achievement of middle school students.* Unpublished doctoral dissertation, Michigan State University.

Elbaz, F. (1983). *Teacher thinking: A study of practical knowledge.* New York: Nichols.

Eyler, J., & Giles, D. E., Jr. (1999). *Where's the learning in service-learning?* San Francisco: Jossey-Bass.

Fenstermacher, G. (1994). The knower and the known: The nature of knowledge in research on teaching. In L. Darling-Hammond (Ed.), *Review of research in education* (Vol. 20, pp. 3–56). Washington, DC: American Educational Research Association.

Forward, D. (1989). A guide to action research. In P. Lomax (Ed.), *The management of change: Increasing school effectiveness and facilitating staff development through action research* (pp. 29–39). Clevedon, England: Multilingual Matters.

Glesne, C. (1991). Yet another role? The teacher as researcher. *Action in Teacher Education, 13*(1), 7–11.

Goswami, D., & Stillman, P. (Eds.). (1987). *Reclaiming the classroom: Teacher research as an agency for change.* Upper Montclair, NJ: Boynton/Cook.

Henson, K. (1996). Teachers as researchers. In J. Sikula (Ed.), *Handbook of research on teacher education* (pp. 53–66). Reston, VA: Association of Teacher Educators.

Hopkins, D. (1993). *A teacher's guide to action research* (2nd ed.). Philadelphia: Open University Press.

Huberman, M. (1996). Moving mainstream: Taking a closer look at teacher research. *Language Arts, 73,* 124–140.

Krug, J. (1991). *Select changes in high school students' self-esteem and attitudes toward their school and community by their participation in service-learning activities at a Rocky Mountain high school.* Unpublished doctoral dissertation, University of Colorado, Boulder.

Lewin, K. (1946). Action research and minority relations. *Journal of Social Relations,* 2(4), 34–46.

Lytle, S., & Cochran-Smith, M. (1994). Inquiry, knowledge, and practice. In S. Holllingsworth & H. Sockett (Eds.), *Teacher research and educational reform* (93rd Yearbook of the National Society for the Study of Education, Part I, pp. 22–51). Chicago: National Society for the Study of Education.

McCutcheon, G., & Jung, B. (1990). Alternative perspectives on action research. *Theory into Practice, 29*(3), 144–151.

McKernan, J. (1988). The countenance of curriculum action research: Traditional, collaborative, and emancipatory-critical conceptions. *Journal of Curriculum and Supervision, 3*(3), 173–200.

McKernan, J. (1991). *Curriculum action research.* New York: St. Martin's Press.

Melchior, A. (1998). *National evaluation of Learn and Serve America school and community-based programs. Final Report.* Waltham, MA: Brandeis University, Center for Human Resources.

Noffke, S. (1995). Action research and democratic schooling: Problems and potentials. In S. Noffke & R. Stevenson (Eds.), *Educational action research: Becoming practically critical* (pp. 1–10). New York: Teachers College Press.

Noffke, S. (1997). Professional, personal, and political dimensions of action research. In M. Apple (Ed.), *Review of research in education* (pp. 305–343). Washington, DC: American Educational Research Association.

Richardson, V. (1994). Conducting research on practice. *Educational Researcher, 23*(5), 5–10.

Rogers, D., Noblit, G., & Ferrell, P. (1990). Action research as an agent for developing teachers' communicative competence. *Theory into Practice, 29*(3), 179–184.

Root, S., Moon, A., & Kromer, T. (1995). Service-learning in teacher education: A constructivist model. In B. Gomez (Ed.), *Integrating service learning into teacher education: Why and how?* (pp. 31–40). Washington, DC: Council of Chief State School Officers.

Sagor, R. (1992). *How to conduct action research.* Alexandria, VA: Association for Supervision and Curriculum Development.

Stenhouse, L. (1970). *The Humanities Project.* London: Heinemann.

Stenhouse, L. (1975). *An introduction to curriculum research and development.* London: Heinemann.

Strickland, D. (1988). The teacher as researcher: Toward the extended professional. *Language Arts,* 65(8).

Taba, H., & Noel, E. (1957). *Action research: A case study.* Washington, DC: Association for Supervision and Curriculum Development.

Wade, R. (1995). Community service-learning in the Elementary Teacher Education program at the University of Iowa. In B. Gomez (Ed.), *Integrating service learning into teacher education: Why and how?* (pp. 41–54). Washington, DC: Council of Chief State School Officers.

Waterman, A. (1993). Conducting research on reflective activities in service-learning. In H. Silcox (Ed.), *A how-to guide to reflection* (pp. 90–99). Holland, PA: Brighton Press.

Weiler, D., LaGoy, A., Crane, E., & Rovner, A. (1998). An evaluation of K–12 service-learning in California: Phase II Final Report. Emeryville, CA: RPP International and the Search Institute.

11

Expanding the Paradigm:
Students as Researchers in Service-Learning

Jeffrey B. Anderson
Seattle University

> Working on our service-learning action research project was a great
> way to learn-by-doing. Not only did I learn more about what it takes
> to make service-learning go but I also improved my understanding of
> cooperative learning, critical thinking skills, oral and written
> presentation skills, and increased my appreciation of how tough it is
> to do good research. The project also met a real need by providing
> the teacher with data about how well his service learning project was
> coming. Doing action research on a service-learning project is really
> doing service-learning.
>
> Dan M. Hathaway
(Personal Communication, March 13, 1996)

This statement from a recent graduate of Seattle University's teacher preparation
program reveals some of the important benefits that can result from teacher
education students conducting research and evaluation on service-learning
projects. This chapter describes the components of Seattle University's Master
in Teaching (MIT) Program related to service-learning and student research,
including a rationale for engaging preservice teachers in service-learning
research. This is followed by two case studies that exemplify the types of
service-learning research projects these students often undertake. Next, positive
impacts of these projects are presented. The chapter concludes with a discussion
of lessons learned that increase the likelihood of successful service-learning
research outcomes.

PROGRAM DESCRIPTION

The Seattle University Service-Learning Partnership was developed in 1993
with the support of a Learn and Serve America: Higher Education grant from the
Corporation for National Service. The partnership has three goals: (a) provide
preservice teachers with the knowledge and experiences necessary for them to

successfully integrate service-learning into their future teaching, (b) provide support to current K–12 teachers in the development and implementation of service-learning projects, and (c) prepare teachers to assume leadership roles in the reforming of public education. This program is described in detail elsewhere (Anderson & Guest, 1995; Wade & Anderson, 1996) therefore this description focuses only briefly on key program components.

All prospective teachers in the Seattle University Master in Teaching (MIT) Program (100 students per year) complete a required two-credit course called "Service Leadership." In the beginning of this course, students receive 15 hours of instruction regarding service-learning as a teaching method and philosophy of learning. After this on-campus preparation, students choose one of more than 20 K–12 teachers to assist in the design and implementation of new service-learning projects with their students. MIT students each provide a minimum of 25 hours of service to the school they choose. Since students frequently work in teams of four, they are able to give classroom teachers 100 hours of free support in the area of service-learning.

MIT students engage in the following activities in their service-learning field placement:

1. Assist teachers and students in contacting community agencies and resolving logistical problems, such as transportation;

2. Monitor and work alongside K–12 students in performance of the service-learning project;

3. Develop and lead the class in reflection activities that highlight what was learned through service;

4. Design and teach whole-class lessons related to the service topic that focus on integration of service experiences and the academic curriculum; and

5. Conduct research and evaluation to help determine the effectiveness of the service-learning projects.

In addition, MIT students lead schoolwide inservice sessions in several schools to introduce K–12 faculty to service-learning.

Throughout the service-learning experience, students engage in frequent written and verbal reflection sessions to help them raise issues, resolve problems, and establish an understanding of why and how service-learning can be effective when conducted from a K–12 school context. The course concludes with a conference, during which preservice teachers, K–12 students and teachers, parents, and community agency representatives share their service-learning project successes and grapple with the myriad of unresolved issues brought to their awareness through participation in service-learning.

Through participation in these activities, MIT students gain a practical understanding of how the principles of effective service-learning they study at the university can be applied in a K–12 setting. They engage in service-learning to learn about the use of service learning as a teaching method.

From 1993 through 2001, MIT students partnered with more than 50 different schools in the Seattle area to help facilitate their use of service-learning. Ten of these schools were partners throughout the entire period and experienced remarkable growth in their service-learning program as a result. The service-learning projects varied greatly from kindergartners involved in nursing-home visits through middle school students serving as cross-age tutors to high school seniors working with the homeless.

RESEARCH REQUIREMENT

Prospective teachers at Seattle University also complete a required three-credit course titled "The MIT Research Project." This course extends over all four quarters of the MIT program. During the first quarter students are exposed to some basic concepts of educational research and read the text, *How to Conduct Collaborative Action Research*, (Sagor, 1992). They next choose a research topic and form groups ranging from two to four MIT students who have agreed to work together in an area of mutual interest. During the second quarter students conduct a literature review, begin data collection, and initiate preliminary writing. During the third quarter students focus primarily on their student teaching experience, with some limited data collection. During the final quarter data collection is completed, as well as data analysis, interpretation, and the writing of the final report. The course concludes with a conference, at which students present their research projects.

The goals of this course include:

- Providing students with knowledge of the research process and the nature of knowledge produced by research;
- Assisting students to read and analyze research with an open but critical perspective;
- Familiarizing students with research journals;
- Preparing students to conduct research on their own teaching and/or schools that they can use to improve their educational practices;
- Helping students to gain an indepth understanding of the educational practice or issue they choose to examine;
- Providing students with one tool to use to facilitate their playing a leadership role in advocating for educational improvements; and
- Providing useful data for other educators to use to improve their programs.

Each research group of two to four students works directly with a faculty research advisor who provides guidance and support for their project. The advisor also evaluates the final research report. Students are free to choose virtually any educational practice or issue to research and many decide to focus on an aspect of service-learning. Rather than limiting the definition of action research to "research in which teachers look critically at their own classrooms primarily for the purpose of improving their teaching" (Hopkins, 1993, p. 9), this project used Noffke's (1995) broader definition of action research as "a set of things one can do, a set of political commitments that acknowledges that lives are filled with injustice, and a moral and ethical stance that recognizes the improvement of human life as a goal" (p. 4). This wider definition of action research makes practical sense for preservice teachers because for three of the four quarters of the MIT Program they are not teaching on a regular basis.

As a result of participation in these two courses, MIT students engaged in two different types of research on service-learning.

1. As a part of the service leadership course, students conducted research on a K–12 service-learning project they are closely involved with in terms of project design, preparation, curricular integration, and reflection; and

2. As a part of the research course students, conducted studies to examine MIT graduates experiences with service-learning during their first years as full-time teachers.

An example of both types of service-learning research projects are presented next in the form of case studies. Data regarding the service-learning research projects were obtained from interviews conducted with MIT students after completion of the research and from the reflections and discussion sections of their research reports. The validity of the research reports as sources of data may be limited because students were writing for the professor who grades them. The interviews, however, all took place after final grades were received by students and were conducted by a research assistant not associated with teaching either the service-learning or the research course.

CASE STUDY 1:
"ALL THIS WORK AND IT'S NOT SIGNIFICANT?"

During the 1995–1996 academic year, four MIT students engaged in a service-learning partnership with a health teacher at a large, urban middle school. This teacher was in the process of implementing a new service component in his seventh-grade health course. As a part of the semester-long course, all students were required to perform a minimum of 18 hours of service related to the health curriculum. Students could choose one or more projects from a list of options developed by the health teacher, the four MIT students, a full time adult volunteer, and an AmeriCorps volunteer who worked full-time at the school. Some of the more popular projects included tree planting, working at a daycare center, analysis of pesticide use at the school, creating and managing an organic garden, teaching organic gardening to elementary school students, and working at a local food bank. Most of the seventh-grade students completed the required 18 hours of service and a few provided more than 50 hours of service; however, 20% of the students completed no service at all.

The MIT students met with the teacher and the adult volunteer early in September to plan what their role would be in the service project. They agreed to develop possible service sites for students, lead in-class reflection sessions, and conduct a substantial research effort designed to determine some of the effects of participation in the service projects on the seventh graders' self-concept, motivation for schooling, and locus of control. Data would be collected by administering the Nowicki-Strickland Locus of Control Scale (Nowicki & Strickland, 1973), and the Conrad and Hedin's (1981) Social and Personal Responsibility Scale (SPRS) on a pre-/post-service basis to all 120 students in the four health classes. In addition, pre- and post-service-learning focus group interviews of seventh-grade health students would be conducted by the MIT students. The teacher agreed that one of the four classes (30 students) would not participate in any service-learning activities but would receive the same health curriculum as the three classes involved in service. This class would then serve as a comparison group. In addition, all 120 students would be given a pre- and post-test covering basic health concepts addressed in the course. This test was teacher-created and scored. The four MIT students and their advisor decided that this evaluation project was sufficient in scope to serve also as their MIT research project. This research study served a second purpose as well. The health teacher had received funding from the Corporation for National Service to conduct this service-learning project and, as a condition of that grant, had agreed to participate in evaluation activities.

The data collection process began in mid-September and soon encountered some snags. It was difficult to arrange times when the Seattle University students were not in class and the health teacher could spare the time in his full curriculum for them to administer the survey instruments in class. Several trips to the school ended without any data collection occurring due to the teacher feeling he was too far behind in his teaching to spare the class time for data collection. Eventually, however, all preservice data were obtained.

Further complications arose when Seattle University students began collecting post-service data near the end of the first semester in January. The adult volunteer had arranged with MIT students to interview students in the health class during the students' other classes (English, math, history, etc.). On several occasions the teachers of these classes refused to release the students for the interviews. It turned out that the health students had been pulled out of these other classes three or four times in order to actually do the service projects and these teachers were fed up with it and decided not to cooperate any more. It took several meetings, apologies, and thank you notes among all involved to resolve the bad feelings this experience created and to conduct the focus group interviews. Part of the difficulty here was due to the fact that these other teachers had little idea what service-learning was and why their students were being pulled out of class to engage in service-learning.

Immediately after all the post-service data were collected, another issue arose. The health teacher revealed that he decided, on his own and without informing anyone, that the health class that was the comparison group really needed to be engaged in service in the same ways as his other classes. He felt the service was a very valuable experience and that it was inequitable to penalize a whole class by not allowing them to begin the service component of the curriculum. He did not think this would make any difference in the research because these students had already completed all the preservice data collection surveys and interviews. The MIT students were upset over this change of events because of having made a concerted effort to work closely with the teacher on all phases of the research design and data collection. They felt the teacher had agreed to that research design and understood why a comparison group was helpful. The MIT students then decided to create a new comparison group using the 25 students from the four classes who had not completed any service at all.

The MIT students either scored all the instruments or used grant funds to have them scored by the publisher that produced them. The MIT students then analyzed the data, compiled demographics and descriptive statistics, and ran several tests of statistical significance. When the results were in they initially experienced great disappointment and confusion. There were no statistically significant differences between the service and the comparison groups on any of the measures. To make matters worse, some scores had actually decreased slightly after students completed their service project.

Fortunately, the students had also conducted focus group interviews of the health students and began to use these data to make sense of the lack of positive statistical results. Interviews revealed that most of the seventh graders were upset with their service projects and would recommend to other students that they not take this course. Their concerns centered on the following elements: They felt the service should be voluntary, not mandatory as it had been, and students needed to be involved in thinking up and choosing their own service projects; rather than having the adults design all the service options with no student input.

Interview data also revealed that most students could not see any connections between the service they performed and the health-class curriculum. In fact, they thought the service really had nothing to do with school at all. All students thought it was okay to offer service in school but only on an optional basis.

The MIT students then wrote a 50-page research report to present their findings. In this report they identified the lack of student voice in the service projects and lack of service integration with the curriculum as essential components of service-learning that were missing in this project. They also noted that the frequency and duration of the service activities (18 hours over one semester) may not have been sufficient to result in changes in student attitudes. They noted the importance of finding out the degree to which a service project is actually implemented, not just how it looks on paper, before drawing any conclusions about the efficacy of service-learning as an instructional method. Finally, they observed that although the quantitative data indicated the service projects were ineffective, the focus group interviews revealed some of the seventh-grade students had expressed their increased understanding of issues related to hunger and homelessness. One of their conclusions was that qualitative research methods, especially individual interviews and journals, might be a more effective way to assess the impacts of service-learning than quantitative instruments.

The following comments from MIT students reflected their learning and frustration.

> My appreciation for service-learning and understanding of its intricacies has grown immensely as a result of this research project. Talking to students and teachers about its impacts and ways to improve its implementation has vastly increased my own knowledge base. Having this background will positively impact my own use of service-learning as an engaging and powerful approach to teaching. I have raised my consciousness most about the impact an individual teacher can have on the success of a project. How that teacher communicates enthusiasm, allows for student input, and sets a tone for the classroom as a whole has an incredible effect on students' attitudes and progress with service-learning as it would with any other teaching strategy. Seeing service-learning as an approach or perspective for teaching rather than an add-on program is integral as well. Overall, my confidence in service-learning is more deeply rooted in my own values of what an education is meant to achieve than ever before.

> Conducting collaborative action research is both challenging and interesting on many fronts. While I now have a much more critical eye and appreciation for research and its interpretations, I am also more skeptical. The power of interpreting statistics is a great one that can easily sway or color results and implications of a research project. My awareness of this fact will help me be more educated in my own readings and applications of educational research in the future. In actually conducting research I learned that collaboration is not always easy but often results in a more powerful combination of various points of view. The struggles of scheduling, personality conflicts, and differing work ethics made working together unpleasant at times.

> It has been some time since the completion of our research project. I am surprised to find that, upon completion, I didn't wipe the information and the project immediately from my mind and my

experience. Although we did the research to fulfill a course requirement, it was valuable to me personally in terms of simply understanding what a research project is and requires. The information gathered and details learned have also been used as personal reference points in recent conversation.

The project, in hindsight, was far bigger than it should have been. I reference the term *should have* not only in terms of the work that we, as a group, undertook, but also in terms of the thoroughness of the project. Despite our initial narrowing of the topic to exclude research pertaining to the Quality Standards of Service-Learning, by the completion of the project I think we all would have preferred a far narrower scope. The quality of the project might also have greatly benefited from having a narrower scope from the outset. Both our data collection and our analysis and write-up would have benefited from less information and more focus.

All of this problem in clearly identifying those students who really performed service-learning made clear the importance of the Quality Standards of Service-Learning. Just because a student is registered in course with service-learning does not mean that he or she will necessarily participate fully or even perform any of the service.

In addition to learning a lot about service-learning in the course of our project, I also learned a lot about doing research; about selecting topics, defining research questions and hypotheses, researching the literature, developing research methods, gathering and analyzing data, and writing a research paper. I gained a tremendous appreciation of how complex it is do high quality research which really provides definitive answers to specific research questions and of what a difficult task it is to complete a project on a large topic within a given time frame. Completing the project has given me a great sense of satisfaction and a much deeper understanding of the complexities of service-learning and of the process of academic research.

In summary many MIT students gained a deeper understanding of complexities involved in implementing service-learning and a greater appreciation of the challenges in conducting successful action research. In addition, they came away from this project with an increased acceptance of their advisors' suggestion to begin with small, relatively simple, clearly focused projects with both service-learning and action research.

CASE STUDY 2: "WHEN IS A RESEARCHER NOT JUST A RESEARCHER?"

A group of seven MIT students was interested in exploring the experiences MIT graduates have with service-learning during their first years of teaching. Through their involvement in the MIT program they were in a position to obtain indepth data from teachers who were exposed to service-learning as a part of their preservice preparation. These students not only wanted to discover the factors that influenced beginning teachers' use of service-learning, they also desired to provide Seattle University faculty with data-based recommendations to help improve the service-learning component of the MIT program.

It quickly became apparent during the first meeting with their advisor that although these seven preservice teachers shared common goals, they had very different ideas regarding the specific research questions they would attempt to answer and how they would go about obtaining the necessary data. After several lively debates regarding the pros and cons of quantitative and qualitative methods of research, students decided to split into two separate groups. One group decided to use a quantitative approach and mail a four-page written survey to 91 MIT graduates and a comparison group of 37 graduates of another university's teacher education program that did not include any preparation in the use of service-learning. The second group took a more qualitative approach and determined to interview six MIT graduates regarding the factors that influenced their use of service-learning. Three of these graduates had employed service-learning in their teaching and three had not.

The survey group experienced many of the challenges faced by most survey researchers, including: gaining access to a comparison group; designing relevant, nonleading questions; keeping the survey relatively short yet still long enough to answer the research questions; obtaining funds to cover duplication and mailing expenses; and obtaining a high-enough response rate to allow valid conclusions to be drawn.

One student contacted the dean of a nearby school of education to obtain permission to survey its graduates regarding their use of service-learning. The student was turned down immediately because the dean felt the results might reflect negatively on her program. The student was also turned away by an administrator at the second program contacted. Finally, at the third institution contacted, the dean gave permission to conduct the survey. This process resulted in a considerable delay in survey implementation. In order to obtain funds to cover mailing and duplication costs, students applied for grant funds from the Seattle University Community Service-Learning Partnership, a Corporation for National Service (CNS) funded agency whose mission is to employ service-learning to expand the positive relationship among K–12 schools, higher education, and community agencies. Grant funds were awarded after students made several amendments to their proposal.

The third primary issue was not resolved so easily. Students were concerned that the second-year teachers they were to survey would be too busy to take the 15 to 20 minutes necessary to complete the questionnaire. They worked hard to shorten their survey and pilot-tested it with 12 MIT students in their third year of teaching in order to make it user-friendly. In addition, they approached a local coffee company with a request to provide a coupon for all respondents good for two free extra large lattes. These coupons were included with the initial mailing of all surveys. With this enticement, a follow up mailing and a phone call, the response rate reached 67%.

Survey results indicated that 21% of the MIT graduates implemented service-learning during their first year of teaching and that this percentage was not significantly different than that reported by the graduates of the comparison teacher education program. The student researchers were perplexed by these results because they had hypothesized that the Seattle University graduates, who had received preparation in the use of service-learning as a teaching method, would engage in far more service-learning than those who had not received this preparation. Based on other survey data they concluded that "factors other than preservice preparation, such as schedule flexibility, availability of transportation and financial support, project planning time, and administrative support are crucial in determining service-learning use" (Connor, Grief, Gunsolus, & Hathaway, 1996, p. 17). The student researchers were relieved to discover that significantly greater numbers of Seattle University graduates planned to implement service-learning in their second year of teaching than did graduates of the comparison group.

The second student research group chose to examine the factors affecting the use of service-learning by six MIT graduates in their second year of full-time teaching. They conducted a one-hour observation of each graduate's teaching and two 45-minute interviews with each graduate, the first in November, and a second in April. This group found it relatively easy to identify six graduates willing to be interviewed. They quickly came to agreement on their research questions and designed a protocol for a semi-structured service-learning interview. At the time of the first interview in November, three interviewees were using service-learning in their teaching, and three were not. When interviewees returned in April for the second interview, two of the non-service-learning teachers had begun new service projects with their students. When questioned about their reasons for starting the new projects, both attributed their renewed interest in service-learning to the November interviews. One teacher noted: "Having you come and ask me all those questions about service-learning was like a wake-up call. It brought me back to some of the things I believe in and what I learned at Seattle U."

One of the student researcher's conclusions included the realization that they (the researchers) were not objective and isolated from the issues and context they were studying. They wrote, "We were really participant-observers because our first round of interviews stimulated changes in teacher use of service-learning which in turn changed their responses to the questions we asked in the second round interview. The distinction between researcher, respondent, and teacher was an artificial one." Both groups of student researchers presented their studies at the National Service Learning Conference in Detroit in 1996 (Hathaway, Dolber, Scobie, Martin, & Anderson, 1996).

POSITIVE IMPACTS ON PRESERVICE TEACHERS' PROFESSIONAL DEVELOPMENT

There are numerous benefits that accrue from having preservice teachers engage in research on service-learning projects. MIT research course evaluations completed by students upon completion of the program indicate that 87% of graduates felt the research project was a valuable experience that should be maintained as a part of the MIT program. Many students interviewed indicated that the experiential learning that occurred as a result of completing the research project was the primary reason for their supporting the research project as an essential component of the program. This quote is representative of the majority view: "Overall, I found this research a valuable learning experience. You can listen to lectures all day on research and read a ton of books, but there's nothing quite like diving head-first into a research project to give you a realistic perspective on what you'll encounter."

Negative comments regarding the service-learning action research focused on two primary issues: the difficulty of implementing either service-learning or action research in a classroom managed by someone else, and concerns regarding the amount of time spent on these activities "that could have been used to learn more teaching and discipline strategies." Positive impacts on preservice teachers' professional development can be clearly seen in three distinct areas: (a) knowledge of research, (b) increased understanding of service-learning, and (c) making greater sense of other MIT coursework and preservice field experiences.

KNOWLEDGE OF RESEARCH

Conducting a research study provides students with a deeper understanding of what research is and how it is performed. After completing a service-learning research project, many students are both more skeptical of others research results and more appreciative how difficult and time consuming it is to conduct high-quality studies. One student commented: "So often in graduate programs we use references from publications without having any knowledge of the work and thought that goes into such research. After this experience, I read with a more critical eye and understanding heart."

Another insight mentioned by many students was their increased understanding of how important it is for teachers to consistently engage in research to answer the question, "Is my teaching effective?" Some indicated they would actually collect written data to address this question and others said just having this question firmly in mind would motivate them to view many aspects of student performance as potential data to analyze in response to this question. It seems clear that student attitudes toward the value of engaging in action research were strengthened as a result of their participation in a service-learning research project. This outcome is in accord with results reported by Arends (1990) and Clark (1992).

Students also gained a greater understanding of specific logistical issues involved in conducting research. For example, several noted that "involving K–12 students in too much data collection in one session greatly reduces the quality and usefulness of that data." These students had administered written tests to seventh grades for more than 90 minutes without a break.

A final revelation pertaining to action research was that "teachers *can* do their own research—it is realistic to do it on your own—in fact, it might even be easier than working with a group of three like we did." Several students took this insight to heart and conducted simple pre- and post-test reading assessments during their elementary student teaching experience. This MIT student perception is notable because very few of the cooperating teachers they worked with during their student teaching experience engaged in any written or systematic form of action research.

Many students intend to apply the action research model with their own future students. One student noted:

> Professionally, this project has given me a framework from which I can continue to apply action research to my interactions with students on a daily basis. As a special education teacher, it is a necessary and useful skill, particularly in behavior modification. This practice will help me avoid some of the common pitfalls of action research and working in a collaborative group.

INCREASED UNDERSTANDING OF SERVICE-LEARNING

Students quickly picked up on several issues that experienced service-learning researchers must grapple with on a regular basis. As the data collection and analysis activities unfolded, students became somewhat disillusioned with their research design and data collection instruments. They raised issues and engaged in a long discussion regarding the need for longer longitudinal studies of service-learning outcomes, the limitations of quantitative data, and the importance and logistical difficulty of focusing on individual students as the unit of analysis. Students had strong opinions on these points:

> I'm not sure the impact of service-learning can actually be measured quantitatively in a meaningful way. First, the impacts may not be seen for years and how can you possibly control for all the other interfering factors that occur in the same time frame? Second, the

impact may be diluted by the sample studied. In other words, service-learning may have a *major* positive impact on 5 to 10 kids out of 100, minor positive impact on 25 to 45 kids, and little or negative impact on the remainder. The major impact may never show up as significant. It would likely be diluted by the rest of the sample. For service-learning crusaders with number-crunching administrators, this is bad.

This is my first experience with research outside of the scientific realm, within which I am so comfortable. I found that I missed the 'hard facts' or science. It was unusual to put so much meaning on scales and measurements that appeared so arbitrary to me.

I learned that 'good teaching' is not as easy to substantiate with research as I thought it would be. I feel research in such a realm would be more effective if we looked longer and harder at what was going on.

Students also noted, frequently with some disgust that the service-learning teachers with whom they worked neglected to include some aspects of service-learning usually identified as essential to project success. For example, the lack of student voice, or ownership, in several service projects and the resulting negative attitude toward service displayed by the seventh graders involved made a strong impact on the student-researchers. "My renewed commitment is to empowering and enabling students. If that piece is missing, service-learning seems to be a lot of hot air and smoke."

Student researchers also felt that the lack of meaningful reflection activities diminished the quality of learning K–12 students experienced. The researchers noted that reflection was either an afterthought, engaged in only upon completion of the service, or it was a somewhat superficial formality, with K–12 students being instructed to reflect by responding in journals to questions such as "What did you do?" and "How do you feel about it?"

MAKING SENSE OF OTHER PRESERVICE COURSE WORK

Preservice teachers in Seattle University's program are taught that interdisciplinary, thematic instruction can be an effective method of teaching. However, instructors in their foundations, educational psychology, and methods courses do not always model this approach to teaching. Through participation in the service-learning action research projects, students experienced a more integrated approach to learning where specific skills and techniques they had learned in isolation were used together in the context of service-learning and evaluation. For example, preservice teachers most frequently mentioned the need for the K–12 students and themselves to engage in the following activities in order to successfully complete their projects: cooperative learning, using oral-presentation skills, letter and grant writing, critical thinking, problem solving, discussion, and conducting needs assessment. It became clear to many that service-learning can be applicable to any academic content area and that good service-learning is good teaching.

Working to collect data from sixth graders helped one MIT student understand what it really means when students are reading considerably below grade level. She administered to sixth graders a group self-concept instrument that was written at the third-grade level. Much to her surprise, 8 out of 28 students in the class just sat and did not complete the assessment. When she realized this, she first had to find out why they could not read it and then had to arrange to read it to them in a small, separate group at a later time. She commented, "maybe it was good the teacher didn't tell me they couldn't read it because this way I learned what I'll be facing during student teaching and I figured out a way to solve the problem—on the spot!"

An increased sense of self-esteem also was expressed in many students' comments about their service-learning research project. One student said, "this shows I'm capable of doing good research. I'm proud of this report and I'm going to bring it with me to job interviews."

This point focuses on an additional benefit of engaging in service-learning action research. As an essential component of most of the research projects, students needed to work collaboratively with practicing teachers, administrators, counselors, parents, and other community members. In one very real sense, every one of these contacts was a job interview. Students who presented themselves well gained an inside edge on future jobs or formed relationships that will help them with the networking often helpful in obtaining a teaching position.

Each year, all MIT students present the results of their research at an on-campus research conference. In addition, a group of six to eight of them also present at state and/or national conferences such as the National Youth Leadership Council (NYLC) sponsored National Service-Learning Conference. Their experience provides them with the opportunity to refine their presentation skills and engage in reflective discussion with professionals prior to their obtaining a teaching position.

LESSONS LEARNED

As a result of our experiences having preservice teachers engage in service-learning research projects, faculty sponsors learned many valuable lessons. These can be divided into two general areas: observations pertaining to enhancing the knowledge students gain from their research projects and observations regarding procedures and practices to make the research process function more smoothly.

ENHANCING STUDENT KNOWLEDGE

Both the research project and the service-learning courses are designed and taught following a constructivist approach to learning. Students engage in a wide variety of rich experiences, and through reflection, construct meaning and develop understandings from these experiences. Some student constructions, however, appear to be less accurate than others. This most often occurs when students misinterpret an experience or overgeneralize one experience as applicable to all similar situations. For example, some students tend to become very skeptical about the validity of all research based on one specific validity issue they dealt with in their project. These students tend to take the jaundiced view that the conduct and interpretation of research is so arbitrary that teachers should not rely on research findings to guide their teaching. These individuals state that teachers should rely on their common sense to guide their educational decision making.

This outcome can be avoided if instructors and research advisors plan their courses in a thoughtful manner. First, students can be immunized against these types of misconceptions by discussing them openly and throughout the research process. This is often accomplished most effectively in small group-discussion sessions. Second, conducting a service-learning or research conference at the end of the projects at which all students and teachers present their research results and discuss their accomplishments and challenges in an open manner helps homogenize student knowledge constructions. In other words, when students who experienced difficulties with one component of their project, such as lack of voice in designing service-learning projects or a low-response rate to a survey, or when they hear about other students who did not have these problems, they begin to put their experience in a broader perspective. In this way, the tendency to overgeneralize can be greatly reduced. Post-conference reflections with students are especially valuable in facilitating their understanding of the essential learning that can be gained from completing a service-learning research project.

Other helpful practices include involving teachers, K–12 students, parents, and other community members in analyzing the research results and process. These populations often thank the preservice teachers for the valuable service they have provided and share specific ways in which they will use research findings to improve their service-learning projects. This type of response tends to reinforce the value of the work for Seattle University students. It is also helpful to provide additional forums for preservice teachers to share their research results. Presentations at state or national conferences, creating a publication of proceedings from the in-house conference, and having preservice teachers present their research results and experiences to undergraduates in "Introduction to Teaching" courses have all been successful practices.

A second area of potential misunderstanding involves student perceptions that qualitative research methods are synonymous with an easy, relaxed approach to data collection and analysis. Some will choose to conduct interviews and observations rather than employ standardized instruments or other quantitative methods because they believe it is much easier, and they are somewhat intimidated by the inferential and descriptive statistics involved in quantitative studies.

In order to help students choose the research method that is the best fit with their research question, it has been necessary to repeatedly teach the importance of maintaining a rigorous approach to qualitative data collection and analysis. This is important not only in the initial class sessions in which research methods are taught but throughout the course of the research project whenever advisors interact with student researchers. Issues of validity and reliability of qualitative data need to be emphasized strongly at the beginning of the data analysis phase of the studies. This heightened emphasis helped ensure that conclusions reached by student service-learning researchers are supported by the data, and all the data are analyzed in as objective a manner as possible. Some student researchers have a tendency to focus quickly and exclusively on quotes or observations that support their personal beliefs regarding service-learning while ignoring conflicting evidence. Continued discussion with the research advisor can help develop in student researchers an appreciation of the importance of following rigorous procedures in data analysis and reporting. This can be discussed as both an ethical and a methodological issue.

A third area to emphasize with student service-learning researchers relates to determining the degree to which a particular service-learning project has actually been implemented. Students had a tendency to assume that a written description of a service-learning project, created prior to project implementation, was an accurate record of what really happened. This was often not the case. Some student researchers drew negative conclusions regarding the effectiveness of service-learning as a teaching method in cases in which students did not demonstrate changes in targeted academic knowledge or in aspects of personal social/psychological development. What these students, and in a few cases their advisors, failed to take into account was the fact that the service-learning activities these K–12 students engaged in were very different from what was originally planned. In some cases, students participated in five to six hours of service when the original plan was for 30 hours. Other changes included eliminating student voice in choosing and designing projects and eliminating reflection activities planned to take place throughout the service-learning project. It is inaccurate to judge service-learning to be unsuccessful in cases in which little or no service-learning was performed. As student researchers heighten their awareness of this important consideration, the importance of incorporating the best service-learning practices into the service-learning projects they develop with their future K–12 students was reinforced.

Fourth, the context in which service-learning research is presented to students can shape their attitudes toward the research project and impact both the quality of research and the amount of student learning. When advisors and the K–12 service-learning teachers stress that engaging in the study of service-learning involves both providing a service and learning for the researchers about service-learning and research skills, students do a better job on the research and learn more. When the service aspect of the research is not emphasized, students are less willing to be flexible with research responsibilities, less committed to the projects, and more focused on "what's in it for them" rather than how they can help meet a real need. This emphasis on service can be accomplished by simply mentioning the service aspects of the projects on a regular basis and by having K–12 teachers and students express their commitment to applying the research results to improve their service-learning projects (see Campbell, Edgar, & Halsted 1994).

FACILITATING THE RESEARCH PROCESS

There are seven ways in which faculty can make the service-learning process run smoothly. First, if students are to conduct research in groups, considerations of individual students' personality, educational philosophy, and school and work schedules are at least as important to successful group functioning as is interest in the topic to be studied. Delays and confusion can be reduced by having students form groups with others with whom they are reasonably compatible and are in classes together.

Second, novice researchers tend to take on large research projects that can easily overwhelm them. Students are often unaware of how much time is really required to collect and analyze data. Many K–12 service-learning teachers also are highly motivated to engage in service-learning research and tend to bite off more than they can chew, unaware of the complexities that lie ahead. A conscientious advisor can respect this motivation but also provide beginning researchers with advice to keep the research a little smaller and simpler than they perhaps believe is necessary. More meaningful research results usually come from examining a limited topic or issue well, rather than doing a scattered, superficial job on a large number of research questions. Students who are skeptical of advisors' suggestions on this issue can be provided with phone numbers of past student service-learning researchers who are happy to share their experiences.

Third, projects progress more smoothly with K–12 teachers and students who are committed to the projects and doing the work necessary to finish the research. Teachers (and preservice teachers) who are involved in service learning are frequently creative, high-energy people who are in the forefront of numerous innovative school reform projects. If they do not have the service-learning research as a clear priority, they can become so busy they do not have time to focus on the logistics of data collection or other aspects of the research. This contributes to communication breakdowns and the resulting confusion and squabbling. It is much easier to work with teachers who have voice mail or e-mail, use them regularly and demonstrate commitment to the project by communicating with student researchers in a timely manner. To inspire teachers' continuing commitment, it is helpful to keep them actively involved in decision making throughout the research project.

Fourth, student service-learning researchers also need to be directly involved in decision making regarding research design, data collection and analysis, and final write-up. In cases in which K–12 teachers used student researchers primarily as data collectors and have not worked with them to enhance their buy-in to the service-learning research project, the students often lose interest and only go through the motions of completing the research without putting their full capabilities to work. This concern can be reduced by all parties involved talking together to develop a clear understanding of the service-learning project, and jointly creating a research design.

Fifth, although they are graduate students, these preservice teachers are usually new to both research and service-learning; as a result they often need a considerable amount of guidance and support to gain the maximum value from their research efforts. The advisor can provide support by having frequent check-in points where student researchers obtain advisor approval before progressing. This structure is important to keep students from making irreversible errors that would dramatically reduce the value of the research effort. On the other hand, this structure needs to be balanced with providing students the freedom to design their own research, to learn from their mistakes, and to leave the project with a feeling it was truly their research, not the advisors' or K–12 teachers'.

The art of successfully balancing structure and freedom can be developed by having new advisors work with experienced mentor advisors on a few projects (Campbell, Edgar, & Halsted, 1994). Advisors also need to be familiar with and committed to principles of effective service-learning, especially the importance of student voice. Conducting student-driven service-learning research in a manner incongruent with best service-learning practices reduces the value of both the process and the final product.

Sixth, collaborate on service-learning research projects that extend beyond one year in length. By building long-term relationships with K–12 service-learning teachers, it is possible to design and conduct longitudinal research studies with a much broader set of possible student outcomes. In these cases, different classes of student researchers can contribute to different components of the research. If this is done, it is important to let students know beforehand that they will not experience all phases of a typical research project. Some student service-learning researchers have obtained teaching jobs in the area and have continued to play a role in ongoing research. The more service-learning practitioners and researchers can network and share challenges and findings, the faster the quality of service learning offered to K–12 students will improve.

Seventh, if we seriously expect graduates to engage in research and assessment of their service-learning project, university faculty must engage in these same practices. Faculty also need to discuss service-learning research challenges and successes openly with students in order for modeling to have maximum positive impact. Gandhi's advice, "You must be the change you wish to see in the world," clearly applies here.

CONCLUSION

Service-learning proponents in higher education have a great opportunity to both expand the types of service-learning in which their students engage and to share their research expertise with K–12 educators and the wider community to improve service-learning K–higher education. The engagement of student service-learning researchers allows both of these opportunities to be realized. Conducting research on service-learning projects can be a powerful form of service-learning for preservice teachers. Teacher educators and service-learning proponents in higher education have a gold mine of service and learning possibilities to tap as service-learning expands in K–12 education and the need for research and evaluation studies continues to be crucial.

REFERENCES

Anderson, J. B., & Guest, K. (1995). Service-learning in teacher education at Seattle University. In B. Gomez (Ed.), *Integrating service-learning into teacher education: Why and how?* (pp. 11–30). Washington, DC: Council of Chief State School Officers.

Arends, R. I. (1995). *Learning to teach*, (3rd ed.). New York: McGraw Hill.

Campbell, P., Edgar, S., & Halsted, A. L. (1994). Students as evaluators: A model for program evaluation. *Phi Delta Kappan, 76*(2), 160–165.

Clark, S. R. (1992). *Research dispositions of teacher candidates.* Doctoral Dissertation. College Park, MD: University of Maryland.

Connor, C., Grief, A., Gunsolus, L., & Hathaway, D. (1996). *Community and the classroom: Beginning teachers' use of service-learning.* Paper presented at the National Service-Learning Conference, Detroit, MI.

Conrad, D., & Hedin, D. (1981). *Instruments and scoring guide of the experiential education evaluation project.* University of Minnesota: St. Paul.

Hathaway, D., Dolber, R., Scobie, L., Martin, J., & Anderson, J. B. (1996). *Service-learning in a middle school health class: Successes and challenges.* Paper presented at the National Service-Learning Conference, Detroit, MI.

Hopkins, D. (1993). *A teacher's guide to action research*, (2nd ed.). Philadelphia: Open University Press.

Noffke, S. (1995). Action research and democratic schooling: Problems and potentials. In S. Noffke & R. Stevenson (Eds.), *Educational action research: Becoming practically critical* (pp. 1–10). New York: Teachers College Press.

Nowicki, S., & Strickland, B. (1973). A locus of control scale for children. *Journal of Consulting and Clinical Psychology, 40,* 148–154.

Sagor, R. (1992). *How to conduct collaborative action research.* Alexandria, VA: Association for Supervision and Curriculum Development.

Wade, R. C., & Anderson, J. B. (1996). Community service learning: A strategy for preparing human service oriented teachers. *Teacher Education Quarterly, 23*(4), 59–74.

12

The Promise and Challenge of Service-Learning Portraiture Research

Terry Pickeral
National Center for Learning and Citizenship

Don Hill
Service-Learning 2000

Marty Duckenfield
National Dropout Prevention Center

INTRODUCTION

Researchers have been collecting and describing quantitative and qualitative data about service-learning programs for several years, but many people in the field feel that current studies have been ineffective in capturing the richness and complexity of what they experience and observe. In 1996, in response to this reality and a growing interest in service-learning stories and to help meet this perceived need, The Service-Learning 2000 Center at Stanford University decided to try to adapt the research approach of portraiture developed by Sarah Lawrence-Lightfoot and Jessica Davis at Harvard University. Center staff believed that their portraiture theory held great promise for creating compelling narratives to engage readers and help inform the service-learning field.

Center staff began this effort by contracting with Lissa Soep, a colleague of Jessica Davis at Harvard University's Project Zero, to translate central portraiture methodologies into a set of concepts and practices to guide Service-Learning 2000 Center research and writing. From 1996 to 2001, Center staff coordinated the research and writing of service-learning portraits for three secondary schools, two middle schools, and six service-learning teacher education programs in California. In addition, two staff members led an institute at Clemson University in South Carolina in July 2001, to help launch a major portraiture project for professors and K–12 teachers from the southern region of the U.S. who shared a common interest in creating powerful narratives about their service-learning work.

This chapter begins by describing the general conceptual framework used in four portraiture projects. Examples are drawn from three Service-Learning 2000 projects to illustrate the framework in action. More attention is focused on the teacher education project because it departed from the Lightfoot-Davis model by asking professors to write about their own work. Faculty members serve not as outside researchers but as key actors in the projects. These professors were, in many respects, portraiture pioneers who tested the possibility that action research could be successfully adapted for portraiture. In addition, they experimented with the value of forming a collegial learning community connecting six teacher education institutions across the state of California. The chapter concludes by describing a fourth portraiture effort centered in South Carolina. Although participants in the South Carolina project received training in the Lightfoot-Davis model, they further adapted the model to serve their unique purposes.

DEFINING CHARACTERISTICS OF PORTRAITURE

Portraiture shares much of its approach with other forms of qualitative research. Ethnographic case studies, for example, assemble details in a similar manner. Whereas the writer's voice is normally absent or masked by the veil of objectivity in a case study, a portrait is marked by the voice of the writer.

Portraiture, like all qualitative research, must be grounded in the data that lead to authentic description via an intense analysis process. The description, like a portrait painting, should capture the essence of the subject. Creative fiction has no place. Portraiture researchers also take a different stance toward their subject than many traditional researchers. They adopt what Lawrence-Lightfoot described as a generous regard for what you study. Instead of probing intentionally for failures from an autopsy lens, portraiture seeks to focus more on process and unashamedly cares about what is being studied and represented. This stance does not mean sugar coating reality but rather means a commitment to uncovering potential goodness.

DOING PORTRAITURE RESEARCH

Using portraiture research to study service-learning requires the following components:

- Agreeing on a central guiding question for research;
- Identifying a small number of dimensions to serve as organizers for data collection and project analysis;
- Identifying from data analysis a small number of themes that guide the writing of a portrait;

- Triangulating data from a variety of sources; and
- Using an outside-in writing strategy that effectively brings the reader into the context of the project.

Portraiture also involves stressing the importance of creating a compelling narrative that uses vivid language and includes multiple voices and perspectives. Portraiture shows rather than tells a story.

GUIDING QUESTION

The central guiding question for portraiture research is similar to traditional research or evaluation questions. Agreeing on a central guiding question for this portraiture research was both crucial and difficult. Many hours of debate focused on fine-tuning questions so that they offer potential both to drive data collection and lead to results that will matter for the service-learning field. Careful attention was directed to reaching agreement on the definition of each word.

The resultant questions were simple and almost self-evident. The middle school portraits focused on the strategies and challenges of integrating service-learning into academic curriculum. The teacher education portraits researched how service-learning impacts the teaching and learning of program participants. One would never guess how much heated discussion and experimentation with alternatives preceded the final decision. Few would disagree, however, that this discussion time was well spent. Portraits need to be grounded in a serious question that matters, that limits the scope of data collection, and that informs the selection of themes.

Central guiding questions made important contributions to Service-Learning 2000 portraiture work. The teacher education project began by inviting professors from seven schools to attend a workshop on portraiture that concluded by identifying a common guiding question for their research. This workshop was followed by Service-Learning 2000 staff support that included one-on-one coaching, conference calls on different aspects of portraiture research, a second workshop to share progress and obtain further training, and a two-day writing retreat with personal writing conferences. Throughout this collaborative work and coaching, the guiding question provided a constant and common focus. In addition, having this common guiding question facilitated cross-portrait analysis at the end of the project and gave the resulting analysis more credibility.

DIMENSIONS

Organizing the collecting, sorting, and analysis of data for portrait writing is similar in many respects to other forms of research. Data collection is organized in a small number of conceptual categories called dimensions that are selected to inform the central guiding question and to reveal themes. Because the culminating goal is to craft a portrait that brings the multidimensional context of a service-learning experience to life, special attention is directed to collecting insightful quotes and examples across dimensions and from a variety of sources and voices.

Research in each of the three projects began by agreement on a small number of dimensions that offered promise for sorting data for analysis and shaping theme selection. Dimensions function much like a temporary storage bin for related data. The high school portraits used four dimensions to collect data.

- The journey of the program defined as origins and future vision;
- The service activity defined as the nature of service provided;
- The environment in which the program operates defined as relationships with and nature of the school and surrounding community; and
- The program structure defined as leadership, funding, and buy-in.

The dimensions for the six teacher education portraits were similar but they included change over time, with an emphasis on flexibility involved in implementing reform within institutions.

THEMES

The most important and difficult challenge of service-learning portrait research is to select two or three themes that capture the drama and reality of a project while providing valid insight into the guiding question. Looking across dimensions for powerful themes is where art and science collide. As a researcher aiming for scientific objectivity, one analyzes all data, looking for generalizations that might explain what was observed, experienced, and reviewed. After reading and rereading interview transcripts, observation and focus group notes, student work, surveys, and other kinds of school and community documentation, the researcher begins to create possible themes to test for explanatory power. When four or five tentative themes emerge, the researcher must then test the capacity of these themes to work as the organizers for the actual writing of a portrait. It is here where the artist meets the scientist. Sometimes promising themes simply do not work—they fail to generate the kind of vivid writing demanded or initial writing efforts gradually reveal that a theme is less powerful and insightful than originally thought.

There is no set way to identify an effective portrait theme. The limited experience at Service-Learning 2000 suggests that themes often emerge from conversations where the researcher talks with one or more colleagues at some length about possible themes and, in a sense, listens to ideas being reflected back and questioned. Final themes often surface at the last moment. Although the process of theme search is grounded in intense, concentrated analysis of data, the final selection has the feeling more of an artistic "aha" experience.

Experience here suggests that researchers consider five questions or criteria to determine the authenticity and power of a potential portrait theme.

1. Are there patterns in the evidence that lead to and support the theme as distinct from single occurrences?

2. Is the theme something that simply appeals to you or does it really emerge from the data? Researchers need to avoid the temptation to settle on a theme that they think they can find data to support rather than something that the data compel.

3. How useful is the theme in generating description? Does it serve as an effective catalyst for your writing?

4. Does the theme make sense and convey authentic insight to people involved in the project? If it does not, the researcher needs to return to start over.

5. How well does the theme fit with the guiding question? Does it have clear potential to inform?

Service-Learning 2000's portraits have used a variety of themes. Some researchers have used quotes from participants to describe a theme; other researchers have created their own language to describe a theme. Although listing some of the themes used in this service-learning portraiture research will reveal little about the identification process, it will, perhaps, offer insight into the range of possibilities that may emerge. Themes from this service-learning portrait research include:

*   The Gift of Community
*   Life on the Sidelines
*   Service-Learning as Instigator of Empowerment and Transformation
*   Gentle Infiltration
*   Weaving Connections
*   Sowing the Seeds of Humanity
*   Multiple Hurdles

Portraits use themes to organize the presentation of narrative data. For example, Gelenian (2001) in a portrait, *Service-Learning in Multicultural Settings*, described a project at California State University, Humboldt. He identified the Gift of Community as one of his themes. He introduces this theme directly. "As I examined and reexamined my students' work and listened to site personnel talk about their students, I repeatedly read or heard comments about community and the importance of caring" (p. 11). He proceeds to cite several examples of community through the words of participants. "The Mural Project required many hands and talents. It also fostered a sense of community among everyone involved" (p. 13). In his journal, Gelenian had this to say about one project:

> The project was teen-centered. It brought together students from various backgrounds and communities who had a chance to talk together. There were no assignments, no grades, and no obligations. Students choose to come, decide what they want to work on, and how long they can work. Tammy (project director and credential candidate) guided the teens by organizing work dates and activities. Teens have designed the mural, raised money for it, and did it. This sense of ownership is extremely motivating for them. Parents seem to be very proud of their teens that are participating, which add to the positive atmosphere. The project is also very open. Anyone can come to help, and this seems to create a cooperative atmosphere. (p. 13)

A second theme in Gelenian's portrait (2001), *Life on the Sidelines*, provided a conceptual coherence for sharing a rich array of data in gallery pieces at the end of his Multicultural Education course. For example, one student composed a song to illustrate his observations and insights:

> Well look at me I'm sittin in the back again
> I'm the one that never volunteers
> I just sit and try to figure out what you want
> Why can't you see I do care?
> You ask me questions that I don't understand
> You interrupt me when I speak
> You tell me what I say has just about nothing to do with what
> It is you want me to say
> Well I can't tell you how many times I've tried to tell you
> What it is I mean
> But I don't speak like you, and you don't speak like me
> Isn't there someplace we can meet? (pp. 8–9)

It is hard to read the first stanzas of this poem without recognizing and feeling the reality of the *Life on the Sidelines* theme.

OUTSIDE-IN WRITING

In order for a service-learning portrait to achieve its overarching goal of helping K–12 teachers and university professors better understand the promise and problems of service-learning pedagogy, it must succeed in engaging the reader and bringing the project context to life. A major strategy for meeting this challenge is what portraiture calls *outside-in* writing. The portrait writer works extraordinarily hard to find language and images that bring the reader up close and into the world of the service-learning experience depicted—to help the reader sense the smells, sounds, and tensions like a participant. In the words of Lissa Soep:

> The narrative begins with a setting of the scene; the reader encounters the site of the study from the outside-in- a picture of the geographic, demographics and ideological setting that helps shape the experiences portrayed. Portraiture makes no attempt to present these experiences through the anonymous, disembodied voice typically associated with research documents. The writer is present in portraiture, in every detail included and omitted, in the themes explored, and sometimes (but not always) in first person accounts that run through the narrative. (Anderson, Swick, & Yff, 2001, p. 105)

Pine (2001 in her portrait, *The Complexity of Beginnings*, provided an example of outside-in writing.

> The carillon from St. Vincent's peals the evening melodies. Birds of many species sing their varied songs above in the exotic old trees as I walk toward the classroom buildings for my elementary education methodology class. Pulling my cart of books, handouts, videotapes, and assorted teaching materials, I wonder what I have forgotten. I take a few breaths to draw in the peacefulness, and nod to students clustered for a quick before-class meal at outside tables. The low drone of freeway traffic is almost lost to consciousness. The is the Doheny campus of Mount St. Mary's College, located in the heart of Los Angeles, two blocks from the busiest LA freeways, clogged bumper to bumper. (pp. 43–44)

> The Doheny campus is a pond of tranquility within the complex, pulsing energy of central Los Angeles. Its history is entwined in the rise of millionaires. A square bloc of Victorian homes surrounded by plantings collected from around the world. The campus was home to the Dohenys, their relatives, and friends. Today it serves the college mission: preparing multiethnic, multilingual students to become leaders in a diverse and changing world. . . . The splendor of past, isolated wealth has been adapted for 21st century work to empower those who have historically been ignored. . . . As I continue toward class I mull over my student's incredibly diverse stories and experiences. One group of students in my class describes themselves

as "two Catholics, two Protestants, and one Hindu. We speak English, Spanish, Hindi, Tagalog, and Vietnamese. Two of us are graduate students, three are undergraduates. One has taught for 10 years, one for two years, one has been a teacher's aide, and two of us have never taught. (Blackwell et al., 2001, pp. 43–44).

This outside-in description paints a picture of the campus while providing introductory background to the themes of Weaving a Team Tapestry and Flexibility is Essential that the author develops in the portrait.

PORTRAITURE: A COLLABORATIVE APPROACH

As part of the W. K. Kellogg Foundation funded *Learning In Deed* (LID) national service-learning initiative, several districts in South Carolina are working interdependently and with the state Department of Education to integrate service-learning into the core education experience of K–12 students. This goal encouraged the LID districts to create collaborations with local postsecondary institution education programs, ensuring that current K–12 teachers gained the necessary competencies to engage students in service-learning, and helping the next generation of teachers gain corresponding knowledge and skills during their collegiate experience. These efforts built on the National Service-Learning in Teacher Education Partnership (NSLTEP) focusing on professional development and integration of service-learning into the core teacher education curriculum.

The initiative in South Carolina is focused on a central guiding question: "How are we moving toward the institutionalization of service-learning into our educational programs?" Each of the K–12 and teacher education collaborations, after training from Service-Learning 2000 professionals, embarked on the portraiture process to share their experiences, document progress, and improve service-learning practice. The training included:

- A basic understanding of the portraiture process and benefits, through formal training, stories, and resources;

- The development of a realistic timeline for completion;

- A commitment to take the risk to try something new;

- Knowledge of appropriate data collection methods, checklists, and formats to effectively implement the portraiture process.

At the conclusion of the training, participants understood that:

- There is a benefit of including multiple voices in analysis of student performance, school cultures, and collaborations;

- Frequent data collection, analysis, and reflection are critical to documenting and improving service-learning practice and programs;

- Regular meetings within the organizations and within the collaborations are critical to utilize the information in a timely manner;

- There should be a focus on equity in the process; and

- The portraiture process would be a catalyst for enhancing K–12 and teacher education (higher education) collaborations.

Participants also identified the following audiences for the portraits.

- Teacher education faculty;
- School and district administrators;
- Service-Learning practitioners;
- Peers (teachers and faculty); and
- Community members.

The South Carolina portraiture process covered 12 months. The coordinators requested the writing teams be composed of members from both higher education institutions and K–12 whenever possible. The teams agreed to a series of working meetings and conference calls to report on their progress, seek assistance, and provide support for one another. They also shared their early drafts via a listserv.

To facilitate the writing process, the coordinators gave the portraiture teams a checklist to help them to conceptualize and begin their writing. This checklist was very effective in assisting the higher education partners, in particular, in moving away from the traditional academic writing style to the more engaging portraiture process. In addition, at a face-to-face workshop, the checklist was used as a tool to critique shared writings, assessing how they could bring more art into their fledgling portraits. Figure 12.1 shows the content of the recommended checklist.

As this group of participants engaged in the portraiture process, they encountered other novel experiences besides the change in writing style. They began to:

- Understand that portraiture is a *process* (someone needs to keep participants on task and time—they need to be motivated and supported with feedback);

- Focus on showing what occurred rather than telling what happened;

- Wrestle with the issue of the authenticity of portraiture so that it is acceptable by peers in the higher education world;

- Be patient with the data collection, avoiding the temptation to settle on a theme that has one or two compelling illustrations without rigorous triangulated analysis; and

- Learn to talk to each other as they were collecting the data ensuring all the perspectives of the partners were in the portrait.

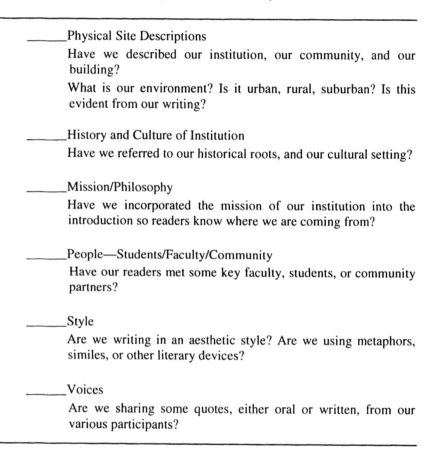

_____Physical Site Descriptions
Have we described our institution, our community, and our building?
What is our environment? Is it urban, rural, suburban? Is this evident from our writing?

_____History and Culture of Institution
Have we referred to our historical roots, and our cultural setting?

_____Mission/Philosophy
Have we incorporated the mission of our institution into the introduction so readers know where we are coming from?

_____People—Students/Faculty/Community
Have our readers met some key faculty, students, or community partners?

_____Style
Are we writing in an aesthetic style? Are we using metaphors, similes, or other literary devices?

_____Voices
Are we sharing some quotes, either oral or written, from our various participants?

Figure 12.1: Suggested checklist for "outside-in" context of your portrait

Over time, the majority of portraiture participants found the process exciting and appropriate for capturing their efforts, outcomes, and improvements. They discovered that the process enabled them to reflect constantly within their partnerships on their progress toward institutionalization.

The following is an example of an early effort to create an outside-in introduction to a forthcoming portrait. The University of South Carolina is a partner with Richland School District Two in Columbia, South Carolina, in the *Learning In Deed* national initiative.

THE UNIVERSITY OF SOUTH CAROLINA: THE BEGINNING

The University of South Carolina's coordinator of student service in the community was addressing about 50 faculty members from various disciplines in a faculty breakfast on service-learning. Some of his introductory comments provided me with a metaphor of "serving and learning together" as symbolic of this large university's commitment to human empowerment. [The coordinator] talked about how thousands of students, faculty, and staff had contributed to the "Carolina Care" holiday giving program to help children and families in need. Later in that same faculty breakfast, a student spoke to the faculty about how powerful her service-learning was in helping her realize that teaching was indeed the profession she wanted to pursue.

Two months later I saw another group of USC students and faculty "serve and learn together" in a Martin Luther King Service Day. Over 700 people gathered to go into the community to help clean up parks, build homes, paint, and clean up child care centers and help in many other different ways. Reflective comments shared later that day tell the story:

"I was amazed at how the senior citizens were so responsive to our clean up work; they were more than thankful—their attitudes empowered us!"

"I saw our students in a different light today (from a faculty member). They seemed so much more committed. Is this because I have not really taken steps to see them in these service modes? I have learned today that I need to change my teaching approach to use more service-learning."

It is this "people rich" university environment in which our College of Education's Service-Learning and Teacher Education Project evolved. As an extension of the College of Education's mission of service to the public, in 1997 the Department of Instruction and Teacher Education created a faculty team that developed a purpose and structure for advancing service-learning in teacher education. This team (Service-Learning and Teacher Education, SLATE) was initially funded by a grant from the American Association of Colleges for Teacher Education and the Corporation for National Service. The grant was awarded in January of 1998, and the work of this team has continued since that time.

From the outset, the USC Service-Learning and Teacher Education team was keyed on the metaphor "serving and learning together" with faculty, students, staff, teachers, and students in our collaborating schools and agencies. All activities of this team focused on strengthening the integration of the "service" function of teacher education into meaningful community contributions and academic learning.

Continuing threads of this "serving and learning together" pattern that under gird the SLATE work are:

- *A group of faculty who meet regularly to develop and use service-learning in their classes and in various aspects of teacher education.*

- *An ever-evolving mission of service within the College of Education to train and educate teachers who are committed to a philosophy of "serving and learning."*

- *Students and faculty put the service-learning philosophy into action in class activities, in partnership work with schools and agencies, and in advocacy and policy making efforts through work with professional associations, communities, and other groups.*

It was within this context that the USC—SLATE Project was selected to be a partner in the South Carolina Kellogg Praise Project with Richland School District Two. Because of its total commitment to "serving and learning together," this partnership was a natural extension of the work started in prior grants and activities. The real thrust of the partnership with Richland Two was and is to empower each other through our service and learning efforts, with particular focus on sharing our talents, resources, ideas, and skills in multiple ways and within varying contexts.[1]

By introducing some of the key actors from the university, sharing their comments, and describing actual events, the authors bring the reader into their world to better understand the context of what follows. This introductory piece also introduces what will likely be a stronger theme of this portrait—serving and learning together.

Another portrait clearly shows the powerful connection between a college and its neighborhood and how service-learning enhances that partnership. Benedict College, a historically black college located in Columbia, South Carolina, is a NSLTEP partner.

BENEDICT COLLEGE: A GLIMPSE

Benedict College finds itself nestled amongst a sprawling metropolis in the midst of a revitalizing neighborhood that once bustled with community activism, high achievers, and black pride. Former community residents include leaders such as civil rights activist Modjeska Simpkins, renowned attorney I. S. Leevy, and Astronaut Charles Bolden, whose mother still resides in the community working actively with area schools promoting education. From a historical perspective, the neighborhood once stood proud; its people, its schools, its streets, and even the multitude of housing structures, each characterized its own unique design. This was the neighborhood.

Throughout the years many things have led to declining conditions that have cast somewhat of a negative shadow over the community. However, in the midst of such a decline, its educational institutions have faced challenges and

---

[1] Kevin J. Swick, Michael Rawls, and Nancy Freeman of the University of South Carolina; Beverly Hiott of Richland School District Two 1–2, 2001.

have overcome adversities to help sustain and revitalize this once prominent neighborhood.

Benedict College, standing tall on the shoulders of the community's products and holding firm as it bears the burdens of the very same community, finds itself in a unique location in the heart of a community rich with history. Embracing a vital component of the college's mission to provide public service and impact conditions in the African-American community, the College seeks opportunities to help maintain this rich history. The College's evolved mission dictates its goal of meeting the needs of the community. On any given day the comings and goings of the College's constituents can be measured by the activities that are helping to forge a new chapter in this community and hopefully have an impact on teaching and learning to help shape the lives of others throughout the state and beyond. These individuals, regardless of backgrounds, are actively engaged in learning and sharing through various service initiatives.

Under the administration of President David H. Swinton, service-learning has become a vehicle for transforming our learning community when in 1995 it was institutionalized as a graduation requirement for Benedict College students in each department. Dr. Swinton says, "Service-learning provides Benedict College students with an opportunity to put what they are learning into practice. It helps them hone their leadership skills and to develop confidence in their ability to provide work of value to society. In addition, it instills in them a sense of personal responsibility for finding solutions to the problems and concerns of society. Service-learning teaches students to take ownership and think in terms of 'us' and 'we' rather than in terms of 'them' and 'they.' While they learn and serve, Benedict students provide incredible resources to help address important social and community issues."

The Service-Learning Program quickly became one of the entities designed to enhance the service component of the college's mission, which states that the College is committed to using its faculty, students, and administrative resources to provide service to impact conditions in the community. Through the service-learning program, students begin to learn and understand why devotion to civic responsibility is more than simply a request.

Within this service-learning community we share many experiences that include successes and challenges. Our success is manifested through a reflection by a teacher education faculty member who shared her experience of developing understanding of the service-learning and its impact through a project conducted with her students. During this project, students were to study social studies as a part of a course. Therefore, the teacher set out to have students learn more about social studies by researching issues of environments and community. The project involved interviewing parents who were tenants of a nearby housing project. She says, "The students were scared to go to the 'projects,' but after going and interviewing the parents they discovered that the parents wanted for their children the same as their parents wanted for them." For this faculty member, infusing real-life contexts to expand course learning is

a natural fit for teaching her education courses, and she is even exploring how it
helps meet state and national standards.[2]

In this portrait, readers are introduced to this community, gaining an
understanding of the institution and its role in the neighborhood. The team of
authors shows, from both the cultural and historical roots of the institution and
the words of the president today, that the environment for nurturing service to
the community is an especially rich one at Benedict College.

As is evident from both portrait introductions, the authors bring the reader
into the setting of the project, creating an understanding that will serve as the
foundation for the stories that will follow. The uniqueness of this technique is
that the authors are key actors, responsible for establishing the process and
caring about what is being studied and represented. Their inside knowledge of
the setting brings a truth to the telling of the stories. The writing teams, by
bringing the diverse voices of various other actors into the portraiture process,
can further enhance this truth.

Various service-learning portrait authors indicate that this process has been
very helpful to improve their practice. The portraits, completed by stakeholders,
provide specific insights into the impact on participants and recommendations
for improvement including:

- Improving the way teachers view their students' work;

- Greater alignment of an assessment approach with program goals and
  purposes;

- Enhanced relationships with community partners;

- Increased capacity to ask critical questions of all stakeholders;

- Expanded scope of the projects through the focus on themes;

- Increased orientation to diversity of participants and their capacities;

- Greater acknowledgement of the political nature of curriculum and
  service-learning pedagogy;

- Greater listening skills to understand students' concerns and teacher
  responses;

- Increased appreciation for uncertainty involved in service-learning and
  willingness to embrace this pedagogy;

- Greater knowledge of the service-learning program, partners'
  contributions and impacts;

- Greater interaction among program partners; and

---

[2] Gwenda Greene, Patricia Dixon, Ruby Blair, and Tondeleya Jackson of Benedict
College (1–2), 2001.

- Increased recognition of the positive effects on students, including self-efficacy.

According to one teacher:

> When I think about it, it seems that portraiture improved my service-learning work in ways that reflect the process. It improved the way that I looked at it. It gave me a view of what my students learn that I believe helps me feel more confident in what I tell students about service-learning when they ask questions like "Why do I have to do this?" I really feel that an experiential pedagogy like service-learning demands an interpretive analysis of learning. You can't measure empathy with calipers.

CONCLUSION

Portraiture is emerging as both an effective and efficient process to help service-learning advocates in their struggles to apply research to collect, analyze, and communicate information about their work.

Portraiture research to study service-learning is organized through the following:

- Agreeing on a central guiding question for research;

- Identifying a small number of dimensions to serve as organizers for data collection and project analysis;

- Identifying a small number of themes from data analysis that guide the writing of a portrait;

- Triangulating data from a variety of sources; and

- Using an outside-in writing strategy that effectively brings the reader into the context of the project.

It also creates a compelling narrative that uses vivid, showing language and includes multiple voices and perspectives.

Portraiture is a method that also aligns with the values of service-learning including a focus on reflection and collaboration. In addition, it provides formal opportunities to use information for continuous individual and program improvement.

The challenges of employing portraiture processes (e.g., a different way of writing including multiple voices, triangulation, and finding time for collaborative thinking and writing) are overcome by developing and nurturing collaborative learning communities that bridge disciplines and K–12 and higher education. Portraiture, thus, offers both an opportunity to tell a story through strategic organizing components and to create deep collaborations within and outside educational institutions. Both leading to improved service-learning practice.

REFERENCES

Anderson, J., Swick, K., & Yff, J. (2001). Service-*learning in teacher education.* Washington, DC: AACTE ERIC.

Blackwell, K., Caesar, J., Donahue, D., Gelenian, K., Hill, D., Jacobson, J., Karayan, S., Kelly, M., Pine, N., & Ryan, M. (2001). *Struggling to Learn Better III: Portraits of six teacher education service learning programs.* Oakland, CA: Service Learning 2000/Youth Service California.

Gelenian, K. (2001). Service-learning in multicultural settings. In J. Addison-Jacobson & D. Hill (Eds.), *Struggling to Learn Better III: Portraits of six teacher education service-learning programs* (pp. 1–18). Oakland, CA: Service-Learning 2000/Youth Service California.

Lawrence-Lightfoot, S., & Davis, J. (1997). The *art and science of portraiture.* San Francisco: Jossey-Bass.

Pine, N. (2001). The complexity of beginnings. In J. Addison-Jacobson & D. Hill (Eds.), *Struggling to Learn Better III: Portraits of six teacher education service-learning programs* (pp. 42–61). San Mateo, CA: Service-Learning 2000 Center.

Pope, D., Batenburg, M., Intrator, S., Verducci, S., & Hill, D. (1998). *Struggling to Learn Better: Portraits of two middle school service-learning programs.* Palo Alto, CA: Service-Learning 2000 Center.

Soep, E., & Pickeral, T. (2001). Capturing the power of service-learning in teacher education through portraiture. In J. Anderson, K. Swick, & J. Yff (Eds.), *Service-learning in teacher education* (p. 9). Washington, DC: AACTE ERIC.

Soep, E., Pope, D., Batenburg, M., Addison-Jacobson, J., & Hill, D. (1994). *Struggling to Learn Better: Portraits of three high school service-learning programs.* Palo Alto, CA Service-Learning 2000 Center.

ABOUT THE AUTHORS

Jeffrey B. Anderson is Associate Professor of Education at Seattle University. He has been a service-learning practitioner and researcher for over 20 years, both as a high school teacher and teacher educator. He recently co-edited *Service-Learning in Teacher Education: Enhancing the Growth of New Teachers, Their Students, and Communities*.

Lawrence Neil Bailis, Ph.D., is an Associate Research Professor at Brandeis University's Heller Graduate School and a Senior Research Associate at the School's Center for Youth and Communities. During the past seven years, he has directed over a dozen studies of service-learning programs at the elementary, secondary, and college level (often in collaboration with Alan Melchior), including a national study of higher education service-learning, a study of community-based service-learning programs in Massachusetts, and evaluation of several national foundation-sponsored initiatives, such as the *Active Citizenship Today* program.

Shelley H. Billig, Ph.D., is Vice President of RMC Research Corporation in Denver, Colorado. She directs the Research Network for the W. K. Kellogg *Learning In Deed* initiative that seeks to give every K–12 student an opportunity to engage in school-based service-learning. She is series editor of the volumes entitled *Advances in Service-Learning* and co-edited *Service-Learning: The Essence of the Pedagogy* with Andrew Furco. She directs multiple service-learning and educational reform projects at the national, state, and local levels and directs several K–12 educational reform projects.

Dr. L. Richard Bradley is Director of the Service-Learning Curriculum Integration Project for small, urban high schools in Ohio for the John Glenn Institute for Public Policy and Public Service. He also serves as Program Design and Evaluation Consultant for four suburban Columbus (Ohio) school districts, assisting teachers in incorporating service-learning and character education strategies into their classrooms. He is the author of a service-learning training manual for Ohio and serves as Ohio's service-learning trainer. He served as program evaluator for Ohio Partners in Character Education. He also teaches graduate courses in service-learning and character education through Ashland University and Bowling Green State University. He has presented at numerous national conferences.

Marty Duckenfield serves the National Dropout Prevention Center at Clemson University as director of publications and coordinator of all Center service-learning projects.

Dr. Carl Fertman, Associate Professor, School of Education, University of Pittsburgh, is the founding director of the Pennsylvania Service-Learning Evaluation Network.

Andrew Furco is the founding director of the Service-Learning Research and Development Center at the University of California-Berkeley, where he serves on the Graduate School of Education faculty. Since 1994, he has led more than 20 studies of service-learning in K–12 education, teacher education, and higher education. He is currently serving a four-year term as a Campus Compact Engaged Scholar and is a member of the Campus Compact Research Advisory Board, Kellogg *Learning In Deed* Research Advisory Committee, the AAHE Service-Learning Consulting Corps, the National Service-Learning Partnership Board of Directors, and the National Review Board for the Scholarship of Engagement. He holds a masters degree in Education from UCLA and received his doctorate in the area of Educational Administration from UC Berkeley.

Deborah Hecht is a Project Director at the Center for Advanced Study in Education, The Graduate School and University Center of The City University of New York. She has a doctorate from New York University in Educational Psychology with a specialization in research and evaluation. Dr. Hecht has been involved in the areas of service-learning, applied learning, and character education for 10 years as a researcher, evaluator, program developer, and trainer.

Don Hill is the Director of the Service-Learning 2000 Division of Youth Service California.

Jeffrey Howard is the Assistant Director for Academic Service-Learning at the University of Michigan's Edward Ginsberg Center for Community Service and Learning. He has taught, conducted research, and published work on academic service-learning for more than 20 years. He is the founder and editor of *The Michigan Journal of Community Service Learning*, and co-editor (with Robert Rhoads) of *Academic Service-Learning: A Pedagogy of Action and Reflection* (Jossey-Bass). He is a member of the National Advisory Council for Campus Compact and the National Review Board for the Scholarship of Engagement. His latest publication, funded by the Corporation for National and Community Service, is the *Service-Learning Course Design Workbook*.

Alan Melchior is the Deputy Director and Senior Research Associate at the Center for Youth and Communities at Brandeis University's Heller Graduate School. Since early 1992, he has directed or co-directed (with Lawrence Neil Bailis) five major service-learning evaluations including the national evaluations of Serve-America and Learn and Serve America. He is currently leading the evaluation of the W. K. Kellogg Foundation's *Learning In Deed* initiative and conducting a study on the institutionalization of service-learning for the Corporation for National Service.

Terry Pickeral is the Executive Director of the National Center for Learning and Citizenship at the Education Commission of the States.

Dr. Susan Root is Professor of Education at Alma College where she teaches courses in Educational Psychology, child and adolescent development, and early childhood education. She was co-author of a W. K. Kellogg Foundation grant that funded the establishment of the service-learning program at Alma College. She is one of seven regional directors of the AACTE/National Service-Learning in Teacher Education Partnership, a project sponsored by the Corporation for National and Community Service, to help teacher education faculty incorporate service-learning into their courses. Dr. Root recently received a dissemination grant from the Corporation to publish *Service-Learning in Teacher Education: A Handbook.* Dr. Root has co-written several articles on service-learning in teacher education, including "Service-Learning in Teacher Education: A Consideration of Qualitative and Quantitative Outcomes," which recently appeared in *Service-Learning: The Essence of the Pedagogy,* and "Building Teaching Dispositions and Service-Learning practice: A Multisite Study," recently published in *The Michigan Journal of Community Service Learning.*

Robert Shumer is the former director of the National Service-Learning Clearinghouse and the Center for Experiential Education and Service-Learning at the University of Minnesota. He has taught courses from middle school to graduate school, and currently is heading research efforts in four states on service-learning and character education. His research interests are in qualitative inquiry, youth development, as well as service and experiential learning.

Fredric Waldstein holds the Irving R. Burling Chair in Leadership and is Professor of Political Science at Wartburg College where he is also Director of the Institute for Leadership Education. He has been engaged in service-learning research and teaching for more then 10 years. His current research interests pertain to the exploration of educational paradigms to foster critical inquiry, civil discourse, and service-learning as means to develop the skills necessary to practice the arts of civic engagement and participatory democracy. Among his service activities, Dr. Waldstein is the chair of the American Association of State Service Commissions, which he helped found while chair of the Iowa Commission on Volunteer Service

Alan S. Waterman (Ph.D., SUNY/Buffalo) is Professor of Psychology at The College of New Jersey. He is a Fellow in the American Psychological Association and American Psychological Society and has published extensively on the transition from adolescence to adulthood. He is serving as the North American Editor of the *Journal of Adolescence.*

Yolanda Yugar, Evaluation Specialist, Fund Development Services, Allegheny Intermediate Unit, works as part of a team that conducts comprehensive program evaluations in education and assists school districts in using data for decision making. She was the former Pennsylvania Service-Learning Evaluator.

Author Index

Thorndike, R. L., 117, *123*
Thorndike, R. M., 117, *123*

V

Van Horn, R., 100, *105*
Van Liere, K. D., 79, *89*
Veninga, J. F., 45, *46*
Verducci, S., *222*
Vogelgesang, L., 4, *10*, *12*

W

Wade, R. C., 14, 17, *33*, 178, *184*, 188,
    205
Waldstein, F., xi, 225
Walsh, B., 48, *72*
Wandersman, A., 150, *171*
Wang, C., 74, *90*, 108, *123*
Waterman, A. S., vii, xi, xii, *xiv*, 25, 27,
    33, 74, 77, *90*, 178, *185*, 225

Watt, J. H., 100, *105*
Weiler, D., 173, *185*
Westheimer, J., 74, *89*
Widaman, K., 59, *71*
Williams, R., 16, *33*
Woehrle, T., 55, *72*

Y

Yates, M., 17, *33*, 74, *90*, 108, *123*
Yff, J., vii, *xiii*, 213, *222*
Yonge, G., 58, *71*
Youniss, J., 17, *33*, 74, *89*, *90*, 108, *123*
Yugar, Y., xii, 225

Z

Zeisset, C., 65, *72*
Zeldin, R., 74, *89*
Zlotkowski, E., 14, *33*

Subject Index

A

Abt Associates, 132
Academic achievement outcome, 22, 138
Academic assessment, 75-76, 82-85
Academic-community integration, 2-3
Academic curriculum
defined, viii
design challenges, 7
empirical research, 114, 115, 116-117
teacher research, 175, 178, 182
Academic curriculum integration
Master in Teaching Program (MIT)
(Seattle University), 192-193,
199-200
portraiture research, 209, 214-216, 220
Academic development outcome, 16, 17,
28-29
Academic engagement outcome, 16-17,
138, 180
Academic learning outcome, 3, 17
Academic performance outcome, 3, 7, 47, 74
Academic service-learning, viii, 2-3
ACT Community Problem Solving Exercise, 140-141
Action process
service-learning conceptualization, viii
Shumer Self-Assessment for Service-
Learning (SSASL), 149-150
Action research
collaboration, 189
Master in Teaching Program (MIT)
(Seattle University), 187,

190, 193-194, 197-198,
199-200
methodology challenges, ix
scientific method, 43, 44
Shumer Self-Assessment for
Service-Learning (SSASL),
155, 169, 170
teacher research origins, 175
Active Citizenship Today (ACT), 127,
129*t*, 133-134, 139-141, 144
ACT tests, 36-37
Advocacy
portraiture research, 208, 211-212
research rationale, 5
social justice, 178, 182
Affect development outcome, 16
Affect management, 53*t*
African-Americans, 218-220
Alienation decrease outcome, 17, 47
Alliance for Service-Learning in Education
Reform (ASLER), 107
Alma College, 179-182
Alternative analysis, *see also* Cognitive
moral development alternate
data interpretation challenges, ix
large-scale/multisite research/
evaluation, 139-141, 147
portraiture research, 208
Alternative Student Service Educational
Trust (ASSET) (Illinois), 127,
130*t*, 133-134, 144
American Association of Colleges for
Teacher Education, 217

uniformity value, 155
University of California–Berkeley, 151
University of Minnesota, 151
usefulness value, 154
utilization variations, 153
value of, 150, 152, 153, 154-156
Wisconsin, 150-151
Simpkins, Modjeska, 218
Simplicity approach
    large-scale/multisite research/
        evaluation, 145
    Master in Teaching Program (MIT)
        (Seattle University), 194, 203
Shumer Self-Assessment for Service-
        Learning (SSASL), 153-154
Single-class initiative, 134
Site-based managers, 144
Site defined, 127n.2, 134-135
Site visits
    large-scale/multisite research/
        evaluation, 132-133,
        136-137, 143
Shumer Self-Assessment for Ser-
        vice-Learning (SSASL), 152
Skill acquisition outcome, 4
Skill development outcome, 74
Social action theory, viii
Social and Personal Responsibility Scale
        (SPRS), 191
Social attitude outcome, 74
Social change agents, 177, 178
Social competence perception outcome, 17
Social consciousness outcome, 177
Social construction theory, viii
Social development, see Cognitive social
        development; Psychosocial devel-
        opment (college); Psychosocial
        development (K-12)
Social isolation decrease outcome, 17
Social justice advocacy, 178, 182
Social justice theory, viii
Social responsibility outcome, 3, 4, 7, 17,
        47, 173
Social science standards
    design challenges, 6, 8
    empirical research, 40-41
    epistemological context, 37, 40-41
    scientific method, 37, 42-43
Social thinking complexity outcome, 4
Soep, Lissa, 207, 213
Software programs, 92, 94, 95, 100

South Carolina
    Benedict College, 218-220
    Clemson University, 151, 207
    Department of Education, 214
    Learning In Deed (LID), 214-218
    Richland School District Two, 216, 218
Service-Learning and Teacher Education
        (SLATE), 208, 216-218
Shumer Self-Assessment for Ser-
        vice-Learning (SSASL),
        150-151
    University of South Carolina, 208,
        216-218
South Carolina Kellogg Praise Project, 218
Splitting hairs phenomenon, 38, 39
Standardization, see also Social science
        standards
    database functions, 93
    empirical research, 40-41, 108
    epistemological context, 36-37, 40-41
    large-scale/multisite research/
        evaluation, 133
Shumer Self-Assessment for Service-
        Learning (SSASL), 151,
        155-156
Standing with the Public: The Humanities
        and Democratic Practice
        (Veninga/McAfee), 45
Stanford University (Service-Learning
        2000 Center), 207-214
Statistical analysis
    empirical research, 38, 40, 43-44,
        109-110, 112-113
    individualized outcome measures, 82,
        85
    large-scale/multisite research/
        evaluation, 143, 145
    Master in Teaching Program (MIT)
        (Seattle University), 192, 193
    outcome variable selection, 74
    scientific method, 43-44
Structural equation modeling, 119
Student ability, 7, 16, 18
Student interest, 7, 16, 18
Student research, see Master in Teaching Pro-
        gram (MIT) (Seattle University)
Subjectivity, 43-44
Subjectwide initiative, 134
Substance abuse decrease outcome, 47
Surveys
    attitudinal measures, 25, 28-29, 82-85

LaVergne, TN USA
23 October 2010
202009LV00011B/10/P